God's Earth

God's Earth

Religion as if matter really mattered

Paul Collins

Gill & Macmillan

Published in Ireland by
Gill & Macmillan Ltd
Goldenbridge
Dublin 8
with associated companies throughout the world

© Copyright Paul Collins 1995
0 7171 2346 4

Designed by William Hung
Cover design by Pierluigi Vido
Cover photograph by Astrovisuals
Typeset by HarperCollins*Publishers*, Melbourne

Printed in Australia by Griffin Paperbacks
First published 1995 by HarperCollins*Religious* (Australia)

A catalogue record is available for this book from the British
Library.

For my mother the late Veronica Margaret Collins
and the late Winifred O'Hehir
and for my father Michael Patrick Collins
and Peter Thomas Collins.

O if we but knew what we do
  When we delve or hew —
Hack and rack the growing green!

To mend her we end her
After-comers cannot guess the beauty been.

Gerard Manley Hopkins
Binsey Poplars (felled 1879)

Acknowledgements

None of us is really original. In both thought and life every one of us owes debts, both intellectual and personal, to many other people. My debt to Thomas Berry is both far-reaching and obvious. Tom is one of the few truly creative thinkers in the contemporary Catholic Church. It was reading him over a number of years and then later talking to him that first helped me articulate what I felt and thought about ecology and theology.

I also owe much to Graeme Garrett. He never let me forget that my context and roots were explicitly and deeply Christian and that it was only within that context that I would make sense to myself, let alone to others. This book owes much to him as a theological sheet anchor whose critique I value highly. Seven years with the Australian Broadcasting Corporation, and above all with the talented staff of *Radio National*, increased my awareness of the need for a critical approach to all ideas and opinions, especially my own!

The Australian publisher of HarperCollins*Religious*, Kevin Mark, offered many helpful comments. Most importantly, he helped me think out what was meant by natural law.

Paul Collins
January 1995

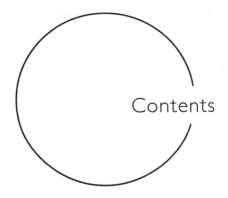

Contents

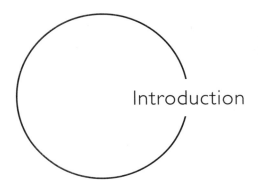

Introduction

It is perhaps odd for an historian to be writing a book about ecology. But it arises out of my conviction that those of us whose lives span the second half of the twentieth century will be among the most despised and cursed generations in the history of humankind. The reason why we will be hated by our children's children and by those who come after them is simple: never before have human beings exploited, damaged, and degraded the earth to the extent that we have. Without regard for the future we have unconscionably rendered the earth less and less inhabitable for both our human future and that of other species of flora and fauna, many of which we have already driven to extinction.

It is our inability to see ourselves in any historical perspective, especially our complete lack of care for the future, that will cause the generations who come after us to curse us most. Despite our advances in many areas and the undoubted generosity of many people, we are still the most psychologically self-engrossed series of all generations. We now seem to have turned our myopic self-enclosure into a permanent attitude.

The preceding paragraphs might be thought to reveal another aspect of my attitude and background: as a priest and preacher I might be expected to express myself through hyperbole! But in this case I mean exactly what I say. Historically, we are part of the most destructive phase of human history ever known. Since about the beginning of the nineteenth century we have carried on a developmental binge that has probably done more damage to the

earth and other species than anything else in cosmic history. This
has accelerated and reached its peak in the period since the end of
the Second World War. As we approach the coming millennium
we are only slowly beginning to glimpse the extent of our
destructiveness. But even with our increased ecological
knowledge, we still largely lack the conviction, will power, and
generosity of spirit to do anything about it.

It is very difficult for us to see this period of environmental
destructiveness in historical perspective because we are usually
educated in a compartmentalized and dichotomized approach to
knowledge. We have largely lost the ability to imagine a broad
historical perspective and to think in a comprehensive way across
a number of disciplines. In this book I try to think both
historically and comprehensively, within a broad philosophical
and theological context, about what is happening to us and to the
world. With a broader vision we may have a chance to escape
from the developmental myopia whereby we imagine that the
only solution to our problems lies in further consumption and
increased "productivity."

Fundamentally this book is about the world, God, ecology,
and us, and the profound interconnections between all four. It
examines a series of pivotal human and religious questions that
arise from the new ecological vision that has developed over the
last three decades. It is clear that in most democratic countries
the majority of reasonably educated people are far ahead of
politicians and institutions in their attitudes toward the
environment. Ecology constantly recurs in public opinion surveys
as the most important long-term issue facing us today. This book
arises out of a conviction that the environment is the central issue
facing the contemporary world and that if we do not face up to
the issues embedded in the environmental crisis we will have no
future as human, ethical, and religious beings. We will be hated
by the people who come after us because we will have denied
them their birthright by destroying so much of the natural world
in our selfish and self-engrossed attempt to take everything for
ourselves. Up until our time, extinctions were the result of

natural or cosmic processes, such as the large scale destruction of species, including the sea reptiles and dinosaurs, at the end of the Cretaceous period sixty-seven million years ago. What is happening now is different: it is an unnatural extinction that results from our human activities and decisions.

Certainly we are the first series of generations who have been able to exploit the natural world to such an extent. We have the technology that people in the past lacked. It is an open question as to whether previous generations would have acted in as destructive a way as we have; that probably would have depended on their cultural, religious, and ethical context. There is no doubt that our individualistic western culture has encouraged a range of attitudes that have led to our present impasse. It has not yet been widely recognized that modern ecology is really quite subversive and challenges much of our cultural and religious underpinning. As such it provides us with a real opportunity to break out of our destructive cultural patterns, to emerge from our contemporary historical amnesia, and to work to recover those aspects of the natural world that are under threat *now*. Tragically, we cannot bring back from extinction what has already been lost.

While the modern environmental consciousness arises from the inter-connection of a number of scientific disciplines, and it is obvious that these will continue to influence it deeply, it is also true that religion and ethics will have to become an essential part of our ecological rethinking. For our self-definition as human beings is derived from two primal sets of relationships. The first is our relationship to each other and to the natural world and all that is in it; this is what we call morals or ethics. The second is our mysterious, intangible, and difficult relationship to the transcendent; it is within this context that we sort out the meaning of our existence. This is what we call spirituality or religion. Although their origins are very different, modern ecology is absolutely central to the future of religion. I contend that religion generally and Christianity specifically will gradually cease to exist if the natural world continues to be devastated at the present rate. There is a deep and dependent inter-relationship between the development of religious attitudes and the sustainment of the natural world.

It is patently obvious that it is human beings and their activities which destroy the infrastructure of the earth and that this destruction will escalate if the increase of the human population is not slowed. If this devastation continues it will eventually lead to the world becoming nothing more than the foundation for a food supply for human beings. Everything will have to be subsumed to this. But human beings, living in a feed-lot world where all wilderness has been destroyed, most species extinguished, and nature driven out, will slowly lose touch with the possibility of the development of culture, art, religion, and spirituality. For, deprived of the natural world in its beauty, multiplicity, mystery, and complexity, we human beings will simply shrivel up spiritually and lose our ability to perceive and experience the deeper issues that give meaning to our lives and the transcendent reality that stands behind the natural world and all that is. For nature is the source of our human origins and the on-going context of our evolution and spiritual development. If we were to lose our natural context we would lose a sense of ourselves as human beings.

The result: the poetic, mystical core of our spirituality and culture would dry up, for there would be nothing to renew and nurture it. Our human imagination would stultify without the inspiration of natural beauty and ecological diversity, and we would lose the ability to conjure up the new possibilities that actually drive us creatively onward. With the loss of the power of imagination we would descend into a hopeless, mad world in which we would most probably destroy ourselves. For it is our imagination that saves us from the paranoid monism that characterizes the essential core of insanity.

I make no apologies for this seemingly apocalyptic scenario. This issue cannot be swept aside. So much of our contemporary religious, political, and economic thinking is short-term and short-sighted. As we move toward the year 2000 and the coming millennium, we *have* to make decisions about the environmental issues that confront us. We already have very little time left, for so much of the natural world in its beauty and complexity has already been permanently lost.

All of the usual sources that provide a constructive approach to human problems have failed us. It is useless to look to democratically elected governments to solve environmental problems. They are still dominated by short-term compromise with conflicting interest-groups and by economists and technocratic planners who lack the breadth of vision to grasp the real issues of our world. Our cultural and intellectual elite has also lost its way and lacks the ability to offer any coherent interpretation of what is happening to us. It has retreated to the particularist morass of deconstruction and post-modernist philosophy. At heart, this nihilist and purposeless ideology offers little in terms of analyzing what is actually happening to our world now. Its denial of the possibility of constructing any coherent "meta-narrative" (or over-all understanding of what is happening in culture) renders it incapable of comprehending the bigger picture.

Our religious traditions too have been at very best less than half-hearted in their response to the contemporary ecological and cultural crisis. There has been some window-dressing in the Christian communities, but the bottom line for all of them is the absolute priority of the human. Everything else in the world plays a secondary role to humankind and its needs. No matter what their rhetoric about ecology, the mainstream Christian churches are infected with an anthropocentrism that dominates their unconscious reactions and guides their value judgments. Since I am going to use this ugly word "anthropocentrism" often in this book I will explain its meaning. It comes from the Greek word "anthropos," meaning "man" in the generic sense. So to be "anthropocentric" is to be entirely focused on humankind and its needs and aspirations to the virtual exclusion of all other species and priorities.

I personally find it sad that the hierarchs and many of the faithful of my own Catholic tradition still seem largely preoccupied with either the moral minutiae of sexual behavior and reproduction, or with the church's struggle to free itself from the self-engrossed and defensive hangovers of the sixteenth century Counter-Reformation and the reactionary and hierarchical preoccupations of the nineteenth century. The saddest aspect of contemporary Catholicism is the widespread retreat by the institutional church into a new conservatism and a narrow orthodoxy that is as contemptuous of the true Catholic tradition as it is of those Catholics who have tried to live their lives in critical harmony with contemporary society. The Catholic community still wastes so much energy on basically insignificant internal struggles about hierarchy and power and the role and function of popes and clerics.

Even the Catholic Church's significant stand on social justice is still focused almost entirely on the needs of humankind. In many ways the social justice tradition is both out of date and engrossed in talking to and constantly quoting itself. At best there is only a very tentative acknowledgment by a small number of Catholics of the fact that there can be no genuine justice between people when the natural world, the source of life for us all, is exploited and destroyed with disinterest and contempt.

One of the more attractive aspects of pre-post-modernist European philosophy was its emphasis on the priority and centrality of the human person. Existentialism was the philosophical context within which personalism developed; many of the key figures in the evolution of personalism were Christians. This philosophy asserted a kind of horizontal transcendence: it argued that human existence and experience is of unique value and is both the primary object and the fundamental source of philosophical inquiry. According to the personalist notion, human beings reach their ultimate fulfillment in relationship with others. This happens, as Gabriel Marcel says, when the person comes to see another not just as a "you" but as a "thou," a beloved with whom I am in committed relationship.

Certainly, personalism has been a very attractive philosophy for Christian theology. Among the followers of Christian personalism is Karol Wojtyla (later Pope John Paul II), who would position himself very much within the tradition of Christian existentialism. While he is not a significant Christian personalist, he has become very important because of his position as pope. However, his approach to personalism is profoundly modified by the neo-scholastic philosophy that he imbibed from his mentor in the late 1940s at the Angelicum University in Rome, the French Dominican Reginald Garrigou-Lagrange.

In his book *Love and Responsibility* (Polish edition 1960), Wojtyla applies his philosophical personalism to sexual ethics. He argues strongly that human beings differ radically from animals and the rest of reality because they have an "interior" life.

> A person differs from a thing in structure and degree of perfection. To the structure of the person belongs an "interior," in which we find the elements of spiritual life, and it is this that compels us to acknowledge the spiritual nature of the human soul, and the peculiar perfectibility of the human person. A person must not be put on the same level as a thing ... Between the psyche of an animal and the spirituality of a man there is an enormous distance, an uncrossable gulf.[1]

One of my main purposes is to show how inaccurate and misleading it is to say that there is an "uncrossable gulf" between human personhood and the other beings of the natural world. In the light of modern science this dichotomy must be seriously questioned, for genetically and biologically we human beings are profoundly connected to the rest of the living world. So why argue for such a radical disjunction? An animal or a plant is not just a "thing" like a machine. It is a living, sentient being. Its life has value and purpose. Pope John Paul's comments are symptomatic of a radical anthropocentrism that has no justification either from the genuine Catholic tradition or in the light of modern scientific knowledge.

This is not to deny that Christian personalism has distinct strengths, not the least of which is the provision of an ethical base for human rights. But there is also something paradoxically myopic about it that makes it blind to the difficult ethical issues we face concerning the environment. Is it true that only human beings have an interiority that sets them apart from all the rest of nature? Is the value of the human person to be exalted at the expense of everything else on earth? Human beings have, in fact, increasingly become the earth's major problem. With the improvement in modern medicine and public health in the nineteenth century, we have been able to breed and survive with great success. But the increase in the human population has placed extraordinary strains on all other natural systems, and we now threaten whole species of animals and plants. Since human action is responsible for virtually all environmental destruction, does this not imply that some serious ethical limits have to be placed on the reproductive activities of human beings? In the light of this you would have to conclude that, in practice, personalism is often little more than the exaltation of the human at the expense of everything else in the natural world.

So if all of our usual religious, social, philosophical and cultural sources have failed us—and I believe they have—then we have to turn elsewhere. We need to turn back to the natural world itself from which we originally sprang, and we have to begin to re-interpret our religious and cultural experience in the light of our interaction with that natural world. So at heart this book is about the deep theological, human, and cultural shift that contemporary ecology inevitably implies.

This shift will involve firstly the way in which we perceive God and God's relationship to us. There are strong traditions running through all religions and theologies, including elements of Christian theology, that posit the natural world as the primary symbol that reveals the presence of the transcendent in earthly existence. What is needed is a shift in the way theology views revelation—and here I take the word "revelation" to refer to the way in which the divine is manifested to us. Actually, ordinary people are already way ahead of the theologians. Many today are finding traces of the transcendent in the world around them, in nature, beauty, and the wilderness. Urbanized people, as they abandon the superficial scientism and intellectualism that underpins so much of contemporary pragmatic culture, are starting to rediscover what indigenous people have always known: that the whole world breathes a sense of an unseen presence, that it points beyond to a spirituality and transcendence that transforms our whole view of existence. It is the theologians and church leaders who need to catch up with what many people today already experience.

Interestingly, the environmental movement is already breeding a cadre of "saints" and "martyrs" who parallel those of the great religions. A deep conviction about and trust in the natural world demands that the committed environmentalist attain a discipline and a willingness to sacrifice the self in a way that is parallel to the ascetic demands of the great spiritual traditions. While it is always dangerously premature to declare someone a "saint" before death, when their lives can be seen within the perspective of all of their achievements and limitations, there are already some environmental leaders whose commitment and asceticism suggest a sanctity that is remarkable. Chico Mendes, the leader of the *seringueiros*, the rubber tappers of Acre province in the Brazilian Amazon, is an example of this. Murdered in December 1988 by a gunman in the pay of wealthy landowners, he and his followers had harvested the renewable products of the rainforest and had fought against the destruction of the Amazon by those intent on short-term profit. Another example is the Australian ecologist and political campaigner Dr Bob Brown. Despite the fact that he has been a successful politician, there is a gentle, ascetic quality about Brown that points to an inner core of deep commitment.

Many people today feel considerable ambiguity about the use of the word "God." Because of historical and cultural accretions, the word comes to us loaded with meanings that are quite antithetical to this discussion. For some, the connotations of the word still refer to a punitive and legalistic judge who notes our failings and punishes us accordingly, both now and in the next life. More recently, certain elements of popular Christian spirituality—elements that are really little more than pop psychology dressed in religious language—have trivialized the word "God" and turned Him (most of this "spirituality" predates inclusive language!) into a kind of divine therapist who nurtures and consoles those who are "hurting." I also feel that there is a sense of artificiality in the references to God as "Father" and "Mother," despite their biblical antecedents. Other Christians, such as the theologian Paul Tillich, want to abandon the use of the word "God" altogether and replace it with various circumlocutions, such as "ground of being."

Certainly we have to admit that often the word "God" comes loaded with undesirable meanings. However, I am loath to abandon such a rich, traditional, and powerful word to the fundamentalist fear-mongers and the psychological trivializers. I will use the word to refer to the transcendent presence that permeates the whole world. For me the words "God" and "transcendence" mean the same thing and I will use them interchangeably. My own inclination is to move toward a content for these words that is benign and loving, concerned with human life but not overly personal nor anthropomorphized, and profoundly and primarily revealed in the natural world.

This book argues that none of our modern religious traditions can turn away from the consequences of contemporary ecology without rendering themselves irrelevant to *the* major issue of our time. As one of the dominant world religions, Christianity will have to face up to some radical shifts of emphasis in its theology in order to remain in touch with the ecological age. The consequences for Christianity will involve a re-focusing of our notion of God and a new definition of the meaning of transcendence. Ecology will also have consequences for the theology of revelation: it will mean that we will slowly come to recognize that we are more likely to encounter the transcendent presence of God in the natural world than in the Bible or the church.

Ecology will also require a shift in the way that theology perceives the position of Christ in human history. For all of Christianity, Christ is central; he is the focal point of history. But ecology posits the natural world and its long cosmic history as the primary given. Theology in an ecological age will see the world as the first icon and sacrament of God and the fundamental source of revelation. In contrast to the history of the cosmos, salvation history (the history of Judaism, Christ, and Christianity) is remarkably brief and limited. Also, if the natural world is the primal revelation, then this implies a relativity in the position of the Bible and the church as revelatory sources. In an ecologically influenced religious world-view, both the Bible and church will be relativized to become specific and supportive sources for the primal revelation of God which will be found in the natural world itself.

It is at this point that some of the most difficult and contentious questions will have to be faced. Despite the fact that Christ himself always pointed outward to the mysterious God who sent him and whose kingdom he proclaimed, many believers will find it hard to cope with a theology that places Christ in a much wider cosmic context. In practice, many Christians today are caught up in a worship of Jesus that is fundamentally idolatrous—"Jesusolatry," as Matthew Fox calls it. The trinitarian nature of God is lost in a myopic focus on Jesus. This loss of perspective on the position of Christ sometimes infects the mainstream churches and certainly dominates the thinking of the fundamentalists. In a theology influenced by ecology, the focus will shift back to God, that mysterious transcendent presence that underpins all reality and that is most manifest in the natural world. Ecology points to the mystery of the divine reality that stands beyond our limited perceptions.

Ecology and science inevitably raise meta-questions that are of their very nature theological. My ultimate purpose in this book is to try to discover something of the transcendent presence that stands behind both the natural world and the cosmos, and which alone gives meaning to all of creation. It was in this sense that the Roman thinker Cicero and the early Christian theologians St Basil and St Augustine saw the beauty of the world as a pointer to God. The poetry of the sixteenth century Spanish mystic St John of the Cross also illustrates the notion that mysticism begins with the contemplation of nature and the discovery of the reality that stands behind and beyond the world. It was this inexorably attractive mystery that "lit and led" St John to the profound "presence" that stands at the core of everything.

So, in a way, this book is an attempt to restate a kind of natural theology within a new context. It moves well beyond the argument from design formulated in the late eighteenth century by the Anglican divine William Paley, which resulted in a limited natural theology that eventually either drove God totally from the world or devolved into pantheism. My aim is to take the natural world seriously as the primal revelation of God and, working from that, to try to find what we can discover of the transcendent from this world.

In all of this we have one thing going for us. As human beings we have a unique ability: we can see ourselves in perspective. Alone of all creatures we can comprehend our context; we can reflect upon ourselves within the parameters of history and culture and sketch the borders that create our world and environment. This possibility has greatly expanded recently as our knowledge of history (cosmic, biological, and human), science, technology, psychology, and culture have increased. Though most of us judge reality from the narrow, parochial experience of our individual lives and cultures, yet the stark environmental choices that confront us at the end of the twentieth century are beginning to press us to see ourselves in this wider context as never before. For our human species is facing a series of decisions, both locally and on a world-wide scale, that will require that rare ability to see ourselves in a broad historical and scientific perspective.

Our modern crisis is both cultural and environmental. It is widely agreed that profound historical shifts are occurring now as the old political, cultural, and economic hegemony of western Europe retreats increasingly back into itself. Within the broad sweep of decolonization and an emerging world culture, we are seeing the development of new constellations of power and influence based on either geography (such as Africa and Latin America) or religious ideology (as in the revival of Islam and the emergence of fundamentalism in all the great faiths). The emergence of fundamentalism across the whole religious spectrum is one of the most frightening aspects of the contemporary world. This primitive religiosity is the antithesis of everything that I will argue in this book. Religious fundamentalism, of any kind, is a profoundly destructive expression of human existence.

But it is not with the geopolitical issues, or even with cultural issues, that I am primarily concerned. My interest is explicitly environmental and ultimately religious. Issues associated with ecology and religion/spirituality have already emerged as pivotal factors in the type of new world that is in the process of emerging. But given the increased rate of destruction of the natural world and the increase in world population, one thing is clear: unless human attitudes and ethical values change, and change quickly in all societies, the natural, environmental, and religious context of the "new world" will be bleak indeed.

It is an illusion to hope that people will just "change." Human beings need intellectual convictions, ethical structures and a fundamentally religious motivation for lasting and far-reaching adjustment to occur. Contemporary ecology is not just talking about tinkering with the edges; it demands a deep-seated shift of attitude, akin to a conversion. This is where religion has a pivotal role to play.

Here I should declare my hand right from the start. It is my view that the underlying theological substratum of Catholic Christianity is probably one of the best placed religious systems in the contemporary world from within which to develop a coherent environmental theology and ethic. Its strength lies, paradoxically, in its notion of tradition. This refers to the idea that Catholic theology and teaching can develop and evolve within a broad interpretation of the parameters of biblical revelation and the church's on-going articulation of its experience of itself and its beliefs in interaction with the world around it. Certainly, as I will admit in detail later in the book, Catholic Christianity has a bad track record in terms of dealing with the natural world. But inherent in Catholic theology is the idea of the evolution and development of doctrine, and, among Catholics in touch with the genuine tradition, there is a unique openness to cultural and historical experience. It is in the interaction between this sense of continuity and the sense of contemporary culture that Catholic Christianity can be most creative. It is far less rigidly tied to an unchanging biblical word than are the more evangelical elements of Protestant Christianity. I will develop these issues in more detail in later chapters.

What I have tried to do in this book is to provide, within a brief compass, a context within which we can begin to look at environmental and religious questions more creatively. I also want to try to articulate some theological principles upon which a practical set of environmental ethics can be based. At the deepest level we need to undergo a form of conversion so that old attitudes can be changed and outdated ideologies jettisoned. Many people feel that the odds against this happening are too high and that it will be impossible to achieve the necessary changes in time to save much of the threatened environment and the many species that are now in danger. There is much to support that view. Often despair seems justified as the facts of on-going contemporary environmental destruction are spelled out and the powerful nature of the forces arrayed against a change of relationship to the natural world are realized.

Even so, we should remember that despair is not necessarily coterminous with surrender. Already an enormous amount has been achieved. Even the most reactionary and pro-development governments have at least felt the need to dress up their policies in environmental rhetoric. Again this is where theology and spirituality step in: the virtue of hope is nothing more than the ability to imagine something different. In this instance, it is the passionate determination to achieve that difference even against governments and the power of the pro-development lobby. So if this book is about anything, it is about hope. If we have this, there is a possibility that we will be able to save something of the natural world for the future. Without it, the descent into the absolute madness of a purely human monoculture is inevitable.

Are We the Center of Everything?

Humankind, religion, and environmental destruction

As the heirs of Freud, Jung and modern psychology, our age is characterized above all by a peculiar self-consciousness. We are aware of ourselves and aware of the superficial levels of our inner lives to a degree that far exceeds the self-absorption of previous centuries. By this I do not mean that we are particularly wise, or have greater insight, or are necessarily more spiritually conscious than the people of the past. It is just that we are engrossed in ourselves and in our inner processes in a way that previous ages never were. We turn to psychologists, psychiatrists, and therapists to give us insight into the meaning of our perceived inner experiences in the way that previous ages turned to sages, gurus, and priests. But our self-absorbed individualism often cuts us off from the wider human and natural worlds that could give a more helpful context to sort out our inner tangle.

Psychology and self-absorption are both a blessing and a curse. They are a curse in the sense that they encourage us, both as individuals and as a community, to confirm the illusion that we are the center of everything. They tell us that the world revolves around us and that everything derives its ultimate meaning and purpose from us and our needs. It is natural, of course, to focus attention on ourselves and on our species. But our modern self-consciousness is often so subjective and so focused on the self that it loses perspective on everything else. The individual becomes his or her own reference point; all else is subsumed to the needs of the self. This sense of assumed superiority over every other living thing feeds our arrogance and self-importance.

But our self-consciousness and psychological knowledge are also a blessing in the sense that they bestow uniquely upon us the ability to stand back and see ourselves in perspective in a way that previous generations never had been able to achieve. The fact that we have a broad historical knowledge also gives us access to a perspective that previous generations never had. The fact that few people ever use it does not mean that it is not there. Our sense of context gives us the facility to begin to see ourselves as other people and the rest of reality experience us. This is obvious enough in the case of other human beings, but when applied to ourselves it is painful: there is nothing more searing than that moment of truth when we finally see ourselves as others have seen us for probably much longer than we care to think.

But by helping us to place ourselves in the perspective of the rest of reality, self-consciousness enables us to discover the humiliating truth that the entire world does not revolve around us as human beings, and never has. The moment of recognition comes when we realize that for almost all of geological history humankind has not existed and has thus been irrelevant to all of the rest of cosmic life (except, of course, that just recently we have become the world's most acute and intractable problem). We begin to see ourselves not just as other people see us, but as all the other species of the natural world view us. We suddenly find ourselves in a broad cosmic perspective. In religious, and especially Christian terms, this recognition of our real place in the whole scheme of things provides a chance for "metanoia"—a dramatic moment of humility and of possible conversion.

For me this moment of insight came one evening some years ago watching television. The program was one of those glorious nature documentaries which have done so much to change attitudes to the environment and nature—television has an immediate visual impact that gives the viewer a sense of intimacy with living realities that is hard to ignore. (In fact, color television has become one of the most potent influences in helping to advance the environmental movement. We do not just hear or read about seal pups being clubbed to death in Labrador or dead dolphins being caught in Japanese and Taiwanese driftnets; we can actually see it happening.)

The particular program that brought me to the moment of truth about the real place of human beings in natural history was about the Antarctic and featured a segment showing the life patterns of Weddell seals. These seals inhabit the borders of Antarctica and the surrounding islands and are named after the Weddell Sea, a vast ice-filled Antarctic bay situated to the south of the Patagonian part of continental Latin America. It suddenly struck me, watching the film, that Weddell seals existed in Antarctica for aeons before homo sapiens evolved and up until very recently were unknown to and totally independent of humankind. They have lived in Antarctica perfectly adapted to the environment and entirely for their own sake.[1] For the totality of human evolutionary history, our existence has borne absolutely no relationship to theirs. Until, of course, humankind arrived in the southern oceans, firstly as sealers in the nineteenth century to kill and exploit them, and then, in the more environmentally "sensitive" late twentieth century, to study and film them.

The Antarctic and Southern Oceans and the species that inhabit them are now reasonably safe in the short term from exploitation and development because of recent international agreements and the declaration of a whale sanctuary. But the isolation of the Weddell seals has gone forever because their environment and existence have now been inextricably linked to our insatiable curiosity and our need to know and dominate everything. It is this restless search to know and to control which has driven us literally to the ends of the earth and out into space. As soon as humankind entered the Antarctic scene, the equation changed for the Weddell seals. Their continued existence now depends upon us and our decisions. Their long independent life-cycle is now subject to the variables built into the processes of human cupidity and greed, as well as to our good will and environmental and ethical responsibility.

Our complete modern dominance over all forms of life, and even over the structures of the earth itself, has led to the development of a contemporary anthropocentrism unique in both biological and human history. As Timothy Weiskel says: "We seek feverishly to meddle with ecological processes and to channel the entopic flow of energy to our own intentions as if the entire handiwork of creation were put in place simply for human needs."[2] The notion that the world exists for us and that the whole of cosmic reality is focused on us is usually traced back to the humanist philosophy of the Renaissance. But according to the American Catholic environmental thinker Thomas Berry, the whole earth has been dominated ever since neolithic times by what he calls "exploitative anthropocentrism."

Anthropocentrism and its results

"Anthropocentrism" refers to our focus on the human and the belief that we are the final purpose of the cosmos. It is the unconscious assumption that the earth exists simply for humankind and that its total meaning and entire value is derived from us. Berry believes that anthropocentrism is rooted in "our failure to think of ourselves as a species" like other species, interconnected with and biologically interdependent upon the rest of reality.[3] Instead, we think of ourselves largely in ethnic, cultural, linguistic, or economic terms, and see all other reality as existing simply to satisfy us and fulfill our needs. Putting anthropocentrism another way, we take ourselves and our needs as the focus, norm, and final arbiter of all that exists. It was the Weddell seals that evening on television that helped me to see the falsity of this anthropocentric assumption!

What is the result of our anthropocentrism? We are facing cataclysmic problems. The earth is dying at an ever-quickening rate. What Berry calls the "slaughter of the innocents" is occurring as animals and plants are simply wiped out; not just individuals, but whole species are becoming extinct at an ever-faster rate. "Between fifteen and twenty per cent of all species will become extinct by the year 2000."[4] The key issue in the loss of species is the destruction of tropical rainforest. Rainforests are being destroyed at the rate of the area of England every year in Latin America, West Africa, the Philippines, Malaysia, Brunei, Sarawak, Papua New Guinea, the Pacific Islands, and Australia. About eleven million hectares (twenty-seven million acres) are disappearing each year.[5] By 2020 all the major rainforests will be gone except those in the west Amazon and west Africa. With the continuing loss of habitat, thousands of species of animals, birds, plants, and insects face extinction. The whole diversity of life— which has taken billions of years to establish—is threatened in a brief period of fifty years. But we are completely blinded to the sheer enormity of our contemporary destructiveness.

It is significant that environmental destruction has accelerated remarkably since the end of the Second World War in 1945. Part of this is due to an enormous increase in population pressures, but the most important component in this acceleration is the vast increase in the use of energy and raw material resources in the developed countries. This is also the period when petro-chemicals have been used on a much vaster scale, with little regard for the consequences for the natural environment.[6] While this increase has been amply documented in economic and social terms, it has hardly ever been commented on in historical terms. In the five decades between 1945 and 1995, human consumption of resources has increased at a staggering rate. There is simply no comparison in previous history. It is not the two world wars that have been the most destructive events ever experienced. It has been the developmental binge of the last fifty years. Even in human terms this has only benefited a tiny proportion of rich people. For the non-human world, it has meant widespread destruction and extinction.

But the earth is beginning to respond to our barbarism. The hole in the ozone layer is exposing people in the southern hemisphere to the dangers of ultraviolet radiation. While there is debate about the exact nature and results of the greenhouse effect, there is certainly ample evidence to show considerable climate change over the last decade. The cause is summed up by *One Earth One Future*: "The rising concentration of greenhouse gases in the atmosphere are [*sic*] a direct response to our actions as we conduct our lives, drive our vehicles, grow our food and run our industries."[7] This change affects local environmental regions that cross international borders. For instance, there is evidence that Indonesian destruction of rainforest in West Irian (Western New Guinea) is already changing the rainfall pattern over northern Australia. Some people maintain that the copper sulphate pollution of the Fly River in Papua New Guinea by the Ok Tedi mine is now threatening the Gulf of Papua, and possibly also that wonder of the natural world, the Great Barrier Reef. Environmental issues are rarely local. Droughts and recurrent starvation in Africa, acid rain and the biological death of thousands of lakes throughout Canada, the leaching, salination, and degradation of Australian soil —all these are the results of human decisions and human actions, sometimes decisions taken in other countries.

Australia is a very good example. It is a dry country, but in the south-east corner of the continent there is a marvelous network of rivers—the Murray–Darling system. These rivers have already been partially devastated by human intervention in their natural flow by damming for irrigation. But in 1992–93 there was an epidemic of blue-green algae that for a period destroyed the life-systems of the rivers. This algal outbreak was the direct result of run-off from agricultural chemicals and cattle waste and the use of the river system as a sewer by the towns that abut it. Thus human action has threatened the destruction of the most extensive river system on the driest continent on earth.

But there are other tangible consequences of our destructive behavior. Thomas Berry puts it bluntly:

> We are the generation when the day of reckoning has come. In this disintegrating phase of our industrial society we see

ourselves not as the splendour of creation but ... the most pernicious mode of earthly being. We are the termination, not the fulfilment of the earth process ... We are the affliction of the world, its demonic presence. We are the violation of the earth's most sacred aspects.[8]

Even allowing for a degree of prophetic hyperbole, the truth of Berry's statement is becoming progressively obvious to those who break out of the autism that blinds so many people today and who honestly face the consequences of environmental degradation.

The failure of contemporary culture

Human beings are the sole cause of our modern environmental crisis. Prior to human intervention, living realities existed in a dynamic and ever-changing balance with each other. Certainly, in the geological past, many extinctions occurred naturally and dramatic events could disturb this balance, but modern human intervention has created an increasingly unnatural and massive dislocation in the world's ecological systems. The modern philosophical basis for this dislocation goes back to the French philosopher Rene Descartes (1596–1650), who split off mind/spirit from the material world, which he defined in purely mechanistic terms. Over time the human ability to exploit and manipulate the natural world has escalated, especially since the beginning of the eighteenth century when the development of science and technology dramatically increased our capacity to interfere with living processes. In addition to this, the incremental growth of the human population over the last few centuries has enormously increased pressure on all natural systems. The problems for the environment begin when we intervene, usually to exploit the animals, plants, or the earth itself for our own advantage. As the most manipulative of all living species, we seem unable to leave anything alone or untouched.

What is the origin of the modern attitude toward the world? At one level, it is rooted in the restless inquisitiveness and self-aggrandizement of the modern western European spirit. This restlessness has come to the fore especially over the last four hundred years. While most pre-modern people (and most contemporary indigenous people) have less sense of a conscious and highly defined individuality and retain a deep sense of their oneness with nature, modern western people exist to an increasing extent in an alienated individualism that is often characterized by a sharp dichotomy between the self and everything else. It is this individualism that has led to an inquisitiveness that is expressed through exploration and the desire to know how the natural world and everything else works. It has also led to an acquisitiveness whereby only ownership, control, and consumption will satisfy our lusts.

Yet paradoxically, many people today seem to feel that they have less and less control over their own lives. Theodore Roszak says correctly that our contemporaries feel that they face a vacuum, when they are confronted with the question of the meaning of existence. Roszak says that secular society has excluded the religious and spiritual responses to the existential vacuum, and the members of the so-called "helping professions" (such as social work, medicine and psychotherapy) have little or nothing to offer. The same is true of that other source of meaning in our society, science. "Both science and technology," writes Roszak, "move toward esotericism and professional exclusiveness," and these exclude most people. When pushed to provide a deeper ethical and metaphysical *meaning* structure, scientists abandon the quest and simply opt out. The result is that our society has "entered an intellectual vacuum."[9]

Many of our contemporaries fill this intellectual vacuum with a kind of absolutization of the technology which increasingly dominates our lives. The problem is that technology further distances us from the natural world. The philosopher Martin Heidegger has pointed out that technology is now so pervasive in our culture that it is part of the very horizon and structure of our being. Fortunately, not all contemporary scientists are dominated by this technocratic attitude. One of the most hopeful elements of the contemporary intellectual dialogue is the willingness of a few scientists to face ultimate questions and to enter into discussion with theologians. One of the pioneers of this is the Australian biologist and religious thinker Charles Birch, whose thought will be examined more closely in Chapter 3.

However, despite these provocative new scientific and religious approaches, the old view still predominates: nature is secularized as an object to be used and exploited rather than a reality to be respected and reverenced. As a result of the prevailing sense of individualism and alienation among so many in our culture, communal values and a personal sense of belonging to and contributing toward society and the wider world are increasingly lacking. Sadly, the atomized self has become the norm for most people. One sees this vividly expressed in modern western art, where alienation and ugly and arcane individualism are dominant themes. Rarely is there any coherent attempt by artists to communicate; lacking any broad, let alone universal values, their works are generally an expression of pure subjectivism.

The movement toward this type of atomized individualism has been loosely characterized as "post-modernism." Symptomatic of post-modernism is the denial of the possibility of universal claims or ideas, or of the general applicability of moral or artistic norms and canons of taste, at least within a specific culture. For post-modern deconstructionists there can be no "meta-narratives," as they call them. All that is possible are subjective, parochial visions that characterize particular groups of people and individuals and their specific experiences. Post-modernism expresses itself most vividly in contemporary art and culture through the abandonment of broader, universal values and ideals and the loss of a sense of genuine reverence.

It is especially striking that post-modernism lacks any sense of the sacred. Instead, it emphasizes the centrality of the personal and subjective and levels all experience as though everything were of equal value. At its crudest, it can be said that in this scheme of things Mozart and pop music are equal in value in that they are judged by the same subjective canons of taste, the value of each being determined by the personal value structure of each individual. The post-modernist excludes the possibility of discerning a cultural norm by which subjective judgments can be contextualized over against broader, accepted canons of taste. In a sense, the modern "yuppie" is an archetypal post-modernist: materialistic, subjective, and self-engrossed. While there are signs that post-modernist orthodoxy is beginning to be questioned from within the cultural elite itself, it is still the predominant view in many universities in the western world and in a significant number of cultural organizations.

A related narcissistic trend can be seen vividly (and more crudely) in the self-improvement movement and in many aspects of "new age" religion. Here again the preoccupation is with the individual and the enhancement of so-called "personal potential." The underlying cause of the growth of the new age movement has much more to do with the profound historical crisis that is affecting our culture than with the so-called discovery of "new ways" of being religious:

> The new age is a *fin d'epoque* phenomenon. Something similar usually appears as historical epochs draw to a close. This explains the apocalyptic manifestations of the new age. An intellectual crisis is usually characteristic of the end of an historical era. As the old orthodoxy breaks down and the old certainties disintegrate, there is an abandonment of coherent thought—in our age represented by the eighteenth century enlightenment. Thus the way is left open for the non-rational alternatives simmering under the surface.[10]

As our traditional and contemporary meaning structures increasingly break down, the seething, unconscious, irrational underbelly of our culture rises to the surface. In our rationalistic and technocratic culture, it is inevitable that the underbelly will be profoundly anti-intellectual. The new age movement is profoundly imbued with anti-intellectualism.

Ironically, a benign ecological attitude is often seen as a major characteristic of the new age. But there are elements in new ageism that are totally antithetical to environmentalism. New agers often emphasize the "spiritual" at the expense of the material world. They talk of the "spiritual oneness" of all reality, but by focusing on this the new age loses all sense of individuality and difference, "all that makes the complex biological web of life interesting."[11] It is our care for individual species and places that helps us focus energy on specific environmental issues. Hard, proactive work to defend specific places and species is much more helpful to genuine environmental sustainability than vague talk of "spiritual oneness." Furthermore, the tendency to split "spirit" from "body" in many elements within new ageism is simply a restatement of the dualism that has infected the western tradition for so long. It is antithetical to a sound ecological approach.

In fact, both the terms "post-modernism" and the "new age" are probably ironic misnomers, because western culture still has a long way to go before it breaks down totally and jettisons the major elements of modernity. We actually live in a difficult age of transition. I have argued elsewhere that the so-called new age is really symptomatic of the tag end of the old *zeitgeist*, rather than a harbinger of the new.[12] The same is true of post-modernism; as the term actually implies, it is a symptom of the decline of the old modernist culture rather than a sign of the emergence of anything specifically new.[13]

The European origins of the myth and dream of development

Historically, we do not really live in "postmodernity" at all, but actually in an awkward interim stage between modernity and what is yet to come. Modernity, the roots of which go back to Renaissance humanism, the philosophy of Descartes, the scientific revolution, the eighteenth century Enlightenment, and the liberal, bourgeois culture of the nineteenth century, was and continues to be marked by four significant characteristics: a commitment to a passionate, almost irrational belief in the myth of progress; the relegation of religion to the sphere of the private and personal; a focus on the importance and the rights of the individual; and a commitment to a rationalistic and technocratic understanding of life. The industrial society that we inherited with modernity was built on the notion of unending progress, an idea that came into its own in the bourgeois, liberal, commercial and intellectual culture of the mid-nineteenth century, even though its roots go back much further to Calvinistic puritanism and the Protestant ethic.

It is a good rule of thumb never to expect consistency in historical and cultural processes, and that is certainly true of the modern era. While the majority of modernism's most obvious characteristics seem reasonable and rational, they are actually based, as cultural presuppositions usually are, on myth and unquestioned belief about the place of humans in relationship to the rest of reality. For instance, the paradox of modern so-called "rationalist economics" is that it is largely the product of a nineteenth century myth—the *myth of progress*.

At the core of this myth is the belief that the historical forces of liberalism and capitalist individualism that had carried European culture and the industrial revolution forward since the eighteenth century would lead onwards to an ever-fuller life. The belief was based on the presumed limitless super-abundance of the earth and the expectation that this would continue into the foreseeable future. It was underpinned by Darwin's theory of evolution (itself a product of the mid-nineteenth century), and it held that science, technology, and capitalism would lead the European countries—especially Britain—toward material happiness and perfection. Paradoxically, the myth of progress is both materialist and utopian—as is Marxist utopian materialism. For the last century and a half, these two intertwined myths have dominated western thinking and strategic, political, and social arrangements. Both myths have been environmentally destructive on a massive scale. Because these myths are based on the same presuppositions and emerge from the same historical matrix, there is probably a close link between their rise and their fall. We have already seen the collapse of Marxism in the old Soviet Union. Serious questions also have to be asked about the future of capitalism.

This European dream of limitless resources has had disastrous consequences in the new worlds of North and South America and Australia. In Australia, for instance, the myth of unlimited development inspired the white Anglo-Celtic settlers to explore and settle the land and to "conquer the wilderness"—and, in the process to destroy seventy-five per cent of the rainforests (which, despite all evidence of damage already done, *continue* to be logged for export wood-chips). It also drove to the edge of extinction (and in some cases into actual extinction) many unique native species of flora and fauna. It degraded much of the land surface and bred attitudes of contempt that led to the dispossession and widespread massacre of the Aborigines.

In fact, the appalling frontier history of Australia is starting to emerge through the work of historians such as C.D. Rowley, Noel Butlin, Henry Reynolds, and more recently Roger Milliss.[14] Butlin has shown that white settlement was disastrous for Aboriginal populations: by 1850 the black population of eastern Australia had declined through disease and massacre to approximately four per cent of the 1788 figure of about one quarter of a million people.[15] Milliss' account of the 1838 Australia Day massacre of about 300 Aborigines near Millie (about fifty kilometres from present-day Moree) by the New South Wales Mounted Police and convict stockmen, and the total failure to punish those responsible (despite the British government's official policy of protection for the Aborigines), demonstrated the ruthlessness and influence of the white squatters and agricultural companies in their determination to hold the land that they had unjustly seized from the original inhabitants.[16] At best, the Aborigines were seen by whites as unfortunate obstacles to the expansion of "civilization," and, at worst, as mere pests to be exterminated like the local fauna.

27

It was the dream of "development" that drove the whites on, however unconsciously. The white men who explored and "overlanded" cattle and sheep into the traditional lands of the Aborigines were seen by most of their contemporaries as the agents of civilization and progress. Describing the archetypal overlander in 1842, the explorer George Grey referred to his activities as:

> [touching] with the wizard wand of commerce a lone and trackless forest, and at his bidding, cities arise, and the hum and dust of trade collect—away are swept the ancient races ... The ruder languages disappear successively, and the tongue of England alone is heard around.[17]

Embedded in Grey's attitude is the assumption that the "lone and trackless forest" had no value in itself until "the cities arise and the hum and dust of trade collect." However, it is worth noticing here that at least one contemporary witness saw the overland cattlemen in a very different light. In 1841, the Catholic priest William Ullathorne referred to them as nothing more than "brutal cattle drivers" who had shot the local Aborigines, taken their land and had literally got away with murder.[18]

In the United States a similar development occurred. The parallel with the cowboy tradition is clear. The seventeenth-century Protestant quest for the establishment of the "new Jerusalem" in North America was secularized in the nineteenth century to become, in the words of historian Frederick Jackson Turner, America's "manifest destiny." The tangible result of both the religious and secular theories of destiny was the constant westward expansion of the frontier of the United States and the consequent destruction of the traditional lives of the native North Americans. By 1890, having destroyed the last vestiges of Indian resistance—of which the massacre of Native Americans at Wounded Knee, South Dakota, was the symbol—the white, Protestant occupiers felt that America's destiny had now shifted to the task of Americanizing and Protestantizing the world.

While the Protestant aspect of manifest destiny was quickly

replaced in the national psyche by the secular myth of "democracy," the United States has never really abandoned the task of "Americanizing" the world. It is achieved in our time through the electronic media, especially television. Modern mass communication technology has vastly increased the number of channels of potential intrusion. Satellites and fibre optics have created a situation in which a couple of hundred TV channels (and even more radio channels) will be available to private homes all over the world. The focus of most of these channels will be narrow (for example, specific types of sport, rock videos, films, fundamentalist religion, or news), and this "narrow-casting" will become even more focused as more channels become available. The source of most of this material is and will continue to be the United States. Unless measures are taken to counter this, American popular cultural hegemony will literally reach to the ends of the earth.

So the myth of development and its racial concomitants lives on. Today its focus has shifted, via the agency of institutions such as the World Bank, to the third world, where exploitation of resources and giant schemes of development (such as dams) have impoverished whole populations and degraded and destroyed vast regions of the natural environment.

In the last decade, however, the myth has finally started to be questioned. In fact, our contemporary culture is being forced to turn away from this crude nineteenth-century commercial and economic value system (a system that the Australian historian C.M.H. Clark has called "the mentality of the counting house") by its sheer cost to the natural world and by its destructive exploitation of so many of the world's indigenous peoples. Ironically, as we begin to leave behind the myths of the nineteenth century, modern western people are being forced by their own spiritual needs to attempt to rediscover the human meaning and significance of what our forebears condescendingly called "the lone and trackless forest." The problem is that, because of the destructive mentality of "the counting house," there is less and less of the trackless forest left.

29

The cult of limitless progress

The roots of the modern myth of progress emerge from several sources. Remotely, they can be found in the Judeo-Christian apocalyptic notion of cosmic and human history as a constant progression toward the fulfillment of all reality in God. Tied up with this is the idea that the rest of reality derives its meaning, structure, and purpose from its connection to humankind and its destiny. Most Jewish and Christian commentators have interpreted the Bible to say that it is humankind alone that is the image of God. With no apparent symbolic value and direct relationship to the divine, the rest of the animate and inanimate world is left to attain whatever worth its use or connection with the destiny of humankind might bestow upon it.

More proximately, the origin of the myth of progress is to be found in the scientific revolution of the seventeenth century. This was the age when, as English historian Geoffrey Barraclough says, "technological progress, introducing a new spirit of inquiry into all branches of knowledge, led with revolutionary suddenness to the perfection and dissemination of a new cosmology and a new outlook on the world."[19] Barraclough is right: the notion of unlimited development and the subsequent myth of unending progress is a *cosmology*. In other words, it is a myth based on a philosophical understanding of the nature of the world and our place in it. Cosmology—the way in which we image the cosmos and our relationship to it—is central to both individual and cultural self-definition.

The cosmology of the modern age of development is both anthropocentric and materialistic, and profoundly underpinned by Darwinian notions of the evolutionary spiral toward ever-greater complexity and perfection. The mythic and religious status of evolutionary developmentalism is made clear by Herbert Spencer, Darwin's immediate predecessor as an evolutionary theorist. With the lack of self-doubt so characteristic of a number of Victorian thinkers, he argued: "Progress, therefore, is not an accident, but a necessity ... As surely as ... evil and immorality disappear; so surely must man become perfect."[20] For Spencer, Europeans, and specifically British males, were the human ideal and norm by which other peoples, such as the Australian Aborigines and the Native Americans, were to be judged. Embedded in this view was an unashamed racism, vividly expressed in the concept of "the white man's burden" whereby the presumed blessings of European culture were to be brought to the world. Certainly, there were some blessings in colonialism; but they were very mixed blessings!

The liberal notion of development also integrated an important element from the eighteenth-century Enlightenment: the idea that the decisive characteristic that distinguished civilized European humankind was reason. "Reason is the faculty that enables one generation to learn from another; it permits the accumulation of knowledge and is thus the postulate behind the idea of perfectibility."[21] The idea of evolutionary perfectibility and the cult of limitless development became the dominant mode of thought in western culture in the late nineteenth century and continued for much of the twentieth century. The myth was spread over the last 150 years in countries like North America and Australia through universal, secular education.

Barraclough stresses that the notion of progress did not really take over as the predominant western ideology until the immense advances in science and technology in the middle of the nineteenth century. He argues that the turning point was London's Great Exhibition of 1851. A similar exhibition was held in Paris in 1855. In subsequent years international exhibitions became popular theaters for the ideas of progress and economic nationalism. Not to be outdone, Melbourne was host to a great Centennial Exhibition in 1888. The theme of historical progress was taken up by historians of the liberal Whig tradition and found full expression in J.B. Bury's *The Idea of Progress* (1920), H.G. Wells' *Outline of History* (1920) (although Wells was later to descend into pessimism about the possibility of the perfectibility of humankind), and the interesting but largely forgotten Australian archeologist and historical theorist,

V. Gordon Childe, who wrote *What Happened in History?* in 1942.[22]

The Christian churches did not deal well with the challenge of modernity in the nineteenth century. As the theological response to the new critical understanding of the Bible and Darwin's *Origin of Species* (1859) showed, the reaction of the Church of England and of Protestants generally was either to retire into the high church traditionalism of aspects of the Oxford movement, or into the biblical literalism of many of the evangelicals. In both cases the evolutionary world-view was decisively rejected through a retreat into the attitudes of the past.

The Roman church was even more complete than the Anglicans and Protestants in its rejection of "the spirit of the age" of liberal modernity, as the *Syllabus of Errors* (1864) and moves toward papal centralism and the declaration of papal primacy and infallibility in 1870 demonstrated. In the *Syllabus* Pope Pius IX explicitly refused to "reconcile himself with progress, liberalism and with modern civilization."[23] The Roman church turned in on itself in an almost sectarian manner. Nineteenth-century Catholic theology revived the medieval notion of the church as a "perfect society," complete and self-sufficient in itself with nothing to learn from the world. To a limited extent both Popes Leo XIII and Benedict XV tried to break out of this mold, but it was not until Pope John XXIII and the Second Vatican Council in the 1960s that the Catholic Church began to admit that it was not totally self-sufficient and that it had something to learn from the world. With the advent of Pope John Paul II some elements in the Catholic Church have progressively regressed to a hard-nosed insistence on doctrinal integrity, somewhat like the anti-modernist attitude of Pope Pius X at the beginning of the twentieth century.

In sharp contrast to these repressive responses, some of the liberal Protestants and a few Catholic scholars (such as Alfred Loisy) became compromised by the spirit of contemporary liberalism and lost their critical edge. Those Christians who did try to steer a middle path between obscurantism and the uncritical acceptance of the modern age were usually rejected by their own churches. This, for instance, was the fate of moderate Catholic modernists such as the Dublin-born Jesuit George Tyrrell. It is only since the Second Vatican Council (1962–65) that modern Catholicism has institutionally attempted to come to grips with the modern world.

In our own age a key element in getting religion to face contemporary reality involves a response to the the modern ecological crisis. Nevertheless, there seems to be a fear-filled fundamentalism sweeping across all of the mainstream Christian churches at the present moment.

Environmentalism versus development?

It is certainly unusual for the captains of industry to put themselves forward as the defenders of western civilization and culture. But that is the role in which the Australian Hugh Morgan, managing director of the Western Mining Corporation, has cast himself. In a newspaper article[24] he describes himself as defending civilization as we know it against a demonic force which has replaced communism as a major threat to the economic prosperity of the west. He makes it clear that he considers that "economic prosperity" is coterminous with social stability and the maintenance of the cultural fabric of western society.

Environmentalism, Morgan says, is now the main threat to western capitalism—and, as a consequence, to western civilization. He argues that ecology is "a religious movement of the most primitive kind, nature worship, coupled with extreme distaste for the human race which in a short space of time has established a dominant position among a powerful and influential group in Western society." He identifies this group as the "chattering class," the talkers and intellectuals, who, he says, "staff the media, the education industry, the churches and has very great influence in our political parties ... bureaucracies and industry." He credits the greens with extraordinary potency: "Contemporary environmentalism, in its pure form, is as radical and uncompromising an attack on the entire structure of Western society as can be imagined."

Paradoxically, Thomas Berry actually agrees with Morgan concerning the seriousness and centrality of the ecological issue:

> Ecology can rightly be considered the supreme subversive science. In responding to the external situation and to the imperatives of our own nature, these ecological movements are threatening all those cultural commitments that have brought about the present devastation of the earth. This rising conflict is beginning to dominate every aspect of the human process.[25]

Both have rightly discerned that the developmental myth is the central issue in contemporary culture, but from very different perspectives and with radically opposed conclusions.

Morgan argues that at the heart of environmental theory is profound opposition to building things. Speaking of the desire to build, he says:

> It is a very important part of the Western tradition, which is based on classical Greek values and on the Old and New Testaments, to want to build things—great cathedrals, opera houses, magnificent bridges, railway stations, even large dump trucks and front end loaders. These things are the result of carrying out the injunction given in the first chapter of Genesis, verse 28, to: "Be fruitful and multiply and replenish the earth and subdue it".

One week after Morgan's article, the very same newspaper was reporting the break-up of the supertanker *Brear*, pouring 85 million litres of crude oil into the North Sea and onto the southern coast of the Shetland Islands. A ship that industrial developers had built and maintained (apparently inadequately) to transport the results of the exploitation of nature (apparently dangerously) had repeated the destructive consequences of the *Exxon Valdez* which had polluted a section of the pristine coast of

Alaska just a few years before with horrendous consequences. Clearly, in both cases things had gone badly wrong with the constructed products of industrial and technological culture, and the environment (as well as the people and life systems of both the Shetland Islands and Alaska) would be suffering the results of these disasters for a long time to come.

While most environmentalists would be amused at Morgan's caricature of them as "chatterers," and certainly many church people would be surprised to learn that the greens had taken over the religious communities, it is very significant that Morgan quotes the Genesis text about "subduing the earth." He clearly casts the environmental "threat" to western culture in religious and apocalyptic terms. As we shall see, the issues surrounding this biblical text are a lot more complicated than he suggests, but it is fascinating that Morgan casts the whole question of developmental capitalism versus environmentalism in direct theological terms.

And to this extent I agree with him: the issue is profoundly religious, and what is at stake here is the role of humanity and the nature of our relationship with the rest of creation. Many in industry and government would certainly not agree with Morgan's extremism and would attempt to argue that "sustainable development" is possible. But Morgan is actually more honest; he does at least highlight the fact that western culture today faces a stark choice between the ethos of development and the ethos of conservation. While the compromise of "sustainable development" is appealing to many in government because it gives politicians the chance to keep the majority of electors on side, it is, like all attempts to back away from hard choices, doomed to failure.

But we should not fool ourselves that to choose the ethos of conservation will be easy. It will require a profound shift in western cultural consciousness which can only be achieved by a form of religious conversion. Ultimately, environmentalism is profoundly connected to the nature of our existence in the world, and it does face us with a stark choice about who we are and why we live. Fundamentally it is about religion and ethics.

How are the world's religions going to respond to the new ecology?

Despite the clear religious overtones of the contemporary environmental crisis, so far the great religious traditions have really done very little to respond to this issue. As the June 1992 United Nations Summit on the Environment, held in Rio de Janeiro, showed vividly, environmental problems are world-wide, but because of narrow nationalism and political expediency, it is almost impossible to get a world-wide response. Similarly, the great world religions are crippled in their response to the environmental crisis by their narrowness and particularity, their isolation and insistence on self-definition. This is not to say that nothing is happening among some religious people but to this point, none of the world religions seems to have clearly recognized the profound crisis we face and to have drawn upon and creatively developed their traditions to confront the issue. All still seem immersed in their intra-mural issues. This is vividly illustrated by the attitude of Pope John Paul II, leader of the world's largest religious community, who treats the environmental issue as quite peripheral to the "real ethical issues," which according to him center around "human dignity."

The major limitation of most contemporary religion is that it starts in the wrong place. Before looking for what they have in common, religious people usually move quickly to define themselves by their obvious differences: "I'm a Muslim, I'm a Christian, I'm a Buddhist, I'm an Anglican, I'm a Catholic, I'm Jewish, I'm a Hindu, I'm an Evangelical, I'm this, I'm that." Even the most irenical believers seem to begin any discussion by describing their unique and differentiating characteristics. This is a very human way to act; we all want to define ourselves and our personalities in relationship to others, and so specific differences seem far more important than the religious search itself. Yet the most mature religious and spiritual people in our world are always profoundly ecumenical: Thomas Merton, for example, who reached out to other forms of monasticism at the end of his life; or Mahatma Gandhi, who acknowledged the diverse religious sources of his inspiration; or great spiritual teachers like the extraordinary Englishwoman Evelyn Underhill.

The most important spiritual task of today's world is to find what the great religions have in common, not what separates them. For the contemporary world needs to harness the common insights that focus religious and spiritual energy on the enormous problems facing our world, rather than dissipating religious power through the definition of difference. The environmental problems of the contemporary world have the potential to unite the diverse religious traditions in confronting a common issue at the experiential level. As I will point out later, the sharing of a common cosmology might be a way of discovering a united approach, not only to environmentalism, but to the other important issues that face both humankind and the cosmos.

It is rare for the religious communities to come to grips with the key, underlying environmental problem—anthropocentrism. Christianity and most of the other great world religions are deeply focused on humankind. At the core of the belief of most of them is the question of the value of humankind and the purpose and meaning of human existence. There is also a failure to recognize the profound and ongoing influence that Christian dualism has introduced into the western cultural tradition. Dualism is the splitting of soul from body, spirit from flesh. In dualism human beings are seen as composites—a body enlivened by a soul. And it is always the spiritual side that is valued at the expense of the physical. As I will outline later, this stymies the ability of religion to respond to non-human needs.

Christians especially need to realize how radical the environmental challenge really is. Developing a theology that takes ecology seriously will require that many traditional Christian views will have to be jettisoned. Most theologians are glib about the profound influence that Christian thinking has had on western attitudes toward the environment and think that they can sweep away quickly and easily the Christian tradition that underpins negative attitudes toward nature. Interestingly, it is

37

often theologians who most underestimate the lasting power of deeply embedded attitudes.

Hugh Morgan and Thomas Berry are both right: this is a debate about the meaning of our existence and our relationship to the world. For environmental and human survival will involve the painful discarding of much that Christianity has introduced into western culture. Theologians who seemingly want to ignore the profound and destructive influence of much of the historical tradition are actually glossing over the stark choices that face us.

But before turning to the direct environmental consequences of many of the religious views that are still deeply entrenched in traditional Christian theology, I want to examine the other great threat to the natural world—the explosion of the world's human population.

How many of us can the Earth sustain and still survive?

Our central ethical problem

Throughout this book I make it clear that it is my view that the greatest threat to the environment and to the natural world comes from human beings. All modern extinction scenarios are attributable, either directly or indirectly, to human action and human decision. US Vice-President Al Gore puts it clearly and bluntly:

> No goal is more crucial to healing the global environment than stabilising human population. The rapid explosion in the number of people since the beginning of the scientific revolution—and especially during the latter half of this century—is the clearest single example of the dramatic change in the overall relationship between the human species and the earth's ecological system.[1]

Gore also emphasizes the speed with which the change has developed: while it has been going on in the west for a number of decades, the major impact has occurred within a single generation in many developing counties.

Serious discussion of population goes back to the second half of the eighteenth century, and Thomas Malthus wrote his *Essay on the Principle of Population* in 1798. There has been an on-going debate since then as to the accuracy of his claims. Despite this, it is only now that ordinary people are starting to realize that the greatest threat to the natural world comes from the increase in the human population and the demand for on-going development to support that population. Certainly this is not the *only* element in ecological destruction, but it is by far the most important one.

It must be admitted that there is uncertainty among experts as to the underlying reasons why human population numbers rise and fall. Some elements are clear: a continuing increase in the age of death and a vast improvement in public health over the last century, linked to better medical knowledge and procedures, have contributed a great deal to the present escalation in world population numbers. But the fact is that it is the developed countries, which enjoy the best public health and the most readily available medical services, that are now at a stable zero population growth, or even a little below it, while the underdeveloped countries, which lack these services, are still increasing in population. So it is clear that these public health reasons do not *fully* explain the modern phenomenon. There seem to be underlying demographic dynamics that at present are still not clearly understood. However, allowing for these contradictions and intangibles, there is no doubt that we face a crisis of human numbers. There are simply too many of us.

Most of the people who read this will not live in overcrowded countries or cities, so the impact of population growth will not impinge in a practical way on their conscious experience. The only way that we can clearly perceive the impact of what is happening—other than by visiting an over-crowded third world city such as Calcutta, Lima, Manila, or Sao Paulo—is by taking an historical overview. Allowing that historical demography is a difficult business, and that only figures for the last few centuries are probably empirically verifiable, it is still frightening to see the historical statistics set out.

Taking the world continent by continent, Colin McEvedy and Richard Jones estimate that the following population increases occurred between 1700 and 2000:

	1700	1800	1900	1975	2000
Europe	120m	180m	390m	635m	710m
Asia	370m	625m	970m	2300m	3500m
Africa	61m	70m	110m	385m	700m
Americas	13m	24m	145m	545m	815m
Oceania	2m	2m	7m	23m	36m
TOTALS	**566m**	**899m**	**1622m**	**3888m**	**5761m**[2]

In other words, the world population in 1700 was approximately 566 million; in 1800, just after the publication of Malthus' *Essay*, it had increased to 900 million; by the year 2000 it will be close to six billion. There are estimates that by 2100 there could be as many as ten to twelve billion people on earth if nothing intervenes to stem the growth of population. Al Gore expresses this in a vivid comparison:

> To put these numbers in a different perspective, consider that the world is adding the equivalent of one China's worth of people every ten years, one Mexico's worth every year, one New York City's worth every month, and one Chattanooga's worth every single day. If these increases continue at the current rate, the impact on the environment in the next century will be unimaginable.[3]

Chattanooga's population in 1990 was 152,494![4]
This growth is, of course, exponential. It took the entire history of the human race to reach one billion in the nineteenth century, but only another century to reach two billion. By 1990 the world population was five billion! It is clear that we are now beginning to reach the stage when the exponential growth has

become so great that we could soon be facing an unprecedented catastrophe.

This is the view of many demographic researchers, including the Club of Rome (the 1972 research group at Massachusetts Institute of Technology that produced the report *The Limits to Growth*), the economist Dennis L. Meadows (from MIT and now the University of New Hampshire), Lester Brown of Worldwatch, and Paul Ehrlich of Stanford University. The titles of Ehrlich's best known books, *The Population Bomb* and *The Population Explosion*, are designed to give readers a sense that we are now living in a very dangerous period in world history. They are meant to awaken us to the danger of runaway population and to warn us of the degradation of the environment that Ehrlich sees looming over us.[5] Ehrlich and these other authors all argue that we must turn away now from the "pro-natalist" views which have understandably dominated both culture and religion for most of world history. I say "understandably" because high infant mortality and an early average age of death have meant that in many places in the past human beings have struggled even to replace themselves. But that situation has now changed radically.

When they first propounded their views in the late 1960s and early 1970s, the doomsday theorists were roundly criticized by many, including the Australian economist, Professor Colin Clark, then Director of the Agricultural Economics Institute at Oxford University. In his short book, *The Myth of Over-Population*,[6] Clark argued that the earth could in fact support a much larger human population than the present one with a resultant increase in economic prosperity. The idea was that human population growth would level out without interference from us as standards of living rose. It is significant in this context that Clark was an economist and Ehrlich is a biologist. While both biologists and economists concede that the world is very crowded and that there is enormous pressure on resources, economists tend to be optimists about the future of population and tend to see each additional human being as adding a unit of production and consumption. Biologists, in contrast, tend to be pessimistic and to see every new baby as another mouth to feed and another human being taking space and resources from other species.

Many technophiles also tend to support the optimistic view. They argue that soon new ways of producing food will give even higher yields, and that genetic engineering and evolving new technologies will allow humans to cope not only with the present population, but even with vastly larger numbers in the future. Julian Simon, apparently reacting against the seemingly anti-human stance of Paul and Anne Ehrlich, says that there are no limits at all to economic growth. The more people there are, the more wealth there will be, and with more people will come more ingenuity to think up new technical solutions. Simon argues that every generation in modern times has lived better than the previous generation. He maintains that we must not lose our nerve, for science and technology can resolve all our difficulties.[7]

However, the technocratic assumptions that underpin the economists' and engineers' approach demonstrate the dominant and pervasive impact of technology throughout our culture. Many people uncritically see technology as a universal panacea for all of the problems that we face. In fact, one of the profound intellectual and practical fissures in the contemporary world is between those who believe that technology is a form of salvation, and those who hold to the much more traditional faith of trust in the rhythms of the natural world and the systems that have been evolved by nature. Those who trust nature are not Luddites who reject technology, but they see it in perspective as an ancillary science that helps humankind and the natural world help themselves.

The optimism of Clark and Simon is not shared by other researchers. For example, the Alan Shawn Feinstein World Hunger Program at Brown University in Providence, Rhode Island, estimated that

> Even if food were equitably distributed (with nothing diverted to livestock), the amount of food produced in 1985—an all-time record—could have provided a minimal vegetarian diet to

about 6 billion people, a number we will exceed by the end of
the century ... A diet consisting of 35 percent animal products,
similar to that consumed by most North Americans and West
Europeans today, could be provided to about 2.5 billion
people—less than half of today's population.[8]

This does not take into account the production lost to pests, the
possible future effects of global warming, and changes in the
hydrological cycle.

The economists and optimists are right in the sense that over-
population should not be seen as an isolated and *total* cause of the
entire ecological disaster that we face. But it is a key factor in all
environmental disaster scenarios. People pollute, even though
more people do not necessarily always mean more ecological
destruction.

For instance, in late 1993 I drove north up the Hudson Valley
from Manhattan on a research matter entirely unrelated to
ecology (in fact, I was looking for the grave of one of the early
priests in Australia, Father Jeremiah O'Flynn).[9] In the process I
visited some of the back-blocks of south-west New York State and
north-east Pennsylvania, an area about 125 miles from New York
City. I was struck by how much of the land in this area was thinly
occupied and thickly forested. It was only after I returned to New
York City that I learned that most of it had previously been
denuded of timber for grazing land and to supply the needs of
New York in the nineteenth century. But with the changing needs
of the city and the collapse of the dairy industry in this area, the
forest had returned, and with it many of species that belonged
there. Yet, at the same time, the population of the area since 1875
had more than tripled.

In other words, here was an area that had recovered from
human depredation. In other developed countries with good soil
this same pattern of recovery has been duplicated.

But such successes have not been achieved in all developed
countries. In Australia, for instance, where the soil is superficial
and land degradation and erosion are constant problems,

people—and the cattle, sheep, and plants that they bring—have meant disaster for many of the eco-systems of the continent since the arrival of Europeans in 1788. It is significant that the north-eastern woodlands of the United States and eastern Canada are extraordinarily fertile. This is simply not true in Australia, where it is estimated that seventy-five per cent of the land surface of the populous state of New South Wales has already been degraded by human occupation and use. The river systems of south-eastern Australia are already badly polluted by chemical and human run-off, as well as by damming for irrigation. In many areas salination is becoming an increasing problem.

In most developing countries the increase in human population has had a disastrous effect. As Vice-President Gore says: "Societies that learned over the course of hundreds of generations to eke out a living within fragile ecosystems are suddenly confronted—in a single generation—with the necessity of feeding, clothing and sheltering two or three times as many individuals within those same ecosystems."[10] These countries cannot afford to care for their environments. Insatiable and unstoppable human needs put enormous pressure on delicate ecosystems, with the resultant droughts, famines, and areas of expanding desert. In these situations it is flying in the face of clear fact to pretend that increasing numbers of human beings, combined with poverty and ignorance, do not have a disastrous effect on the environments of these countries.

It is true that population growths are beginning to slow down. The growth rate—which is the difference between birth and death rates—has dropped overall from two per cent in the late 1960s to 1.7 per cent now. However, in the developing world, where thirty-seven per cent of the population are under fifteen years of age, the demographic facts give cause for grave concern. These young people are only now coming into their prime reproductive years.

In sub-Saharan Africa the average annual population growth rate is over 3% a year; in Kenya it is 4.2% a year. India has a much lower annual population growth rate, 2.2%, but this still translates into an additional 16 million people every year.[11]

The consequences of levels of population growth such as those of Africa or Latin America are already quite disastrous for the environment, and this situation will get worse as the material expectations of people in developing countries increase. This pattern of rising expectations is already apparent in China as economic development gains pace.

The ethics of population

Embedded in the population debate are a whole range of acute ethical issues. The most widely recognized is the imbalance between both the capacity and actual food supply of developed areas (such as North America, Western Europe, and Australia), and the twenty to thirty per cent of the human population of developing countries that is seriously under-nourished. Does this imbalance create an *ethical* demand that developed countries dispose of their food glut to needy countries at concessionary prices? Or is the question more radical: is there a basic ethical and human right, overriding the powers of nation states, to allow migration from countries of over-population and chronic shortage to those with apparent space and surplus food? Then there is the ethical issue involved in inter-generational rights: if we consume so many resources now that the quality of life of future generations is deeply compromised, are we acting in a morally responsible way? Do the generations yet to come have rights—as, for instance, many argue the unborn child has rights? How do we decide on these rights?

And what about the right to reproduce: what limit can the general community place on the presumed rights of individuals to decide their own fertility? What are the rights of the community in controlling family size? Some countries such as China, India, and Bangladesh are already trying to manage their fast-growing populations through radical fertility control. While their policies are understandable, given that a third of the human race live in these countries, are these programs working? Is it racist or chauvinistic for developed countries that have already achieved zero population growth, or are close to equilibrium, to demand draconian control as a prerequisite for economic assistance to underdeveloped nations with growing numbers?

The simple fact is that no one has yet developed the ethical apparatus necessary to confront these issues. Virtually all of the major religious traditions are very divided over the question of the desirability of fertility control—and, above all, over the means of achieving it. Most of the great faiths have only the most rudimentary views on the question of the limitation of population. Official Catholicism is certainly not the only faith clearly opposed to artificial contraception. Thus, because the religious traditions have not applied their ethical apparatus to this issue, the population debate has been largely carried on in secular and economic terms by biologists and economists. Few religious ethicists have applied their minds to it. The reason for this is simple: it is a theological and moral minefield.

But even among secularists there are sharp divisions as to how population equilibrium, or more moderate rates of population growth, especially in third world countries, might be achieved. The basic spectrum of opinion is between *Malthusian pessimism* at one end (best represented by Paul and Anne Ehrlich) and *naturalistic optimism* at the other (best represented by Julian Simon). The optimists contend that the earth and humanity are very adaptable and that equilibrium will be reached again through the natural process of market forces without regulatory intervention.

Lying midway on this ideological spectrum is the notion of *interventionism*. The interventionists maintain that it is only through one or other form of interference that the population balance will be righted. This can be through:

1. *Distribution of world resources* on a more equitable scale and the donation of resource surpluses to those most in need. This is the social justice solution that is much favored by many in the

Catholic Church (although, on its own, it is not clear how this would be effective in stemming population growth, let alone protecting the environment). In fact, the emphasis in this argument is not on ecology at all, but on social justice. Ecology is, at best, a by-product.

2. *Coercive, compulsory measures*, legally enforced by governments, whereby individual fertility is drastically limited through sterilization, contraception, or abortion. This is the solution that is seemingly being forced on governments with populations that are now out of control. This approach tends to be opposed by those with a strong emphasis on human rights, or by institutions like the Vatican, with its strong pro-natalist position and vested interest in maintaining a tradition of moral guidance over the reproductive morality of Catholics.

3. *Persuasive institutional change* whereby people are educated that high fertility is not necessarily "natural" or (in a religious context) "the will of God." This approach uses existing institutional structures (such as churches and educational organizations) to change attitudes. (It is here that the tragedy of the papal condemnation of artificial contraception in 1968 lies. This was a major chance to use the church's moral authority and persuasion to change attitudes, especially in developing countries with large Catholic populations.)

4. *A reduction of economic growth* and an attempt to lower the expectations that people have of high standards of living through education. This is based on the recognition that we simply cannot continue to use resources at the present rate. Even if the world population stabilized in the year 2100 (at about four times the present population), no one could expect to continue living at the standards that at present obtain in the developed world. Resources would simply be exhausted.

These four approaches are by no means mutually exclusive, and it is clear that it is only by combining variations of all of them, with adjustments appropriate to the local area, that we might begin to stem the population explosion.

Along with this must go programs for the on-going education

and liberation of women in developing countries. Women are central in the population debate, for it is they who control fertility. There is considerable evidence to show that women use any education that they gain to improve standards of living for their families; then, with a consequent reduction in child mortality, they are more willing to limit conception. As Ehrlich says, "when women have sources of status other than children, family size declines."[12]

This view is supported by Paul Harrison in his book *The Third Revolution*.[13] He says that the position of women in the control of population is "pivotal." "The number of children that women choose to have is usually lower when they are educated, have equal rights to property and equal access to work with equal pay."[14] Harrison points out that in Cuba, China, Thailand, and the state of Kerala in India, women have the right to inherit property, and in all of these areas the birthrate has been reduced. This is confirmed by work done by demographers at Canberra's Australian National University.[15] Access to cheap and efficient contraception is also a key issue.

While religions such as Catholicism and Islam are often blamed for imposing oppressive conditions on women that maintain a high fertility rate, the actual oppression that women experience in places like Latin America, Africa, and Islamic countries such as Saudi Arabia and Iran is just as much the result of tribal and patriarchical cultural attitudes as it is of religious conviction or teaching. It is simply that religion is used as a major component in the enforcement of the social mores of male control, lack of female education, and high fertility. It is, of course, difficult to sort out which comes first, religion or culture. But there is no doubt that they reinforce each other.

Religious responses to the modern population increase

I said earlier that the great religious traditions have had little to say *ex professo* about the problem of population. Generally all of them are characterized by a traditional pro-natalist stance, especially when it applies to their own membership.

At the core of the Jewish view is the command to "be fruitful and multiply and fill the earth" (Genesis 1:28). Given the terrible losses that the Jewish population in Europe suffered in the Nazi holocaust, some modern Jewish thinkers have encouraged an increase in the Jewish birthrate. But there seems to be no consensus as to whether the command of Genesis applies to the human race as a whole. There is no explicit theological or rabbinical reflection on the population problem as such.

Through the theology of Martin Luther, Protestantism introduced the notion of the importance of individual salvation and of each person's right to a free and conscientious relationship with God. It is out of this matrix of ideas that the notion of individual human rights emerged. Because of this notion of individual autonomy, the Protestant tradition has not had a great problem confronting the issue of artificial contraception. Certainly, puritan evangelicalism in the Victorian era was utterly opposed to any form of sexual license, and contraception was viewed as opening the way to promiscuity. But by 1930 the Lambeth Conference of the Church of England had approved the limited use of contraceptives. This position became increasingly liberal throughout Protestantism, and by the 1960s the discussion of the morality of contraception had been superseded by reflection on the ethics of population. For instance, the 1958 Lambeth Conference said:

> Family planning ought to be the result of thoughtful and prayerful Christian decision. Where it is, Christian husbands and wives need feel no hesitation in offering their decision to God and following a clear conscience. The *means* of family planning are in large measure matters of clinical and aesthetic choice, subject to the requirement that they be admissible to the Christian conscience.[16]

In fact, the most creative thought on the population question in the Christian tradition has come from Protestant ethicists. However, even here the focus has been on broad statements such as responsible individual freedom and the maintenance of equity so that the burden of reducing population should not fall exclusively on certain groups. The general Protestant view is that the right to fertility cannot be denied and there is considerable suspicion of government-inspired coercion. There is agreement that an individual can voluntarily seek sterilization, but this should never be imposed. The traditional Protestant emphasis on the conscientious, autonomous exercise of one's individual moral responsibility is maintained.

Eastern Orthodox thought has followed Protestantism in a slow liberalisation of the stance against contraception, although the strong notion of extended family among the Orthodox would not necessarily encourage family limitation. Orthodoxy has very little to say on the population question as such.

The Muslim response to population is two-edged. Firstly, the large majority of the world's Muslims live under governments that have officially adopted family planning projects. Islam is traditionally not opposed to fertility control. However, the religious view is that the right to apply the ethic of limitation is exclusively vested in individual couples. As Basim F. Musallam writes:

> Muslims are free to control births, and governments are not. As long as compulsion is avoided, the provision of information, clinics, services, and devices can all be accommodated within the dominant interpretation of religious law without damage to its spirit.[17]

However, there seems to be a gulf between rhetoric and practice. The problem is that in many Muslim countries, and especially in fundamentalist circles, the whole business of family planning is seen as a western imperialist plot to reduce the Muslim population. As a result, it is as difficult for many Muslims as it is for Christians and Jews to take the population question seriously. An odd axis of interest between the Vatican and fundamentalist Muslims has formed around United Nations policy on population control.

The Catholic Church and population

So where does the Catholic Church stand on the question of population? While it has many admirable things to say in the area of social justice, Catholicism, like most of the other great religious traditions, has a very poor record in developing a creative approach to the issue of population. The fact is that the church has said very little on the question, and what it has said has been quite inadequate. In fact, the Catholic church's whole approach to the issue of population is distorted by the question of the morality of contraception and the implications of this teaching for the role of papal authority. But it is not only the Vatican that is to blame for this. With few exceptions, there has been no serious Catholic ethical reflection on the issue of population control in the English-speaking world over the last three decades.

One of the outstanding exceptions to this is the work of the English Mill Hill missionary, Father Arthur McCormack (1911–1992).[18] After periods as a missionary in West Africa and as an expert at the Second Vatican Council, McCormack worked for six years in the Pontifical Commission for Justice and Peace in Rome until "it became painfully clear that his views of the problems of world population were an embarrassment to the Holy See."[19] His opinions were quite conservative: he argued that the church had to confront the issue of population and that population growth would only be slowed through the elimination of poverty and the introduction of natural family planning. He also argued that population growth should be taken into account before the church condemned artificial contraception. Like many creative thinkers in the church, he was eventually forced to turn outward. He worked for the United Nations and in many other international capacities between 1971 and 1984, publishing five books and many articles on third world development and population increase.

The sad thing is that so much Catholic ethical energy over the last twenty-five years has been expended, not to say wasted, on the issue of the morality of contraception. In addition to this, although it would never be admitted publicly, many Catholic moralists have avoided the issue of population because of their fear of punitive and repressive interventions in their academic lives and work if they were seen to have disagreed with the official Vatican line on contraception. All of this has meant that there has been no real development of Catholic social doctrine in a direction which might have offered something constructive to the population debate. As the Boston priest J. Bryan Hehir succinctly puts it: "The detailed discussion of contraception in Catholic moral theology has at times conveyed the impression that this one issue constituted the whole Catholic position on population ethics."[20]

Historically, the Catholic Church has always been pro-natalist. This makes eminent sense if it is seen within the historical context of its theological view of marriage. Until the 1950s, moralists consistently argued that the purpose of marriage was the reproduction and nurture of children. The relational aspect of the union was mentioned, but in practice it was accorded a very secondary place. And indeed, for much of human history this has been what human sexual relationship has been principally about: the reproduction and nurture of children. So this was primarily a genetic and cultural imperative that was reinforced by religious sanction. But from the pontificate of Pope Pius XII (1939-1958) onwards, the change of attitude that had been going on in the wider world for much of this century started to permeate Catholic thought. After considerable theological debate, a more contemporary view of marriage emerged in which the mutual fulfillment of husband and wife was recognized as being as important as—if not more important than—reproduction and nurture. After much debate, this stance was largely accepted by the Second Vatican Council.

When the pill first came on the market in 1960, the whole context of the debate about marriage changed. For the first time in history an accessible and reliable contraceptive gave women freedom from the biological consequences of intercourse. The relational aspect of marriage became more and more important in church discussions and in the wider community. But there was still very little connection made between the debate about contraception and the issue of population. The moral battle about contraception which raged in the church throughout the 1960s and 1970s remained very much at the level of personal ethics.

However, there were exceptions to this. During the pontificate of Pope John XXIII (1958–1963) and the period of the Second Vatican Council (1962–1966) there was a real consciousness of the population problem (as well as the issue of the pill) in countries like Belgium and the Netherlands. As with so many contemporary issues, it was the Belgian Cardinal, Leon Josef Suenens, who confronted the issue of population at Vatican II. Talking at the third session of the Council in 1964 about the papal commission set up to study birth control, he said:

> It is up to this commission to deal with the immense problem arising from the population explosion and over-population in many parts of the world. For the first time we must proceed with such a study in the light of faith.[21]

One of the few Catholic ethicists at that time who at least recognized the interconnection between fertility control and population was the French Jesuit, Stanislas de Lestapis. Since his views are typical of the Catholicism of this period, and still strongly influence official Catholic attitudes, I will outline them in some detail. One still sees many of his arguments repeated among conservative Catholics today. His book *Family Planning and Modern Problems* set out both to analyze and to argue against modern attempts to control population through the family planning movement. In practice, De Lestapis, identified family planning and the promotion of government policies of birth control in developing countries like Nehru's India with contraception, sterilization, and abortion. De Lestapis wrote the French edition of his book in 1958, just before the pill became generally available.[22]

De Lestapis maintained that a "contraceptive civilisation" was emerging[23] and predicted the results of such a culture. The "large family" would be viewed as "an unnatural monstrosity"; there would be a decline "into spiritual old age and premature sclerosis"; the idea of "family happiness" would be debased; there would be a collapse in moral standards; sexuality would be fixated at an adolescent stage; there would be an attack on male virility and on women's femininity; there would be increasing tolerance of homosexuality; divorce rates would rise; a new concept of sexuality would emerge in which "sex is first and foremost for pleasure."[24]

Allowing for Gallic exaggeration and the social conservatism that was typical of Catholic ethical thought on these issues at that time, it must be admitted that some of de Lestapis' predictions have come true. But the actual causes of these social changes are much more complex than his notion of a "contraceptive civilisation" suggests. A more serious criticism of his work is that none of these issues really touches the problem of population. His point of view remains squarely within the context of a conservative Catholic approach to personal and community ethics. But the question of population takes us beyond these issues into a whole new order of moral magnitude.

The same problem arises with de Lestapis' explanation of the Catholic position on contraception. Following Pope Pius XII, he carefully distinguished "birth control" from what he called "birth regulation." By "birth control" de Lestapis meant the use of artificial contraceptives; by "birth regulation" he was referring to natural methods of avoiding pregnancy.

> Birth regulation presupposes ... complete or temporary continence, periodic or lasting for a considerable time practised by mutual agreement, ... and organized in accordance with nature and the actual characteristics of the female organism.[25]

How was all of this to be applied to the problem of control of population? De Lestapis argued that the population problem was *not* world-wide, but that it was confined to specific countries and zones:

> There are zones where the population figures are by no means excessive and where the economy is steadily expanding ... There is no threat of over-population, but there are *distorted and dangerously irregular developments.*[26]

While he admits that official corruption and inefficiency in the developing countries are real problems, de Lestapis says that the essence of the solution to the issue lies in the wealthy developed world. He argues that the west has to evolve a real generosity of spirit by giving low interest loans and free technical assistance and allowing immigration from over-populated to (apparently) under-populated countries. This all constitutes what he calls a "gift economy"—something which, he comments, "would be a great advance on capitalism"![27]

I have outlined de Lestapis' approach because what he spelt out in the late 1950s is reflected in the teaching of Pope John XXIII in his great encyclicals *Mater et magistra* and *Pacem in terris*. The pope argues that there is no single population problem but a variety of problems in different countries that will require economic, cultural, and demographic adjustments. (It is probable that de Lestapis had a hand in writing these encyclicals.) These views continue to be reflected by *official* Catholic theorists on the population issue. Among them there is an absolute unwillingness to shift on the question of contraception, while they maintain a strong, positive emphasis on the need for international social and distributive justice. In practice most ordinary Catholics support social justice, but the vast majority of those of fertile age in developed countries ignore the teaching on contraception. And where contraception is not readily available in some strongly Catholic areas, the abortion rate is very high (as it is, for instance, in Poland at present).

Nowadays, what official Catholic discussion there is of the question of population seems to hover between a strong emphasis on social and distributive justice and an unyielding opposition to artificial contraception on the one hand, and an odd, disjunctive connection between these two and the population issue on the other. Most Catholic theorists never seem to confront the question of population head-on; it is as though official Catholicism can never sufficiently escape from the twin poles of contraception and social justice to see population as a legitimate ethical question in itself. In the Second Vatican Council's document on the church in the modern world, *Gaudium et spes* (1965), in Pope Paul VI's encyclical *Populorum progressio* (1967), and in other official Catholic statements throughout Pope Paul VI's pontificate, the problem of population was seen as part of a complex, interlocking series of political, social, and economic issues. The argument is always that population pressures would be lessened if there was a more equitable distribution of the world's goods. There is also an emphasis on the fact that the population question should never be isolated from this context of distributive justice.

The furthest that any pope has gone in the recognition that there can be a limitation on reproductive rights is Paul VI in *Populorum progressio*. Discussing the social role of the state in the business of economic development, the pope at least admitted that some third world countries might have to limit rapid population growth. He said:

> It is certain that public authorities can intervene, within the limit of their competence, by favouring the availability of appropriate information and by adopting suitable means, provided that these be in conformity with the moral law and that they respect the rightful freedom of married couples.[28]

There is a sense in which the emphasis on social justice is profoundly correct. A broad and integrated approach is required to all complex problems, and there is no doubt that the population problem is complex! As J. Bryan Hehir points out:

The population problem is one strand of a larger fabric involving questions of political, economic, and social structure at the national and international level. While acknowledging the existence of a population problem, this view asserts that it is morally wrong and practically ineffective to isolate population as a single factor, seeking to reduce population growth without simultaneously making those political and economic changes which will achieve a more equitable distribution of wealth and resources within nations and among nations.[29]

Hehir's article in the *Encyclopedia of Bioethics* is a very balanced one and he sets out the Catholic position with clarity. This position is based on the right of every person to dignity and integrity and the freedom to marry and have a family. Catholic social ethics places these personal rights within the context of the common good on both a national and international level. As Hehir says: "At both the national and international levels the categories of common good, social justice and freedom of choice for individuals and families in society are used to define the population question."[30]

But there is a problem here. The fact is that, for all their discussion of justice and individual rights, Catholic theorists never actually get to the problem of population because they are stymied by the issue of contraception. It makes little sense for official Catholicism to talk about population control while excluding the most effective means of achieving that control. There is a disjunction in Catholic ethical thought whereby the strands of the issue are never actually brought together in a focused way on the problem of population.

The real issue is that we face an intractable, practical problem *now*. For those who are concerned about the population problem, the issue is not focused through theoretical questions about human reproductive rights. The reality that we confront is that we cannot feed the people who are on earth now, let alone those who will be born in the near future. It is correct that there must be redistribution, that there are outrageous inequalities in international distributive justice, that many countries are overflowing in food while others starve. Nevertheless, as the number of human beings continues to grow, hunger increases, enormous pressure is put on the environment, whole ecological systems are destroyed, and other species continue to slide into extinction. There are clearly profound ethical issues embedded in these extinction scenarios, but the anthropocentrism of Catholic ethics (and most religious ethics generally) prevents the church bringing its power of moral persuasion to bear on the problem of ecological destruction and species extinction *now*. In other words, the whole thrust of the Catholic approach to the population question remains in the realm of the anthropocentric and the theoretical.

The most important issue for the papacy in the condemnation of artificial contraception is consistency in moral teaching. The problem is that popes are restricted by the teachings of their predecessors. In fact, this is the very reason why the medieval popes rejected the idea of infallibility; they wanted to enjoy their sovereign freedom intact! From Pope Pius XI (who condemned artificial birth control in his 1932 encyclical *Casti conubii*), through Pius XII and Paul VI, there is a consistent condemnation of any form of contraception. As the American Jesuit moralist John C. Ford warned both the Roman Curia and Paul VI during the discussions leading up to *Humanae vitae* (1968), any change in attitude toward the contraceptive pill would expose the papacy to the accusation of inconsistent teaching and thus threaten papal teaching authority.[31] For the Vatican, the real issue in the contraceptive debate was the question of papal power over the moral lives of Catholics and the reliability and consistency of papal teaching. There seems to be a real failure on the part of official Catholicism to grasp the fact that the extremely pressing moral needs of the common good of both nature and humankind might override personal reproductive rights and the seeming importance of the role of the pope as a consistent moral teacher.[32]

Pope John Paul II and the issue of population

Throughout the long pontificate of John Paul II, which began in 1978, there has been a failure to confront the population issue. The pope knows from personal observation the terrible consequences of over-population; he has traveled more than any other pope in history and has seen some of the worst over-populated hell holes on earth. In fact, he has probably traveled more than any other political figure in the twentieth century, with the possible exception of Queen Elizabeth II! In his 1988 encyclical *Solicitudo rei socialis*, he almost grudgingly admitted that there was a population problem:

> One cannot deny the existence, especially in the southern hemisphere, of a demographic problem ... One must immediately add that in the northern hemisphere the nature of this problem is reversed: here the cause for concern in *the drop in the birthrate*.[33]

But Pope John Paul has no suggestions to offer as to how this problem might be confronted, except to caution that it cannot be by contraception, abortion, or government decree (which would normally involve a program of sexual education, including contraceptive education). The tragedy of the Catholic Church is that throughout this long pontificate the whole discussion of population control has been obstructed by the peculiarities of the papal agenda. There have been passing and superficial references to ecological values, but no serious attempt to relate them to the problem of population.

There is no doubt that obedience to the official church teaching on contraception has become a litmus test of loyalty for Pope John Paul II. I have explained the origins of his views in *Mixed Blessings*.[34] The foundation of his strictures against birth control are rooted in his view of the dignity of the human person. Since he has become pope, he has consistently lumped contraception in with divorce and abortion and maintained that all are part of an "anti-life" mentality. Even if one were to admit that these three very different moral acts were somehow of the same ethical species, one would still have to comment that his definition of "anti-life" is extraordinarily circumscribed. Surely war, the economic and social injustice that so often leads to exploitation and starvation, and the business of ecological devastation are moral acts that are far more important and destructive in their effects on a complete ethic of life than divorce or artificial contraception.

The papal emphasis seems fixated on moral acts linked to sexuality. The BBC Rome correspondent, David Willey, maintains that on one of his South American visits "the Pope used the word 'contraception' no less than sixty times in ten days of public speeches."[35] Willey also describes the 1988 Vatican celebrations of the twentieth anniversary of *Humanae vitae*, when western countries were accused of a form of "contraceptive imperialism" which imposed on developing countries (in the words of the final report) "vast contraception and sterilisation programs, thus harming family life, threatening women's health and violating human rights."[36] However, it struck many as hypocritical for the Vatican to talk about "human rights" when it itself had not signed the European Declaration on Human Rights. The reason for the failure to sign was that Rome would have had to come to grips with elements of canon law that contradict a range of human rights included in the European Declaration.

The papal opposition to contraception has not abated. In the encyclical *Veritatis splendor* (5 October 1993), Pope John Paul states clearly:

> With regard to intrinsically evil acts, and in reference to contraceptive practices whereby the conjugal act is intentionally rendered infertile ... If acts are intrinsically evil, a good intention or particular circumstances can diminish their evil, but they cannot remove it. They remain "irremediably" evil acts; per se and in themselves they are not capable of being ordered to God and to the good of the person.[37]

In other words, contraception is an intrinsically evil act and it remains so, no matter what the intention of the doer. In no circumstances can it be morally justified. But, as usual in Vatican theology, contraception is treated as an isolated act, the moral species of which is determined only within the sphere of personal morality. Above all, contraception is never considered within the broader context of world population and the overwhelming moral need to protect the environment. In fact, as Sean McDonagh has pointed out, despite the opening sentence of the encyclical ("The splendour of truth shines forth in all the works of the Creator"), there is no discussion of the ethics of ecology in this letter.[38] The ethics of *Veritatis splendor* are, once again, very anthropocentric.

The Vatican and the Cairo Conference (1994)

The Vatican's continuing concern with reproductive issues was brought into focus by the September 1994 United Nations International Conference on Population and Development in Cairo. This was the third in a series of UN Conferences on population questions in which the Holy See participated. The first was in Bucharest in 1974 and the second in Mexico City in 1984. The Vatican had refused to accept the conclusions of both of these conferences, but it was still determined to play a major role in 1994. While the ultimate outcome of the Cairo Conference was positive, the lead up and the Conference itself revealed a lot about both Vatican attitudes and the attitudes of the major population control pressure groups.

It needs to be emphasized that the whole discussion about population has moved on since the 1980s from an emphasis on *control* of birth rates (especially in developing countries) by whatever means necessary, to a more cooperative approach that stresses the participation of couples in the process of deciding fertility. This is linked to the need for women's education, liberation and health care, and ecological conservation through "sustainable development." But the problem that emerged prior to the Cairo Conference was that the International Planned Parenthood Federation (IPPF) and Family Planning International Assistance, with strong support from the Clinton administration, were determined to include the right of women to safe abortion on demand in the Conference Document. The IPPF was numerically well represented at Cairo and its founder and President, Dr Fred Sai from Ghana, was a major committee chairman at the Conference. The emphasis on abortion and women's rights in the preliminary text was considered very provocative by the Vatican.

The Holy See had been working hard through its diplomats, both before and after the Cairo Preparatory Committee meeting in New York City (4–22 April 1994), to influence governments. *The Tablet*, for instance, reported that early in 1994:

> The Holy See ... embarked on a major diplomatic effort to modify substantially the proposals in the draft document for the United Nations international conference on population and development to be held in Cairo in September. The Holy See is concerned that the conference gives far too little attention to "integral development" and tends to promote birth control methods unacceptable to the church—even by force of law—and in particular "the right of access to abortion on demand."[39]

The focus of Vatican criticism centered on the failure of the Draft Document to promote "integral development," by which it meant improvements in health and eduction services. But the real core of the issue was that the UN Fund for Population Activities itself proposed the promotion of a program of contraception, reproductive health and access to safe abortion—or, as Pope John Paul saw it, "an internationally recognized right of access to abortion on demand." There was concern in the Vatican as to what the term "reproductive health" really meant. Could it be interpreted to refer to abortion? This was the nub of the issue for the pope: population policy must not promote abortion, and, more broadly, such a policy should be subject to the Vatican's view of contraceptive morality. It is precisely this attempt to impose one moral view that the Conference at Cairo resisted strongly.

In New York in April, the Irish Monsignor, Diarmuid Martin, of the Pontifical Council for Justice and Peace, had argued that the Draft Document was "individualistic" and based on an "ethical vacuum." This criticism was too harsh. Certainly, phrases in the Document needed clarification, including terms like "family planning," "responsible sex," and "reproductive and sexual health." But there was much to be praised. In fact, a Jesuit priest, David S. Toolan, editor of the prestigious Catholic magazine *America*, argued that the Draft Document was "people centered" and in broad agreement "with Catholic social teaching, particularly with Pope Paul VI's 1967 encyclical 'On the Development of Peoples'."[40] This was clearly not the view of the Vatican. The Colombian Cardinal Alfonso Lopez Trujillo, President of the Pontifical Council on the Family, complained about what he called "contraceptive materialism," linked it with political corruption, excessive military spending, and the lack of development, and claimed that coercion was still involved in contraceptive programs. (It is worth noting that the Pontifical Council on the Family is a creation of John Paul II and is one of the most reactionary bodies in the Roman Curia. Lopez Trujillo, the former Archbishop of Medellin, is an outspoken opponent of liberation theology. His predecessor was the Canadian Cardinal Edouard Gagnon.)

However, by the middle of 1994, the Vatican seemed to have realized that its position would be untenable if it continued to link contraception with abortion. Nevertheless, as the Conference approached, the Pope did not hesitate to put direct pressure on President Clinton, the Executive Director of the UN Population Fund and Secretary-General of the Conference, Dr Nafis Sadik, and other world leaders to drop all reference to abortion. In this he was not successful.

By the time the Conference met in Cairo (5–13 September), the Vatican delegation was focused, in practice, almost exclusively on abortion. The position of the majority at Cairo was made clear in the speech of Norway's Prime Minister, Gro Harlem Bruntland. She said bluntly that religion should not be used to prevent women from having access to family planning services: "Morality becomes hypocrisy if it means accepting mothers suffering or dying as a consequence of unwanted pregnancies and illegal abortions."[41] The moderate Muslim view was expressed on the first day of the Conference by the Prime Minister of Pakistan, Benazir Bhutto. Referring to Pakistan's escalating population, she said:

> At present it is 126 million. By the year 2020 it may be 243 million ... Pakistan cannot grow if we cannot check its rapid population growth ... It is not the future of the people of Pakistan to live in squalor and poverty condemned to a future of hunger and horror.[42]

At the same time she emphasized that Islam rejected abortion as a method of population control and that there was no possibility of compromise on the traditional family unit. She said: "Islam aims at harmonious lives built upon a bedrock of conjugal fidelity and parental responsibility." While her views clearly do not represent the fundamentalists, who argue that contraception is a vast western plot to limit the population of Muslim countries, Prime Minister Bhutto's views clearly reflect mainstream Islamic opinion. US Vice-President Al Gore said that the United States did not seek to establish an international right to abortion since abortion law should be established by each government.

In the position paper delivered to the Conference by Archbishop Renato Martino, head of the Holy See's delegation, there was a broad emphasis on development. He said the Vatican supported "the advancement of women's level of education and health care" (paragraph 2) and made the significant admission that "the Holy See does not support procreation at all costs" (paragraph 3).[43] But he spoke at length about the danger of establishing "abortion as an essential component of population policy" and warned that "unrestricted access to abortion might be elevated to the level of a right" (para 6). The issue that is hardly mentioned in Archbishop Martino's text is population. Instead, he seems to have turned the Conference theme on its head: "Population policies have a particular place in development policies" (paragraph 3).

The predicted "Holy Alliance" between the Vatican and Muslim countries never materialized, and support for the Holy See's position came mainly from Honduras, Ecuador, Guatemala, and Malta. Other countries, of course, had reservations about abortion, especially as a birth control measure. On the ground, the Vatican delegation played it tough. It seemed at times to try to hijack the Conference, forcing several days debate on abortion and infuriating many of the delegates. Development and population issues were forgotten. Vatican delegation member, Australian Monsignor Peter Elliott, from Lopez Trujillo's Pontifical Council on the Family, blamed it all on "feminists": "Feminists are responsible for the abortion issue. They put abortion on the agenda."[44] The key problem chapters in the Conference document for the Holy See and some Catholic and Islamic states were Chapter 7 (reproductive rights and reproductive health) and 8 (health, morbidity and mortality).

The objection to Chapter 7 centered around the question of reproductive health and rights. To some these terms seemingly opened the way to abortion by saying that men and women had a right to have access to methods of "fertility regulation." In the end, compromises were reached and a new text agreed on. Chapter 7 now sets out "the right of men and women to be informed and to have access to safe, effective, affordable and acceptable methods of family planning of their choice, as well as other methods of their choice for the regulation of fertility which are not against the law." The central issue in Chapter 8 was the right to a safe abortion. The Holy See was also concerned about the approval of the use of condoms to prevent the spread of HIV infection. After several days of often acrimonious debate, the key text of this chapter now reads:

In no case should abortion be promoted as a method of family planning. All governments ... are urged to strengthen their commitment to women's health, to deal with the health impact of unsafe abortion as a major public heath concern and to reduce the recourse to abortion through expanded and improved family planning services. Prevention of unwanted pregnancies must be given the highest priority and all attempts should be made to eliminate the need for abortion.[45]

In the end the Vatican endorsed the Cairo Document statement of principles and several of the chapters. It still refused to accept Chapters 7 and 8. However, consensus was reached at Cairo on a *Program of Action* on key issues such as the need to stabilize the world's population, an emphasis on women's health, education, rights and empowerment, support for the family, and the enhancement of reproductive health.

What did the Vatican ultimately achieve? In hindsight it forced the international community to take human reproductive rights and development issues more seriously. It also focused attention on the foolishness of seeing abortion merely as a means of limiting population. As *The Tablet* correctly pointed out:

[The Vatican's] function at Cairo was to insist that fundamental ethical principles must not be abandoned in the face of the urgency of the population problem. Only the Vatican could have stood out in this way, and fair-minded delegates were willing to acknowledge the fundamental improvement achieved in the text.[46]

Other commentators were not so positive. The Conference has been seen as a diplomatic disaster for the Vatican. It is clear that the Vatican delegation was largely made up of men of single-minded and limited vision who often "came across as condescending, as if they had sole access to truth."[47] The *National Catholic Reporter* continued:

The result was an erosion of ecumenism in some circles and breaches of diplomatic etiquette in others. Rome was right to state its beliefs but dead wrong in its approach. In short, the church may well have damaged itself as a moral force on the world scene and prevented itself from reaching a wider audience beyond the hard-rock conservatives who eagerly endorsed its ways.[48]

This is a tragedy. The sad fact is that it is not just the Vatican that suffers as a result of the limited intellectual vision of some of its representatives. The whole church and its moral tradition is perceived by outsiders to be cast in the same mold: fundamentalist, simplistic, sectarian and myopic. Unfortunately, the behavior of Vatican functionaries affects all Catholics.

Is a Christian population ethic possible?

So where does this leave us? Despite the Vatican, is it possible to develop a *genuine* Catholic-Christian ethic which confronts the question of population? I think that it is not only possible, but that it is the most pressing moral issue facing the church now. What can be creatively recovered from the Catholic tradition to assist in the development of a population ethic? What are its outlines? And how should this relate ecumenically to a more broadly Christian ethic?

There is no future for an exclusively Catholic or Protestant ethic of population control. Christians need to find basic and common moral foundations upon which a practical ethical approach can be developed. The issue is too important for the particularity of the different church traditions. The Catholic emphasis on moral principle emerging from natural law, always informed by pastoral care, needs to interact with the Protestant emphasis on the importance of individual moral choice made before God and informed by God's word.

Keeping both these traditional Christian principles in mind, I want to try to sketch out some bases upon which this ethic might be based. Given my background, it will be the Catholic element that I will emphasize.

The first element in developing an ethic of population: the good of the planet

I will make it clear right from the outset where my moral emphasis lies: I will always place the emphasis on the moral imperative of the *good of the planet* and of care for it, rather than on the *good life* for as many people as possible. Thomas Berry argues that the ethical framework that we need today must be provided by the larger context of the earth and the natural world. Human ethics must be subsumed within this cosmic context.

> The human community is subordinate to the ecological community. The ecological imperative is not derivative from human ethics. Human ethics is derivative from the ecological imperative. The basic ethical norm is the well-being of the comprehensive community, not the well-being of the human community. The earth is a single ethical system.[49]

In some ways this is alien to both the Catholic and the Protestant approach to ethics, which are still profoundly anthropocentric. The core of the traditional Catholic and Christian approach to population ethics has emphasized the injustice of the unequal distribution of the world's resources and the need for further development so that the poor are no longer excluded. The core aim of the Christian ethic is to offer the good life to as many as possible through sacrifice on the part of the rich and the redistribution of resources to the poor. (This is also the aim of Marxist theory.)

However, I think that a new ethical starting point needs to be developed. Bluntly stated, this is that *the good of the planet should come first.* The assumption underlying this is that the earth does not simply exist for the good of humans, but that it has an ethical significance in itself that far outweighs the value of all of us. It existed billions of years before us and some present trends could be interpreted to indicate that it will survive us, albeit with considerably diminished life forms. I am not suggesting that the social justice argument ought to be ignored or excluded, but rather that it become secondary and subservient to the far more important issue of the survival of the earth itself.

It is not only the planet that must be preserved, but there also has to be a commitment by human beings to the care and nurturance of other species ahead of our own, especially those species that are endangered. There has always been a hierarchy in our moral judgments. We see some things as ethically more important than others. Traditionally, we have always placed our own species at the head of this hierarchical arrangement. Like all living things we are species-centric. But we are also the only species with the power of self-reflection and with the ability to universalize and see ourselves in a perspective broader than the mere satisfaction of our own needs. As a result we have an ethical obligation to recognize the rights of other species, especially those that are endangered by our activities or by our manipulation of the earth's environment and ecological structures.

Despite the distance that we have come in recognizing the rights of other species, it still seems frightening to say that, ethically, the survival of endangered species, such as certain whales or the Bengal tiger or the migratory orange-bellied parrot, could well be more important than the survival of specific human beings or even groups of human beings. For our survival as a species is not under threat. It could well be that the survival of endangered species is so important that resources might need to be taken from human priorities. It is easy to argue, for instance, that the inconvenience and dislocation caused to people who are displaced or lose their jobs in the timber industry is of little ethical consequence compared to the preservation of a rainforest and the species within it. It is more difficult, but nevertheless necessary, to argue that endangered species may have priority over human needs and even at times over human lives. Christopher D. Stone of the University of Southern California has discussed the ethical and legal issues raised by the protection of what he calls the 'nonperson' in his book *Earth and Other Ethics*.[50]

Usually the tough moral choices between people and species do not have to be made because species are actually endangered by the trivial demands of wealthy elites (often the Asian elites whose trade in endangered species through places such as Singapore has reached large proportions). These elites use rare animals for hunting or animal products for natural medicine, decoration, or even for aphrodisiacs or taste. It is these exploitative elites that need to be reigned in. Other extinction scenarios result from the developmental mania that still grips so many nations. It is not usually the poor and the vulnerable who are the exploiters.

But sometimes the tough choices do have to be made between the needs of human beings and those of vulnerable and endangered species. In these cases I would argue that natural law demands that the survival of endangered species is more important than the needs of human beings who are very much more adaptable and who, with help, can certainly change.

The second element in developing an ethic of population: the natural law tradition

The theory of natural law has been very unpopular among many Christian thinkers over the last few decades. Part of the problem is that the argument from natural law has been recently applied in inappropriate circumstances. The best known is Pope Paul VI's argument in *Humanae vitae* against artificial contraception, which he says is contrary to natural law. In my view this argument is specious because the pope embraces a very narrow definition of "nature." The encyclical argues that artificial contraception is wrong because conception is the natural result of intercourse and the processes of nature cannot be artificially vitiated. Some Catholic ethicists, such a Karol Wojtyla and John Finnis, argue that this is a perfectly reasonable conclusion.[51] But many others, both Catholic and non-Catholic, would hold that to apply the pure theory of natural law in such specific circumstances is to distort it.

Until the early 1960s, the theory of natural law was a dominant one in the Catholic tradition. It has always been far less influential among Protestants because of a strong theological belief that morality was determined by the will of God mediated to us through biblical teaching and applied by an individual to his or her own life. Catholic moralists were much more likely to appeal to natural law and to apply natural reason as the foundational source of morality.

But because of the tendency of Catholic moralists over the last couple of centuries to trivialize natural law through focusing on the minutiae of moral behavior, especially sexual behavior, contemporary Catholic theologians have tended to abandon natural law as a primary source for the ethical reflection. They have moved in a much more biblical direction. The crunch came with *Humanae vitae*. Pope Paul VI's point was that any form of artificial or chemical intervention in the natural rhythms of human reproduction was against natural law and therefore immoral. (Actually, if one were to take the pope's teaching literally and extend it to the whole of nature, we might be able to argue that *any* intervention at all in any natural process was intrinsically immoral. That might please the more radical wing of deep ecology!)

I have always thought that natural law is worth rescuing from the extremes of both the conservative moralists and the radical ecologists. In fact, I would argue that natural law could serve as a secure foundation for an environmental ethic.

Interestingly, both the Roman philosopher Cicero, who first developed the classic formulation of natural law, and the medieval theologian St Thomas Aquinas, who used it so successfully in his ethics, emphasized that the foundation of natural law is rationality. Aquinas says unequivocally in the *Summa Theologiae*:

> The specific constituent element of humanity is human reason. Therefore, whatever is contrary to the order of reason is against the essential nature of human beings. What is in accordance with

reason is in accordance with human nature.[52]

Later he is even more ethically specific: "The rule and measure of human acts is reason."[53] In other words, human nature is constituted by reason.

Aquinas' emphasis on the rational content of the natural law would surely demand a broader setting for the ethics of contraception (and population) than a mere emphasis on the sheer physicality of the act. Human sexuality operates in a complex context, and part of that is the totality of the circumstances of the human agents involved. Any rational discussion of human reproduction must surely include the question of the full circumstances into which the child will be born, and a key element in that equation is the question of world population and the demands that human population growth place on the ecological structure of the world. To decide to have a child is not a purely subjective, personal act; it is essentially social and even has an ecological element in it. Given that human beings are the major agents of ecological destruction, it seems to me that it may be argued that the limitation of human reproduction could be construed as not only *not* against the natural law, but even in profound accordance with it!

The church and most democratic states still maintain the very recently developed fiction that reproduction is a purely private act. The fact is that historically the act of reproduction and birth has never been seen as a purely private act between consenting adults. A new-born child is not just the private offspring of a particular couple. In the past, the birth of a child was seen as the arrival of a new member of the tribe, clan, or community, maintaining its numbers, contributing to its common well-being, and extending its ability to protect and develop its territory. Throughout human history to reproduce has always been a social act endowed with religious and ethical connotations. It has not merely been the right of the particular reproducing couple, let alone the right of a single, individual woman seeking her personal "fulfillment" (whatever that might be).

The social aspect of reproduction is even more important today. To decide to reproduce (and it usually is a *decision* in modern developed countries with the ready availability of contraception) is always a social act, not just a private decision to fulfill and complete oneself or one's relationship. Of course, the personal and relational aspects have importance, but the right to reproduce must be re-situated back within the context of the common good. Clearly the community has rights with regard to reproduction and the increase in the number of human beings. To decide to have a child is not an isolated ethical act. Such a decision must be taken within the context of the ability of both the couple and the community to care for and support that child. It must also be taken within the context of the present population crisis and the rights of nature and other species. Some limit must be placed on the voracious human appetite to reproduce and to consume at the expense of other species and nature itself. Surely the natural law involves the protection of nature.

Let us now broaden the discussion from this rather narrow focus on the human. Aquinas also says that natural law cannot be in conflict with the unchanging, eternal law of God. In the *Summa* he defines eternal law as "the divine providence by which the world is ruled and the divine reason by which the whole community of the universe is governed."[54] What, then, according to Aquinas, is natural law?

> Everything God plans obeys the standards of his eternal law, and bears the imprint of that law in the form of a natural tendency to pursue whatever behaviour and goals are appropriate to it ... This distinctive sharing in the eternal law we call the natural law ... Even creatures without reason share eternal reason in their own way.[55]

Aquinas further clarifies this:

> Everything created ... is subject to the eternal law ... And just as man by utterance imprints inner principles of behaviour on

men subject to him, so God imprints principles of behaviour appropriate to them on all natural things, and in so doing commands all nature. So that *every movement in nature is subject to God's eternal law* (my emphasis).[56]

What Aquinas is saying here is that natural law lays down the general guidelines for the whole of reality whereby God's eternal law is applied to life. Within the general guidelines of natural law as applied to human beings, there is room for legislated law and what Aquinas calls the "prudential judgement." "Prudence," he says, "is reasoned regulation of conduct, reasoning well about the whole business of living well."[57] The virtue of prudence demands that we always act cautiously and wisely and make sure that all our actions are appropriate to the demands of natural law.

It is significant that Aquinas extends natural law to the whole of creation and says that "every movement in nature is subject to God's eternal law." In other words, nothing in nature happens that is not determined by God. If human beings have to make ethical and prudential judgments about their own behavior and cannot step outside the general guidelines laid down by natural law, surely the same applies to the rest of God's creation. *All* of our actions in nature must be "subject to God's eternal law." How, then, could it possibly be argued that the extinction of whole species, or the partial or total destruction of God's creation, could be in accordance with God's eternal law? We can certainly make prudential judgments about nature and our own participation in its functioning, but we are clearly subject to nature's own law which Aquinas argues is an expression of eternal law in action.

As a result, it can be further argued that we cannot continue to reproduce and consume at a rate that threatens the very existence of other species in nature. Natural law and the exercise of prudential reason clearly impose a limit on our numbers. It could hardly be supposed to be in keeping with natural law that we out-breed other species into extinction. A broader concept of natural law, one which includes the rights of the whole of nature, demands that we act prudently (and quickly) to limit population and that we transfer resources and protection to those species and areas that are most under threat. Aquinas says clearly that humankind is not the sole expression of eternal law. The whole of nature gives expression to God's law and must therefore be respected.

But Aquinas also perceives that human laws and values change constantly. So within natural law he distinguishes primary, unchanging principles and secondary, mutable principles. "The fundamental rule of reason is the law of nature ... All human law has the status of law in so far as it is derived from the law of nature." [58] In this way, natural law theory is given a flexibility which some of its modern protagonists do not seem to recognize. It is not an immutable set of practical laws that apply to the most detailed circumstances and that can never be changed, regardless of circumstances. Instead, it is a complex of mutable, practical human laws based on a set of unchanging, fundamental principles. It seems to me that the inherent confusion in *Humanae vitae* is to identify and thus confuse a very specific ethical circumstance with an immutable, primary principle of the natural law. At most, contraception fits into the category of mutable, secondary principles.

I will now apply this to a pressing modern problem. Legislated law ought to be an expression of natural law. Therefore, it ought to give expression as much to the rights of nature as to the rights of humankind. I have already indicated that the right to reproduce is not an *unlimited* right; it can only be exercised within the context of the common good of both the human and natural community. And we have noted that Pope Paul VI, at least in principle, admitted in the encyclical *Populorum progressio* that the state can exercise some restraint over its citizens' reproductive rights. But the tragedy of the church is that it missed the opportunity to help people make ethical decisions about limiting reproduction and thus to neutralize the draconian necessity of the bureaucratic intervention of the state, with all of the economic, social, and cultural prejudices that that involves. The church could have acted as an educative agent of moral persuasion to help poorer people form their own consciences about the control of their fertility. No one with a sense of the democratic tradition wants to grant even to the democratic state more power than it already has to intervene in the private lives of its citizens. Above all, no one wants to see the coercive power of non-democratic and dictatorial states extended. But given the myopic fixation of the official church on the mechanics and chemistry of reproduction and its failure to act responsibly to apply natural law in a wider ethical and cultural context, many states with burgeoning populations have no other option than to intervene directly in their people's reproductive lives to limit population.

A good contemporary example of this is the Philippines. Here the Protestant President, Fidel Ramos, facing a population galloping out of control, has introduced a family planning program. He faces the opposition of many in the Catholic hierarchy, led by Cardinal Jaime Sin of Manila. Yet the population figures of the Philippines (with a total land surface of about 300,000 square kilometres) tell their own story. In 1982 the population was just over forty-eight million. In 1990 it was sixty-five million. That is an increase of just over two million per year. At that rate, the population of the country will double in twenty-five years.

The Philippines has already experienced two ecological disasters of the first magnitude and population pressures were major components in both. After it had lost four-fifths of its original tropical rainforest to the loggers, the landless poor moved into the less fertile parts of the logged areas to farm; the best cleared land was quickly taken by the multinational food corporations to produce cash crops for export. The country's coral reefs are now being devastated by polluted water that results from run-off from the eroded soil washed down from de-afforested areas. Ironically, it was the ecological devastation of the Philippines that led the Catholic bishops to issue their famous Pastoral Letter, *What is Happening to Our Beautiful Land?* in January 1988. They admitted then that "The poor are as disadvantaged as ever and the natural world has been grievously wounded." But despite their own Pastoral, the bishops still seem unable to make any connection between this and the issue of population.

Cardinal Sin claims that he is not only protecting moral values by opposing family planning; he is also safeguarding the Filipino cultural tradition of large families. A similar assertion has recently been made by Archbishop Nicodemus Kirima of Nyeri in Kenya. Speaking to the Special Assembly of the Synod of Bishops of Africa (April 1994), he said that family planning was a weapon used by western governments and elites to promote a new set of values favoring small families.[59] But while it is true that birth control is not an issue of major importance for most Latinos and Africans, for they have traditionally seen fertility as a blessing, this does not mean that the wider, international common good does not demand that these cultural traditions be judged in a broader ethical context and that these nations exercise control over their fertility. It is precisely the failure of the church to confront the causes of the population explosion in the Philippines and Africa with moral arguments in favor of fertility control that has forced the state to intervene. This failure by the church has already produced the terrible consequences for the poor and the environment that I have outlined. Under the influence of the Vatican, the church now seems determined to compound the problem.

So any serious Catholic-Christian attempt to control fertility will admit that in the emergency situation in which the world finds itself today, the state may well be forced to intervene to control fertility for the sake of the common good and to uphold the natural law. The church would do well to support state efforts by humanizing the more harsh, impersonal, and bureaucratic aspects of state policy. It sometimes seems to me that the state is more in touch with God's eternal law than is the church. If the church and its leaders knew its own moral tradition better, took it more seriously, and applied it more creatively, Christians might be able to take a more positive role in confronting the problem of population.

There is a further element in the natural law tradition which needs to be considered. The tradition distinguishes between the way in which non-human reality is governed and the way in which human beings work out their ethical affairs. The whole of non-human reality is said to be subject to the "law of nature" which guides it according to inexorable laws and unchanging patterns. Following the seventeenth-century French philosopher Rene Descartes, the whole of non-human reality is seen as totally lacking any rationality or possibility of choice. Within the philosophical context of Cartesian dualism this view made sense. According to Descartes, animals, for instance, were mere machines totally lacking any self-consciousness or inner life, let alone any ability to make choices.

Our expanded contemporary knowledge of the non-human world makes it clear that Descartes' view was simply wrong. We know that there are differences in the way in which different parts of the natural world works. Physical laws are obviously immutable and predictable; for instance, Bernoulli's principle assures us that the aerodynamic shape of an aircraft's wings will lift it into the air if sufficient airspeed is attained. But once we move beyond physical laws into the realm of sentient beings, a far more complex situation arises. Anyone who says a cat is merely a machine governed by an inexorable law of nature obviously has never lived with one! As our knowledge of nature expands, we encounter complex social structures among insects, birds, and mammals that indicate an inner, relational life and an ability to choose among different objects. In this context, Aquinas' term "rational" might well have its meaning extended to include the higher mammals. The distinction between the rest of the sentient world and humankind is not as watertight as was previously believed.

Thus I would suggest that the sharp division between the operation of the law of nature and natural law can no longer be maintained. In the contemporary world the two are more conjoined, so that the fundamental principles of natural law can be extended to at least the sentient part of nature. As we slowly leave behind the anthropocentrism that led us to distinguish and isolate ourselves completely from the rest of the natural world, the distinction between the law of nature and natural law makes less and less sense. All the beings of the natural world have evolved for a purpose and have a value in themselves, just as human beings are purpose-oriented and intrinsically valuable. Natural law will be just as ethically concerned about nature itself and the survival of the natural world, as it is about the moral minutiae of human ethics—and even more concerned. It would be ironic if "natural law" had nothing to do with nature!

This will mean that human beings are not the only creatures that can appeal to the basic principles of natural law. In practical terms this will mean that *all* living beings—not just humans—will have a natural right to life and to the resources needed for that life. Thus the destruction of natural habitat will not be ethically judged merely by the norms of "rational" economics, or even so-called "sustainable development," but by the natural right to survival of the communities of living species that occupy an area. The lives and well-being of animals and plants will acquire a value in themselves that is parallel to that of human beings. Natural law is a special kind of knowledge and ethical judgment about the whole of nature, not just the moral behavior of human beings. It is the law that is "written in our hearts," which assures us that as human beings we are not isolated creatures who have a right to destroy nature to sustain ourselves. Rather, we are *part* of the fabric of being and our own survival essentially depends on the survival of all the other parts.

The third element in developing an ethic of population: an extended notion of "justice"

The third element in any population policy will have to center around the reality of justice. As we have seen, the word "justice," especially in its distributive form, is already an entrenched element in the Christian discussion of population control.

Christian ethics draws strongly on the classical tradition which, in turn, is expressive of natural law. In the *Nicomachean Ethics* (Book V, 6), Aristotle defines justice as "a kind of mean ...

justice is that in virtue of which the just man ... will distribute either between himself and another or between two others not so much as to give what is desirable to himself and less to his neighbour ... but to give what is equal in accordance with proportion."[60] For Aristotle, justice is a form of equity between people, and it is significant that he describes it in practical, distributive terms.

However, Aristotle's notion is rather ethically limited, and so Christian morality also draws upon the biblical tradition which has a much richer and more complex notion of justice. As the *Dictionary of Biblical Theology* says: "In comparison with biblical language, modern religious usage of words pertaining to justice seems extremely restricted."[61] One biblical approach is parallel to the Aristotelian and focuses on justice as a moral virtue which entitles us "to a just reward before God." God is the model of integrity for all of humankind and acts with a "supreme sense of proportion" as the ultimate dispenser of justice, punishing evil and rewarding good. But another, more profound biblical theme actually identifies the justice of God with the mercy of God. "The justice of God, which man attains through faith, ultimately coincides with [God's] mercy."[62]

This biblical theme, however, is not restricted to mercy, love, and justice toward humankind; it extends to the whole of creation. This notion comes through particularly strongly in some of the Psalms: "[God] loves righteousness and justice; the earth is full of the steadfast love of the Lord" (Psalm 33:5). This is also reflected in Psalm 96:11–13, where justice, mercy, and cosmic themes all come together:

Let the heavens be glad, and let the earth rejoice;
let the sea roar, and all that fills it;
let the field exult, and everything in it.
Then shall all the trees of the forest sing for joy
before the Lord; for he is coming,
for he is coming to judge the earth.
He will judge the world with righteousness.

Perhaps this biblical emphasis is best summed up in Psalm 85:10–11:

> Steadfast love and faithfulness will meet;
> righteousness and peace will kiss each other.
> Faithfulness will spring up from the ground,
> and righteousness will look down from the sky.

The essence of the psalmist's view is expressed in the simple statement: "[God] will judge the world with righteousness" (Psalm 98:9). A strong cosmic emphasis runs right through the Psalms and is integrated into a deep sense of God's justice and mercy.

It is this broader biblical emphasis on cosmic justice, linked to mercy, that should be applied to population policy. As all of the churches have emphasized, distributive justice demands that the goods of the earth be more equally spread among all people. However, usually the churches have seen the "development" of resources as a key element in the process of achieving this equity. For instance, the title of Pope Paul VI's encyclical *Populorum progressio* is usually translated "The Development of Peoples." Pope Paul himself, speaking at the United Nations in October 1965, invited all the poor nations to share in "the banquet of life." But this notion of distributive justice must be seen within the biblical context of God's justice and mercy toward the *whole* of the world, not just toward humankind. If there is to be a more equitable distribution, it has to be in terms of sustainability and respect for all the planet's life systems.

But if distributive justice means indulgence in a gross developmental binge in an attempt to bring the rest of the world to the level of overdevelopment that is characteristic of the west, it cannot be ethically justified in the light of biblical teaching. In fact, the Bible's strong emphasis on a broad distributive justice means that it is the western levels of development that have to fall. For we are now at a point where we can see that the reality of "development" has brought us to a situation where the very structures of the earth itself are under threat. There is no way that the enormous populations of China, India, Africa and the rest of the third world can live at the same level of overdevelopment that has been attained by countries like the United States, the United Kingdom, and Australia. Nor can the developed world sustain the use of resources at the same level. All of this is well known.

The head-long rush toward aping crass western development by the so-called "tiger economies" of Asia (South Korea, Taiwan, Singapore, and, to a lesser extent, Thailand, Indonesia, and Malaysia) has to be viewed much more critically. Several of these countries are experiencing wholesale devastation of their tropical forests, with the resultant extinction of species. Industrialization brings in its wake appalling pollution and the exploitation of the poor. It is especially ironic that they are referred to as "tiger" economies: they use the symbol of an animal that is now on the verge of extinction in the wild in Asia! These countries are really ugly symbols of what headlong development will mean for other third world nations.

The fourth element in developing an ethic of population: the use of an "ascetical exchange"

A contemporary ethical and biblical approach demands that what needs to happen in the contemporary world is a two-way *ascetical exchange* between first and third world countries. This will probably have to be brokered by the United Nations.

Firstly, let us look at such an exchange from the point of view of the developed world. While maintaining populations at or below zero population growth, first world countries would have to begin rapidly to slow their use of non-renewable resources, to halt to some extent further infrastructure development that is destructive of the natural environment, and to abandon the notion of expansion and development as the only way to manage their economies and measure their success. Developed countries would also have to begin to share their knowledge, experience, and know-how with the third world. There would have to be an amnesty on all third world debt. At the same time western nations would have to guarantee that there would be no further exploitative use of the environment in the third world and that individuals and corporations would face severe penalties for violations of this commitment.

In exchange, third world countries would have to guarantee to achieve targets in limiting population. A key issue in this process, as the Cairo Conference pointed out, would be the link between education, especially the education of women, and fertility. Focus on this issue as a central determining factor is explained by Dr David Lucas of the Australian National University's National Centre for Development Studies:

> What happens when education increases is that the marriage age goes up, the period of breastfeeding decreases and the use of family planning increases. In the short term these determinants operate in different directions. The higher marriage age means that women start child-bearing later and the increased use of family planning means that within marriage they can regulate fertility. However, the breastfeeding period becomes shorter and this means that women are more likely to become pregnant as they lose to some degree the protection against pregnancy that breastfeeding provides.[63]

Education also reverses the wealth flow in a family: it means that children are a long-term cost (in terms of educational needs and financial support) rather than a source of income through childhood work and a prop for their parents as they age (usually prematurely in third world countries). But there is also a wide range of local cultural factors that influence fertility: these have to do with religion, family and clan pressures, local practices, language and communication taboos, and economic demands. These local issues also have to be taken into account when developing a population control policy.

No one can pretend that the evolution of an ascetical exchange between western and third world countries will be easy. There are so many vested interests. But unless something like this begins to happen, there is no hope of reversing either the population explosion or ecological destruction. It has to be a two-way exchange.

Nor can anyone pretend that the development of a population policy will be easy. Dr Ralph B. Potter, Professor of Social Ethics at Harvard Divinity School, has indicated some of the complexities involved in applying a concept of equity and justice to the ethics of population policy.[64] He points out that public debate about these issues will be divisive because deeply held philosophical and religious convictions underlie all approaches to the population explosion. Given that the debate is about the *control* of fertility, it touches everyone. Potter says that because "population policies entail the restraint of accustomed liberties, they require explicit justification." He continues:

> The divisive potential of population issues becomes yet more apparent and explosive when it becomes evident that policies are likely to bear differently upon various social, economic, ethnic, and religious groups within a society. Policies may be seen to favour one way of living and handicap another ... Deep aspirations and anxieties touching upon questions of identity, self-perpetuation, prosperity, and survival may become engaged.

As a result, politicians (especially in democratic countries) will generally avoid making decisions about population like the plague!

Although there is more agreement now that we are facing a disastrous situation with the world population out of control, there are still those who assert that this is not happening and advance various arguments to support their claim. As Potter says: "Those who emphasize policies designed to decrease, halt, or reverse rates of population growth must deal with rejoinders that insist upon the value of 'freedom' and 'autonomy' or 'self-determination' in procreative matters." Ecologists can be remarkably naive about the apparent obviousness of the population explosion. They have to confront the dangers to human freedom embedded in draconian measures to control population as well as face the danger of being accused by their opponents of 'environmental fascism' as they insist on the need to both cut back consumption in western countries and develop strategies for population control in the third world. As Potter says: "The population issue is not only a menacing and difficult practical problem but also an intractable intellectual, moral, and spiritual problem."

I have claimed that it is only by intellectual and ethical conversion that we will come to see the world in a different and creative light. But before we do that we need to answer the assertion that Christianity is to blame for environmental destruction.

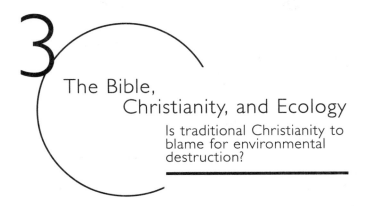

3

The Bible, Christianity, and Ecology

Is traditional Christianity to blame for environmental destruction?

Christianity and its derivative, western European culture, have both been blamed by many contemporary ecological thinkers for being the major causes of the development of exploitative and negative human attitudes toward the natural world. The most influential argument supporting this particular interpretation of the western Christian attitude toward nature was mounted in 1967, when the American medieval historian Lynn White accused the Judeo-Christian tradition of being largely responsible for the dichotomy between humankind and nature.[1] Following this, a fascinating controversy broke out. White's point was that Christianity was the most important element in the resistance of western culture to the development of environmentalism. He held that the Judeo-Christian insistence on the supremacy of humankind over the rest of creation caused a disjunction in human thought that made "Christianity the most anthropocentric religion the world has seen." This is a view that would still find much sympathy among environmentalists today.

White contended that in the Christian understanding of the cosmos, the whole of nature was created exclusively to serve humankind, the one and only true image of God. He said that the biblical assumption, an assumption taken up vigorously by

Christian theology, was that human beings have the right to "subdue" and "use" the whole of creation in order to "build" things (as Hugh Morgan would say). White's point was that real change in human-cosmic relations would never occur "until we reject the Christian axiom that nature has no reason for existence save to serve man."

So what truth is there in White's arguments? How much is Christianity to blame for contemporary exploitative attitudes toward the cosmos and the environment?

Recently, Rupert Sheldrake has argued that White's views are too simplistic; he holds that the real problem is "much deeper."[2] Sheldrake traces human antagonism to nature back to the ancient Greeks and even further in terms of humankind's constant need to manipulate and sometimes destroy our environmental surroundings.

> Cultures differ in the strength of their impulse toward mastery and in the countervailing sense of kinship with the natural world. But the whole of human history—ever since fire was first tamed, tools first made, metals first used, animals and plants first domesticated, cities first built—has involved man's domination of nature to varying degrees.[3]

Sheldrake is correct in that even those cultures that lived in harmony with nature inevitably changed their environments. This concurs with Thomas Berry's argument that humankind ever since neolithic times has been constantly motivated by "exploitative anthropocentrism." Berry points out, for instance, that traditional China had an exalted view of nature, but this did not prevent the Chinese from destroying much of the forest cover of China long before the Christian era.[4]

Sheldrake and Berry's point about the link between extinction scenarios and humanity can be illustrated by the arrival of the Aborigines or their predecessors in Australia. Prior to their coming there were many mega-marsupials, such as the massive wombat-like Diprotodon and the large kangaroo-like Procoptodon. The extinction of these large marsupials roughly parallels the probable arrival of human beings on the continent. There is no doubt that the Aborigines modified the flora and fauna through the widespread use of fire. Australian archaeologist and historian Josephine Flood says that "directly or indirectly, Aboriginal occupation of the Continent had as great an impact on Australian fauna in the Pleistocene as European settlement was to have in recent times."[5] She concedes the possibility that the "huge browsers that survived the initial impact of man the hunter finally seem to have met their end during the Great Dry at the end of the Pleistocene." However, after examining available evidence against human agency as the major cause of mega-faunal extinction in Australia, Flood concludes:

> The main period of extinction precedes the main late Pleistocene climatic change. The only new element in the equation was man, who may have caused the extinctions by a combination of hunting and his use of fire, which drastically altered the animal's habitats. The weight of human evidence favours human hunters as the decisive factor.[6]

Thus the position represented by Sheldrake and Berry has much to recommend it. There is a certain glibness in the view that blames the biblical tradition for our entire western history of alienation from nature. In fact, consciousness of the distinction between humankind and nature probably goes right back to an early level of human evolution, as people asserted their will over some animals and domesticated them. Certainly the development of agriculture, cultivation, and the early evolution of urbanization indicate a distinct human sense of separation and alienation from nature. Towns and cities are essentially artificial environments which cut human beings off from direct links with nature. Historically, such activities and attitudes predate the Bible by thousands of years. From primordial times there was a continuous interaction between humankind and the environment. At first, human beings were almost completely dependent on the environment. It determined the way in which they were to live. But slowly ancient peoples gained the ability to modify their environmental surroundings and to create artificial dwellings which they controlled and in which they felt safe.

Allowing for this qualification, let us examine Lynn White's accusation about Judeo-Christianity and look at the biblical evidence. Is the Bible primarily responsible for human alienation from nature? To take the issue further: is there any sense in which the Bible has anything at all to offer to contemporary religious thought on environmentalism?

The biblical evidence

Certainly the sheer number of recent books on the topic of the Bible and the environment would seem to indicate that the scriptures have a lot to say on the issue. My own view is more cautious. Those who take the Bible as their *sole* source of revelation are obliged to search for and tease out every biblical detail about nature if they want to say anything theologically coherent about ecology. They simply have to make the most of the biblical evidence. Those who are not so single-mindedly biblical are freer to see the Bible as simply *one* source for reflection on environmentalism.

While it is my view that the Bible only has a limited amount of support to offer to a more positive view of ecology, I want to emphasize that my comments are not an exhaustive treatment of the biblical evidence. What I will do here is to try to select those texts and biblical emphases that have been most important in subsequent interpretation for both Jews and Christians. No single individual person or historical period assimilates all the themes that thread their way through the Bible. All religious writers and scholars select those texts and themes that suit their particular theological purpose. What I want to do here is to select those ideas that have been most influential on subsequent religious thought.

It must be admitted that Lynn White is certainly correct that the Christian church inherits a tradition represented by the two primary biblical texts concerning humankind's relationship to nature. The first is Genesis 1:26–28.

> Then God said, "Let us make humankind in our image, according to our likeness; and let them have dominion" ... So God created humankind in his image ... God blessed them, and God said to them, "Be fruitful and multiply, and fill the earth and subdue it; and have dominion."

In this unfortunate text, which so vividly represents early Judaism's own antagonistic relationship to its difficult and arid desert environment, we have a fundamental source of many modern ideas of exploitative development and anthropocentrism. The second text comes from the second and still more ancient description of creation in the book of Genesis: Genesis 2:4–25. In this passage man and woman are actually created from the soil, but the emphasis in the text is still on the separate and unique significance of humankind. The very act of naming all the other creatures gives humankind a special sharing in the divine nature, for, in the biblical mentality, to name something implies that one is part of the formation and definition of that reality and consequently has power over it.

> So out of the ground the Lord God formed every animal of the field and every bird of the air, and brought them to the man to see what he would call them; and whatever the man called every living creature, that was its name (Genesis 2:19).

Both accounts in Genesis set humankind above and beyond the rest of God's created world.

The underlying theological notion in both of these texts is also significant: humankind has dominion over the earth precisely because we share in the very life of God. We are, in the truest sense, the 'icons' or images of God. In the biblical understanding, only human beings—and more specifically (despite the gender-neutral language of the New Revised Standard Version translation) only *male* human beings—are "like God." The early biblical writers' preoccupation with the dangers of idolatry led them to deny any sense of divine iconography to the rest of creation. The biblical fear was that to concede that anything other than human beings could reveal something of God opened the way to setting that natural reality up as an idol to be adored and worshiped. This fear is revealed vividly in the second of the ten commandments ("Thou shalt not have strange gods before me") and in the story of the golden calf in Exodus 32. At the core of the biblical writers' consciousness was the fear that the Jewish people would adopt aspects of the fertility religion of the Caananite people who surrounded them.

The result is that in the two accounts of creation there is no recognition that the animals, plants, birds, and even the earth itself mirror the Creator and are, in fact, also icons of God. There is a denial of any sense of consciousness to creation. The natural world is seen largely as an inert, mute reality that is there simply to be subjected to human guidance and subjugation. The dominant view of creation in Genesis is that nature's only true value is to be found in its relationship to humankind and that its connection with God can only be brought about through humankind. This is not a very positive view of the natural world.

The image of God that is presented in the creation accounts is deeply anthropomorphic in that God is seen almost exclusively as a person like us. This view has also set the pattern for subsequent theological development and biblical exegesis. Even now, most Jewish and Christian believers see God almost exclusively in personal terms, however undifferentiated—someone who exists "out there." Among believers God's personhood is seen as the foundation of all that is good about divine love, fidelity, forgiveness, and acceptance of us as we are. Of course, believers are right: the nature of God is personal, but theology correctly emphasizes that God is personal in a *transcendent* sense. Popular belief tends to obliterate the theological fact that our knowledge of God is analogical, only an extrapolation from our own personhood and human experience.

But to return to the creation accounts in Genesis. While allowing that these accounts of creation in no way exhaust the Judeo-Christian understanding of the relationship between humankind and nature, and that there is much more about the natural world in the Bible, it does have to be said that both mainstream Judaism and Christianity have subsequently interpreted the meaning of the creation accounts to support an attitude in which nature has been valued almost exclusively within the context of subservience to the needs of humanity. It is often forgotten that the *interpretation* of biblical texts is actually far more significant and influential than the texts themselves. This certainly applies to the creation accounts in Genesis. Clarence Glacken, in his interesting history of cosmology, *Traces on the Rhodian Shore*, has commented that the Genesis account of creation is characterized above all by brevity. He then elaborates on the consequences of this brevity:

> Words are used so sparingly in describing the successive acts in the creation of the cosmos that, with the growth of Christianity and the continuing strength of Judaism, an enormous exegetical literature was inevitable ... The intense otherworldliness and rejection of the beauties of nature because they turn men away from the contemplation of God are elaborated upon far more in the theological writings than in the Bible itself.[7]

Glacken argues that the commentaries and interpretations have become much more important than the actual texts themselves.

But at the heart of the discussion about creation and nature in the Hebrew scriptures is the problem indicated by Lynn White: the fact that the Bible is profoundly suspicious of the danger of idolatry. Its entrenched monotheism leads it to see humankind and humankind alone as the only possible image or icon of God. Nature's value is derived entirely from its relationship to human beings. Thus our human needs and preoccupations become the arbiter and the norm of ethical judgment about everything related to nature. The natural world lacks any intrinsic value in itself. In later Christian thought, even the moral demand that we not be cruel to animals is derived primarily from the need to act according to our human dignity, ethical standards, and intelligence, rather than from an acknowledgment of the intrinsic value of the animals themselves. Beyond the animals, there has been hardly any recognition in the Christian theological tradition that sub-animal reality has any intrinsic value at all except to be exploited by and for humankind.

However, as a number of contemporary writers have indicated, there are also many positive visions of nature running through the Hebrew scriptures.[8] My comments about the Genesis accounts of creation must be seen in the light of the fact that it is very difficult to make generalizations about the attitude of the Bible on specific issues. The Hebrew scriptures are a collection of different pieces, in varying styles, written over a very long period of historical development. In fact, there is no overall understanding of the natural world running through the Bible. The most general thing that can be said about the scriptural view of nature is that the biblical text is not abstract, but rather geographically particular. In other words, the biblical writers were not interested in "nature" or the "cosmos" as abstract notions; they were interested in this piece of land or desert, or that mountain, or this river, or that valley. In this, biblical cosmological views are akin to those of most ancient people and contemporary indigenous people whose attitudes are largely shaped by their relationship to a specific place.

The Anglican Bishop of Salisbury, John Austin Baker, sums up the attitude of the Hebrew Scriptures to nature in six points.[9] Firstly, he writes that the earth belongs primarily and uniquely to God. Secondly, under God humankind has a position of some control over nature "which is meant to be exercised in a spirit of respect and responsibility." Thirdly, the world is "desuper-naturalized"; that is, it is neither divine nor demonic. As a result, humans can deal with it rationally, factually, and as it really is. Fourthly, the greater part of the world is created for its own sake and humankind will never fully understand God's intentions in creation. Fifthly, the world and nature reflect something of God's wisdom; therefore, human beings must respect the natural order and be ready to learn from it. Finally, nature, like humankind, will not come to completion until the end time: "Nature is not perfect; there is a work of salvation to be done in it, as well as in humanity."

This fits in perfectly with what I think is the most positive text in the New Testament about the role of the natural world: Romans 8:22–23:

> We know that the whole creation has been groaning in labor pains until now; and not only the creation, but we ourselves, who have the first fruits of the Spirit, groan inwardly while we wait for adoption, the redemption of our bodies.

In this extraordinary text St Paul links our human fate to that of the whole creation and says that all of reality is struggling through a birth-process toward a spiritual redemption that is bodily and material. Although Baker is not sanguine about the extent and depth of reflection on the natural world in the New Testament compared to the Hebrew scriptures, the text in Romans stands out as a shining light in the New Testament.

Another passage which deserves careful scrutiny in this context is Colossians 1:15–17.

> [Christ] is the image of the invisible God, the first-born of all creation; for in him all things in heaven and on earth were created, things visible and invisible, whether thrones or dominations or ruler or powers—all things have been created through him and for him. He himself is before all things, and in him all things hold together.

In this passage Christ is seen as the medium through which creation occurs. He is himself a product of the invisible God's creativity and, as such, is an icon or image of that God. The passage actually sets up a striking trinity: God-Christ-Creation. It suggests an intimate link between Christ and the cosmos so that one may well be able to argue that to destroy the natural world is to destroy the image of Christ, who is himself the image of God.

Certainly, in the Hebrew scriptures there is much that can be applied to the development of a more positive theological approach to the environment. Already a number of writers have begun to develop these themes. But the point that needs to be re-emphasized here is that the predominant historical view in the Judeo-Christian interpretation of creation and nature, and the one which still influences the majority of believers, is that which emphasizes that the world exists to serve human beings. Its raison d'etre is subservient to humankind, which alone is in the image of God.

The loss of the biblical view of nature

While it has to be admitted that the Bible is, at best, a mixed blessing for environmental theology, the fact is that throughout its history Christianity has injected a negative approach to the natural world into its theology. The basic reason for this is that Christian tradition has also failed to deal positively with the human body. There is an intimate connection between our attitude toward our own bodies and to nature. It is our bodies which tie us most closely to the materiality of the earth. If we despise this most intimate aspect of ourselves, then there is little hope that we will value nature. Our attitude to our own material selves becomes the norm of our attitude to the world.[10]

Over the last few years Christian writers on environmental theology have tended to gloss over and even ignore the dominant and on-going dualistic tradition at the core of Christianity, with its negative attitudes toward the natural world. These writers move on quickly to attempt to rediscover and re-articulate what they see as the more positive aspects of the Christian tradition on ecology. They dismiss the theological attitudes of the past as though these can be simply jettisoned without pain. I think that this rush to renewal is premature. It presumes that one can somehow simply abandon the major western Christian theological emphases of the last nineteen hundred years—which denigrated the body, nature, and the material world—and replace these emphases in one quick swipe of the pen with a whole new approach which is more ecologically "friendly." These writers fail to recognize that the Christian tradition is deeply compromised and scarred by the body-soul dualism inherited from Greek thought. It is simply misleading to pretend that this is not the case. I strongly disagree with those who ignore the past; it is impossible to abandon deep-seated Christian dualism so easily. It is not just a matter of articulating a new, more ecologically sensitive attitude, nor of highlighting the views of a tiny minority of Christians such as Hildegarde of Bingen or Francis of Assisi. The task for Christian theology is much tougher.

I will argue later that what is required for a genuine ecological theology is a profound inner change which is akin to religious conversion—and that this change is not achieved superficially or merely through the articulation of another attitude. Change can only occur when the old way of thinking is understood in both its positive and negative perspectives; it is only then that the decision can be taken *consciously and deliberately* to move beyond it. In order to come to this decision some historical perspective is needed. What follows is a brief sketch of the origins of the deep-seated and on-going Christian "problem" with materiality and the world. Only when this history is understood will we be in the position to abandon it and move toward a whole new approach to the natural world.

For most of its history Christianity has dealt badly with human sexuality. It has often promoted a spiritual ethos which has denigrated the body and has generally had an indifferent attitude toward the natural world. At the core of this is a profound suspicion about matter; materiality has been seen as antithetical to spiritual growth and to the search for God. The origin of this suspicion lies in the answer to the question: "What is the human person?"

For centuries, Christianity (and much of European culture) has answered this question by defining the person as a body enlivened by a soul. The soul is identified with the spiritual and higher faculties of the person and the body with the lower animal and material aspect. The body has no personal form unless enlivened by the soul. In popular Christian belief, the soul has been viewed as the individual form that gives personal shape and individuality to each human being; the material body has been seen as a mere repository for spirit. This dualistic definition is the key source of the on-going Christian ambivalence about the body, matter, and sexuality.

The roots of Christian dualism are not found in the Bible but in the post-New Testament adoption of pagan Greek philosophy to underpin theology, as Christian apologists in the second century tried to develop a coherent apologetic for their belief. The integrated Hebrew notion of human beings as animated bodies quickly transmuted into the Greek notion of incarnated souls. The ingrained Christian suspicion of matter focused attention more and more on the spiritual aspects of personhood. And, of course, only human beings were persons. Christianity became more and more anthropocentric.

The Catholic end of the Christian spectrum, of course, has always held that the Bible is only a relative source for theology and belief—relative, that is, to tradition. But tradition, when defined in the narrow sense of past church teaching and theology, gives even less encouragement than the Bible to theologians interested in an alternative view to the prevailing anthropocentrism. John Carmody, in *Ecology and Religion*, after a survey of both biblical and traditional theological doctrine says in something of an understatement:

> The early and later fathers, the medievals, the reformers, the moderns and our contemporaries have reworked the biblical data in the light of the science and spirituality of their times. Seldom, however, have they overcome the somewhat anthropocentric cast of what seems to be the mainstream of the Christian tradition.[11]

If a fundamentally problematic pattern was set by elements within the biblical tradition and its interpretation, it has been above all the importation of pagan philosophical concepts into theology which has most distorted and biased Christian belief. So what happened to Christianity once it moved out of its Jewish matrix and into the cosmopolitan world of Greece and Rome?

Changes in belief as Christianity moved into the Greco-Roman world

Very early in its history Christianity had to leave the Jewish cultural milieu in which it had been born. From the first half of the first century onwards it moved progressively into the Greco-Roman world. In order to interact with this already declining but still deeply cosmopolitan and international culture, it had to discover new ways of articulating Christian thought. To communicate its message and develop its apologetic, the church had to adapt to and adopt the language and cultural patterns of the people of this broader world. In this sense, early Christianity was neither fundamentalist nor biblically literalist in its attempt to evangelize the Greco-Roman world. In its laudable attempt to make itself understood in contemporary terms, it was willing to use the religious and philosophical patterns that were at hand in the culture into which it had moved.

As I said, it was a declining culture, even in the second century AD, and not all of its cultural elements were especially healthy. The fundamental religious milieu of the second and third century Greco-Roman world was gnostic, and Christianity had to struggle to define itself over against this curious religious movement. There is no doubt that through a process of osmosis Christianity was influenced by it. Gnosticism was a complex of teachings and movements, a veritable sub-culture in the second and third century Roman world, somewhat like the new age movement today. Its origins are obscure and are certainly pre-Christian, but it had considerable interaction with the early church. There is a sense in which gnosticism is the primal heresy: it attempts to disembody religion and to spiritualize it. Throughout church history many Christian movements have been gnostic—and thus heretical—in tendency.

J.N.D. Kelly has described gnosticism as a "bizarre mixture of speculation, fantasy and mysticism." It taught that there was a dualistic chasm between the spiritual and material worlds. The latter, the gnostics said, was not the creation of God and was consistently and intrinsically evil. Human beings yearned to be free of materiality and to ascend to their true heavenly home far away from matter.[12]

Applying these notions to early Christianity, the gnostics rejected the Old Testament's depiction of God as involved in the time-shaped pattern of history and in the daily lives of the Jewish people. The gnostics argued that Jesus only had the appearance of a body and that redemption could only be achieved by esoteric knowledge, not in and through the flesh of Christ and especially not through his death on a cross. Gnosticism was clearly an anti-worldly spirituality in the fullest sense. But despite its opposition to it, the early church absorbed elements of this otherworldliness into its own tradition. It seems to be an ironic aspect of history that the church often absorbs elements of the very heresy it condemns!

At the same time as Christianity was attempting to resist the tempting spiritual blandishments of gnosticism, theologians were seeking a meaningful philosophical underpinning for their theology. The earliest Christians stuck more or less to Jewish theological patterns, but by the middle of the second century Christian thinkers had begun to borrow the philosophies that were at hand: Stoicism, Neo-Platonism, and Epicureanism. Through both its theology and apologetic, Christianity absorbed elements of all of these philosophical systems; and all were, at best, ambivalent about matter and life in the body.

This is most vividly expressed in the attitude to the flesh which emerged in the philosophical currents of the third and fourth centuries. As Rosemary Ruether has written:

Late antique culture is obsessed with the fear of mortality, of corruptibility. To be born in the flesh is to be subject to change, which is a devolution toward decay and death. Only by extricating mind from matter by ascetic practices, aimed at severing the connections of mind and body, can one prepare for the salvific escape out of the realm of corruptibility to eternal spiritual life. All that sustains physical life—sex, eating, reproduction, even sleep—comes to be seen as sustaining the realm of "death," against which a mental realm of consciousness has been abstracted as the realm of "true life."[13]

For the philosophers of the late Roman world the dualism of body and soul was a central theme: the fullness of life was to be found in the soul which had been captured, dragged down, and degraded by contact with the body. Asceticism was construed as the only way of escape. The best minds of the late Roman Empire (such as the Emperor Marcus Aurelius and the philosopher Plotinus) saw the natural world as a place of illusion, a joke, "a dream, a delirium" (Marcus Aurelius). The historian E.R. Dodds observes: "Much the same feeling underlies the long and splendid passage where Plotinus in his last years, drawing on both Plato and the Stoics, interprets the grandeurs and miseries of human life in terms of a stage performance."[14] A similar theme is taken up in Shakespeare's *As You Like It*, where Jaques assures a gathering in the Forest of Arden that "All the world's a stage, and all the men and women merely players" (Act II, Scene VII).

Of all these philosophical currents in the late Roman world, the most important was Neo-Platonism. Neo-Platonism was an on-going development of the thought of Plato (c. 428–348 BC) by several thinkers in the late Roman Empire, of whom Plotinus (AD 205–270), who conducted a philosophical school in Rome, was the most important.

The American philosopher Arthur O. Lovejoy has distinguished "two conflicting major strains in Plato and in the Platonic tradition."[15] These two strains are other-worldliness and this-worldliness. It is the other-worldly strain that has particularly affected Christian theology and spirituality. Lovejoy explains what Plato meant by other-worldliness: it is "the belief that both the genuinely 'real' and the truly good are antithetic in their essential characteristics to anything that can be found in man's natural life, in the ordinary course of human experience." [16] In other words, to the other-worldly Platonic mind, the passing reality of this world has no real substance. The good, which is sought by human reason and will, can only be found through contemplation in a higher realm.

Lovejoy comments that other-worldliness has been the persistent strain and, in one form or another, has been "the dominant official philosophy of the larger part of civilized mankind." He makes the penetrating observation that while it has been the "official" philosophy (and by this he means the belief of the educated elite), most ordinary people have never really believed it "since they have never been able to deny the things disclosed by the senses." The on-going historical influence of the Platonic ideology of other-worldliness is pervasive, especially among the traditional elite of the church—the clergy and the celibate members of religious orders. Lovejoy comments:

> It is through [Plato], as Dean Inge has said, "that the conception of an unseen eternal world, of which the visible world is but a pale copy, gains a permanent foothold in the West ... The call, once heard, has never long been forgotten in Europe"; and it is from [Plato's] writings, it is to be added, that the belief that the highest good for man lies in somehow translocating himself into such a world has been perennially nourished. [17]

The other other-worldly aspect of Platonic philosophy centers around the problem of knowledge. Plato asked: how can we have true knowledge? He argued that true knowledge subsists in universal forms or ideas and that these cannot be apprehended by the senses. These forms alone are truly real. They can be perceived only through the soul or spirit, which exists prior to the body. While the soul is in conjunction with the body it has to struggle to remember the forms and thus to know in any true sense; the body and the senses simply cannot apprehend what is really real.

In this way, as Platonic thought developed in the Greco-Roman world, the body came to be viewed as more than just a hindrance to the soul; it actually weighed it down and prevented it from attaining knowledge of the truth. Eventually it came to be seen as the prison of the soul. Excessive Platonic intellectualism drove a wedge between spirit and body and situated the heart of life in the mind. It prevented the soul from attaining a true knowledge of the forms and especially the supreme form—the One. As Christians gradually adopted Platonism as a theological substratum, the One became identified with God.

In the late Roman Empire, Neo-Platonism saw the ascetic life as a preparation for real life, the life of the soul. Many in the philosophical and religious elite of the ancient world tried to live as if they did not have a body. E.R. Dodds comments:

> Pagans and Christians (although not all pagans or all Christians) vied with each other in heaping abuse on the body ... Plotinus appeared ashamed of having a body at all. St Anthony blushed every time he had to eat or satisfy any other bodily function. Because the body's life was the soul's death salvation lay in mortifying it.[18]

In the worst sense, Neo-Platonism created a dualism between soul-spirit on the one hand and body-world on the other. The unity of human reality was lost.

As I have already emphasized, the early Christians were determined to find a philosophical basis for their faith. Neo-Platonism was not only readily available, but it seemed to be the philosophy best adapted to underpin their apologetic. Clement of Alexandria (c. 150–215) and Origen (c. 185–254) were the first to attempt the task of expressing their Christian faith in terms of philosophy. Both were associated with the great Christian catechetical school of Alexandria, so their theology was not purely speculative but was meant to help converts understand their religion. Both these theologians knew that faith had to be integrated into a specific cultural milieu; they saw that the mere assertion of a fundamentalist biblicism and a blind commitment to faith were insufficient. Their purpose was admirable, but the problem was that in seeking a rational ground for belief they imported Neo-Platonist philosophy into the heart of Christian theology.

Thus, body-soul dualism, a down-grading of the value of the body and the material world, an asceticism rooted in the denial of sexuality, and ultimately a profound denial of the finality of human death became rooted in Christian theology and, through the church, flowed into the western European cultural tradition. Without doubt other elements have entered into the traditional Christian problem with the body, but it is these Neo-Platonic themes that have created the models that have become normative for our culture. This is the source of the powerful tension that underpins the whole of the western philosophical tradition. As the philosopher A.N. Whitehead has pointed out, all western thought is really just a footnote to Plato![19]

At the heart of the Platonic philosophical matrix is a strong, even manic denial of death. For Platonists, immortality was achieved by jettisoning the body and returning to the pure, limpid life of the soul. But our actual human experience of reality is different, for it is only when we admit and embrace bodily existence that we can face the ultimate facticity of death. Genuine Christian theology has always understood this and has never accepted "immortality" in the Platonic sense. The Christian view is subtly but decisively different. The facticity of death has never been denied in the Christian tradition. Christ, after all, "was crucified, died, and was buried," as the creed says. But for the Christian, as for Christ, death is seen as opening out to a transforming process of union with God and a profound sense of continuity with this life, rather than as a disembodied terminus. For Christ rose to glory with God *in his body*. And the Christian teaching is that Jesus' followers will also rise to union with God in their bodies. The Christian doctrine of the resurrection of the body confronts the Platonic denial of body head on and refutes it. This is why the doctrine of the resurrection of the body created so much difficulty for Platonized theologians. Augustine, for example, had great difficulty integrating it into his theological corpus. Many people today are still confused about life after death. They tend to identify continuing existence with the Platonic notion of the immortality of the soul, when Christianity is really talking about a continuing life in the glorified body. The tragedy of early theology was that it too was unable to distinguish clearly enough between the Christian teaching about life after death and the Platonic philosophical notion of immortality.

While Platonic dualism has been part of the theological tradition from early on, the key figures in introducing this dualistic streak into Christianity were St Gregory Nyssa (c. 335–395), who applied Neo-Platonic thought to Christian spirituality and mysticism, and Augustine, who confirmed its position in western theology. According to Dodds, Gregory Nyssa's "entire work is penetrated by a deep feeling of the unreality of the sensible world."[20] Yet, at the same time, Nyssa is increasingly recognized as "one of the most powerful and most original thinkers ever known in the history of the church."[21] Nyssa's influence is especially strong in eastern spirituality, and the fifth century spiritual classic, the *Celestial Hierarchy*, applies his notions to mysticism. These ideas flowed into the western European spiritual tradition through the translation of the *Celestial Hierarchy* and the teaching of Hugh of Saint Victor in Paris in the 12th century.[22]

Augustine, of course, has been blamed for the whole western tradition of the rejection of the body and especially for an excessive rigidity in sexual morality. The Harvard historian, Margaret Miles, has produced two interesting studies on Augustine's views on the human body.[23] It is clear from her work that the tradition of Christian rigidity comes as much from those who followed Augustine as it did from him, and, as we have already seen, it was part of both the spiritual and theological tradition before him.

Miles shows that Augustine had a deep ambiguity about the human body. In the years immediately after his conversion to Christianity in 386, he seems to have been preoccupied with overcoming the body, but in the final fifteen years of his life he was profoundly occupied with the theological question of the resurrection of the body. This was the Christian teaching that most profoundly disturbed Neo-Platonized theologians: how can you reconcile a philosophy which sees the body as evil with a theological belief that it was in and through the body that human beings experience the ultimate transcendence of union with God? This was a great puzzle for Neo-Platonized Christianity. As both an honest Platonist and an honest Christian, Augustine did not shy away from trying to deal with it.

There is a paradoxical element in his thought on this issue: at the very time that he strongly asserted the dignity of the human body in resurrection, he was most negative toward a primal expression of existence in the body—sexuality. As Miles points out, it is easy to quote passages from the Augustinian corpus that are pejorative to bodily existence while forgetting the reason for this prejudice. Given his Neo-Platonic framework, it is inevitable that he stressed a mystical union with God that is only possible by a withdrawal of energy inward to the central core of being where, he believed, the soul was united with God.

Christianity in the late Roman Empire also strongly believed in the superiority of virginity and celibacy over marriage. The exaltation of virginity and a commitment to a life of sexual abstinence also arose out of a Neo-Platonized religiosity. The growth of the ideal of virginity was influenced by the notion of the great efficacy of the prayer of virgins. Both Tertullian and Origen argued that purity gave the virgins a unique intimacy with the Christian mysteries and sacraments.

The late Roman period saw the beginning of the demand for celibacy for the clergy of the church. While this clearly emerged from the prevailing emphasis on virginity, it is also rooted in the Jewish and pagan notion of ritual purity. In fact, Edward Schillebeeckx has argued that cultural purity was the "dominant reason" for the early introduction into the church of the demand for priestly celibacy.[24] Ritual purity meant that priests who celebrated the eucharist must have abstained from sexual contact with their wives because of the possibility that the woman may be ritually impure through menstruation. The taboo associated with menstruation is based on the mysterious flow of blood which the ancients could not explain. Because of its close connection with birth, it was thought to have magical properties. Among Christians, the idea was that this demonic magic might pollute a priest preparing to celebrate the eucharist if he had contact with a menstruating woman. The notion obviously entered Christianity through the law of Leviticus (15:19–24; 18:19; 20:18), but the origin of the taboo is more ancient and primitive. Wolfgang Lederer argues that women initially imposed a kind of taboo to protect themselves from male sexual demands during the period of menstruation. In response, "men lost no time in reversing their exclusion from things feminine by proclaiming that such matters were abhorrent because un-clean."[25] Certainly the menstrual taboo, and the demand for virginity, were not the only elements in the development of priestly celibacy, but they were very significant.

The most important contemporary study of early Christian attitudes to the human body is Peter Brown's *The Body and Society*.[26] The book shows how the elite of late Roman Christianity, deeply influenced by the spiritual theology current in their milieu, came to see sexual renunciation as the profoundest symbol of Christian commitment. Slowly the views of the elite permeated down through pastoral teaching to ordinary Christians, although it seems that elitist views were by no means universally accepted. Brown also shows how committed Christians developed a deep ambivalence about sexual relations. All of this led to a change in the way in which they came to view their own bodies.

> It is not sufficient to talk of the rise of Christianity in the Roman world simply in terms of a shift from a less to a more repressive society. What was at stake was a change in the perception of the

body itself. The men and women of later centuries were not only hedged around with a different and more exacting set of prohibitions. They also came to see their bodies in a different light.[27]

The practical consequence of this was that the nude (male) body was no longer something to be displayed when the young men of the Greco-Roman world went to the baths to enjoy the games during the years of bisexual play before commitment to marriage, with its civic responsibilities to the emperor and the state. The gradual growth of the influence of Christianity meant that "No longer were the body's taut musculature and its refined poise, signs of the athlete and potential warrior, put on display as marks of upper class status."[28]

Instead, Christians were filled with a yearning for the coming of the kingdom of God, a desire for the transformation of the decay that was inherent in material existence. For them the human body existed primarily to be transformed through the sacramental rites of the church and through the exercise of the human will in imposing discipline on the always wayward passions, so that the Christian could "take on the lineaments of the risen Christ."[29] Brown points to the glorious mosaics of the period around AD 400, especially those that can still be seen today in Ravenna in all their glory in the churches of San Vitale, San Apollinare Nuovo, San Apollinare in Classe, the Arian Baptistry, and the Mausoleum of Galla Placidia. All of these show Christ and the saints with risen bodies of exquisite classical grace and proportion. They seem lighter than air as they stand "effortlessly alive" on the green grass of paradise. "The dull weight of death has been lifted from them and, with that, their physicality."[30] So the very physicality that had been the boast and ideal of the classical world had now been paradoxically transformed, through physical and sexual renunciation, into the glorious body of the risen Christ and his Christian followers. Augustine's ambiguity about the resurrection of the body was ultimately resolved through his belief in the transformation of ordinary human bodies into, as Paul says, "copies of [Christ's] glorious body" (Philippians 3:21).[31]

However, as Rosemary Rader has shown, not all late Roman views of sexuality were negative. In fact, she argues that there was an important relationship between celibacy and heterosexual friendship among a large number of prominent religious figures in the period of the third to the fifth centuries.[32] Rader demonstrates that, despite the difficulty of placing these relationships within an accepted social framework of the late Roman world, a remarkable range and variety of friendships developed between men and women committed to celibacy. This had social consequences. "Celibacy mandated a reshifting of the social structure so as to allow mutual supportive relationships outside the marriage bond."[33]

Rader stresses that this was particularly liberating for women in the period:

> Although celibacy was predicable of both sexes it was of particular importance sociologically for women. By adopting celibacy as an integral part of the ascetic life women became participants with men in striving toward perfection. In so doing they acquired a position of equality which mandated the creation of a new space for women other than that allotted to wife, mother and courtesan. The rationalized confinement of women to the domestic sphere was no longer valid when a life of celibacy offered an option to marriage.[34]

She also points out that the fact that both men and women were celibates tended to break down the notion of women's natural inequality with men. Celibacy and the friendships associated with it also freed people from the oppressive familial, clan, and social structures of the late Roman Empire.

With the complete collapse of the western Empire in the fifth century, the early Middle Ages inherited the negative view of the body and the world which predominated in the tradition of the church. But these views of the human body and its place in

spirituality did not stand alone. They have to be seen in the light of
the development of notions about nature and the natural world.

The historical development of Christian views on nature and the natural world

I have stressed the importance of Greco-Roman ideas on the
development of European theology and thought. This influence is
also important in the development of western ideas about nature
and the natural world.

For almost all of Christian history, the dominating idea of
nature has been that it was a kind of book in which we could read
something of the purpose of the Creator. It was the Stoics who
first expressed this notion. In Stoic philosophy nature is arranged
according to a divine order which indicates a sense of purpose in
the world. The eclectic Roman philosopher Cicero takes up this
idea and develops it in his dialogue *De natura deorum*. Cicero
argues that nature "progresses on a certain path of her own to the
goal of full development" unless interfered with by human
agency.[35] These same ideas are also found in the Roman writer
Apuleius (*De mundo*) and in the thought of the philosopher and
statesman Seneca.

Cicero argued that humankind can contemplate the world and
discern order and purpose within it. However, his view is strongly
anthropocentric, for he says that the world was created primarily
for those beings that have the use of reason: thus it was made for
the gods and for us. We are the caretakers of the world, and our
work in nature adds to the beauty and purposiveness of the world.
There is also what today we would call a "developmental
mentality" permeating his thought:

> Man cooperates with nature and ever improves on its pristine
> condition; the changes which he has made and is to make are in
> fact part of the divine purpose in creating the world. This
> conception is significant ... because [of the influence] of the
> immense prestige of Stoicism in the Hellenistic period.[36]

These Stoic ideas were influential during the Roman Empire, throughout the medieval period and the Renaissance, and right up until the seventeenth and eighteenth centuries.

It is significant that even in the fourth century church they were picked up by Christian writers such as the Roman presbyter Novatian and Gregory Nyssa.[37] Novatian gives a detailed description of the natural world emphasizing the concordance between the various elements of air, earth, and water. But God is seen as the one who holds the whole thing together:

> God, holding all things together, leaves nothing empty of himself ... He is always present in his work, penetrating all things, moving all things, connecting in order to achieve concord between the discordant matter of all the elements, so that from the different elements, one world, both single and firm, should be forged by the harmony of the elements brought together.[38]

If it is the concordant reason of God that creates the unity of all cosmic matter, then that matter must contain something of God and be somehow symbolic of at least an important aspect of God. Novatian never loses his sense of God's transcendence, but in *De trinitate* he speaks of "God, holding all things together ... and leaving nothing empty of himself, penetrating all things, moving all things and connecting all things."[39] Novatian uses the image of the cosmic chariot (and here he draws on the Old Testament prophet Ezekiel and both Plato and Cicero); the chariot is the natural world and God is the driver. In this way Novatian creates an intimate link between the divine and the natural world as God penetrates, moves through, and connects all things. It is God who ties the world together. It is significant that at such an early level of theological development God and the natural world are intimately connected.

The Ciceronian argument from purpose is also appealed to by early theologians. Augustine believed that the order of nature revealed God's plan at work on earth. Among the early theologians, the notion of nature as a second book backing up the revelation of the Bible is a common one. St Athanasius says that the creatures revealed in the book of nature proclaim the glory of God who is the creator of the ordered world. St John Chrysostom says that the ignorant and illiterate Christian and even the unbeliever can read the book of nature.

One of the most interesting of the early theologians of the Christian church was St Irenaeus, Bishop of Lyons (c. 130–200). His theology is quite different to the fall-redemption tradition inherited in the West largely through Augustine. As Denis Minns points out, Irenaeus "offers to those more used to a Catholicism overshadowed by the figure of St Augustine a remarkably fresh and different outlook."[40] Fundamentally, Irenaeus' theology was profoundly opposed to speculations which today we loosely call "gnostic"; they were the heretics against whom his *Adversus Haereses* was directed.

In reaction to heretical denials of the value of the material world, Irenaeus strongly emphasized the involvement of God in the creation of the cosmos. Minns comments that the heretical denial of God's creative work "most severely abraded [Irenaeus] religious sensibility."[41] H. Paul Santmire, in his interesting history of the Christian theology of the natural world, *The Travail of Nature*, says: "[Irenaeus] saw nature, as he perceived the scriptures to see it, as humanity's God-given home—blessed, embraced, and cared for by the very God who took flesh in order to redeem a fallen humanity and thereby also to initiate a final renewal of the whole creation."[42] According to Irenaeus, God's whole purpose in creation was to bring all things to a final fulfillment and consummation. Christ, in his view, did not come simply to undo the disobedience of Adam and Eve, but was a seal of God's profound commitment to the world. Because Adam's sin and fall was incidental rather than central to God's plan to bring the world and humanity to fulfillment, Irenaeus argues that nature retains its created goodness; it is not scarred and in need of redemption. His opposition to gnosticism leads him to exalt the value of flesh and matter which he says will be brought to its ultimate consummation at the end of the world, when all creatures will revert to a peaceful and mutually fulfilling co-existence.

However, Irenaeus' positive assessment of the world and the flesh was exceptional in the Roman world, and his more positive view of creation lost out in later Christian theology to Augustinian pessimism. The complete collapse of the Roman Empire in the west in the early fifth century and the chaos which followed the collapse of the Carolingian Empire in the ninth century meant that a very negative view of both the natural world and humanity dominated what theology there was. The brutal conditions of ninth and tenth century life (when Europe's population reached its lowest numerical level between the Roman Empire and today) meant that many of the complex riches of patristic theology were lost to sight. Typical of the period is the *Occupatio* of Odo, the second Abbot of Cluny (927–942), who taught that the end of the world was approaching, that the earth was foul with sin, and that the deepest human anguish lay in the loss of the sense of the presence of God. This attitude remained the predominant view of the created world held by the majority of the religious and clerical elite right into the Middle Ages.

As the medieval period developed, however, there were major figures from that same clerical and church elite who were able to break out of this pessimistic mindset. This is especially true of the high Middle Ages. The medieval historian Friedrich Heer comments that a more positive appreciation of nature was characteristic of the intellectual renaissance of the twelfth century:

> Everywhere in Europe during the twelfth century ... men's hearts and minds were waking to a new appreciation of the world, its colour, its vastness, its perils and its beauty. There was curiosity about the world in all its aspects, the world of men, the world of the spirit, the world of the cosmos and the world of nature.[43]

Heer describes the fascinating speculations of several of the twelfth-century scholars (all of whom were clerics and several of whom ended their careers as bishops) of the school attached to the newly built cathedral of Chartres, south-west of Paris.

The thought of the school of Chartres was underpinned by supreme confidence in the power of logic and by a fascination with numbers. While there was a strong Platonic influence at work in the school, there was also a confidence that all of reality could be understood. Heer says:

> The aim was to construct a pellucid, rational theology, light and clear like the Gothic cathedrals, in which the number, light, music and architecture of the cosmos—all based on numerical relationships—showed forth the nature of the Godhead itself.[44]

The scholars of Chartres argued that there was an essential *intellectibilitas*, a deep intelligibility, in everything. This meant that God, humankind, nature, and the cosmos could be "examined, reasoned about, comprehended and measured in their proportions, number, weight and harmony." Nature was seen as a cosmic power, the mother and source of all reality. The Bishop of Lincoln, Robert Grosseteste (c. 1168–1253), espoused similar ideas when he was a lecturer at Oxford. He emphasized the experimental method and the study of mathematics and the physical sciences. He had considerable influence on the man who was perhaps the most important medieval scientist, Roger Bacon.

Unfortunately, this twelfth century interest in nature quickly became exceptional among clerics and theologians. In the thirteenth and fourteenth centuries, natural science had, at best, a profoundly ambiguous position in intellectual life. Despite the fact that the German Dominican St Albert the Great (1206–1280) was interested in both astronomy and Greco-Roman classical ideas of science and the environment, and the Oxford Franciscan Roger Bacon (c. 1212–1292) engaged in the empirical investigation of nature, science continued to be closely linked for a number of centuries with subcultural speculations such as alchemy, astrology, magic, and sorcery. "Theology frowned on any attempt at reaching into the secrets of nature, an unlawful invasion of the sacred womb of the Great Mother."[45] Notions such as these continued to prevail until the development of modern science.

In contrast to this negative attitude toward science, another more positive stream can be found that continued the tradition of the twelfth-century renaissance. Matthew Fox has recently shown that the greatest of the medieval theologians, Thomas Aquinas, understood the cosmos to be a form of revelation of God parallel to biblical revelation.[46]

> Sacred writings are bound in two volumes—that of creation and that of the Holy Scriptures ... Visible creatures are like a book in which we read the knowledge of God.[47]

Among the medieval mystics there was also a much more integrated understanding of the connection between theology and the natural world. Francis of Assisi, Hildegarde of Bingen, Meister Eckhart and many of the medieval and post-Reformation mystics and saints freed themselves from the prevailing destructive, body-denying, anthropocentric tradition.

However, these religious geniuses were really the exception in the medieval period. Clarence Glacken points out (after warning of the dangers of generalization about the cosmology of the Middle Ages) that the predominant idea of the world in the medieval period was that humankind "assisted God ... in the improvement of an earthly home even if the earth were, in Christian theology, only a sojourner's way station."This shows the continuing influence of Ciceronian ideas of nature. Glacken continues:

> The most compelling reason for the observation and study of nature, however, was that it led to a greater understanding of God. It was part—but only part—of the proof of the existence of God, of God's plan for a designed world, and of the truth of the Christian religion.[48]

This is hardly a ringing endorsement of the value of the world in itself, but at least it does show that the medievals did not have as negative a view of the world as most of the early church fathers. But world weariness and the concept of the earth as a "vale of tears" was still the predominant view in monastic circles in the Middle Ages. This reaches right up to our own time, as the popular compline hymn and prayer *Salve regina* illustrates: "Ad te suspiramus, gementes et flentes in hac lacrimarum valle" ("To thee do we send up our sighs, mourning and weeping in this valley of tears").

Rupert Sheldrake has argued in *The Rebirth of Nature* that a much more accepting attitude toward nature was to be found among the inarticulate medieval rural masses. The medievals saw nature as "animate and mother-like," and Sheldrake links this with the medieval teaching that all living creatures had souls.[49] Here he is emphasizing the on-going influence, especially in popular medieval religion, of ancient pre-Christian views rooted in the idea of the earth mother and the sacredness of nature. But while there is truth in his observations, medieval historians on the whole would probably be less sanguine about Sheldrake's views. Popular medieval religion was a very complex reality about which we do not know a great deal. As Jonathan Sumption and Rosalind and Christopher Brooke point out, popular religion in the Middle Ages quickly crystallized into material images such as relics, miraculous statues, or pilgrimage shrines.[50] While the centrality of the role of Mary, the Mother of God, was emphasized in the Middle Ages, and this has obvious connections with the on-going notion of the earth mother, I think that Sheldrake pushes his point too far in the light of the available evidence about medieval popular religion.

Early modern developments in the theology of nature

Sheldrake says that these notions of nature as mother-like and animate were finally destroyed in the sixteenth century by both Humanism and Protestantism which, he argues, released the dual forces of skepticism and iconoclasm. Both Protestantism and Humanism saw an apparently instinctive religion in touch with nature as nothing more than superstition and idolatry.

Sheldrake is right to blame Protestantism for iconoclasm and the elimination of the notion of natural revelation, at least to the extent that it focused almost exclusively on the question of the salvation of the individual through personal faith and emphasized the centrality and uniqueness of the biblical word and the disembodied intellect rather than sacramental, instinctive, and natural symbols. Protestantism effectively lost all sense, especially in its puritan forms, of the sacramental.

But the question becomes more complex when it is focused on Humanism and the Renaissance. Certainly European humanism was anthropocentric, intellectualist, and self-engrossed, as so much of its art reveals. But, in Italy especially, it quickly transmuted into the baroque. An instinctive, dramatic, and almost operatic quality survived in baroque Counter-Reformation Catholicism with its simultaneous emphasis on the formalistic and the sensual. The baroque is profoundly characteristic of Latin and especially Italian Catholicism. It bespeaks a certain psycho-spiritual attitude to life which, while very difficult to define, is certainly characterized by "a feeling of anticipation, of something yet to come, of dissatisfaction and restlessness rather than fulfilment."[51] While the massive frontality of the baroque usually seems far too confronting for our modern taste, and its almost gaudy use of color seems showy and superficial, it actually uses the material and the sensual to draw the viewer into a world that transcends the self and points to something beyond. In this sense, it is a form of the materialization of the spiritual rather than the spiritualization of the material. And it is the former that is closer to the true doctrine of the incarnation than the latter. Nature and the natural world seem to be much more at home in this baroque milieu than in the exaggeratedly bibliocentric view of reality that is characteristic of Calvinistic Protestantism. The influence of the baroque can also be seen in popular devotions such as those to the Sacred Heart and the passion and death of Jesus.

A parallel tendency existed in seventeenth-century French Catholicism. Emerging from a complex cultural, religious, and spiritual matrix, it was certainly more restrained than the Italian baroque and its influence has flowed right through until our own time. In its origins this religiosity can be characterized as more reformist, puritan, even more "Protestant" in tendency. It finds its origin in the great spiritual writer Cardinal Pierre de Berulle, and continued in the writings of Jean-Jacques Olier (who really began the modern idea of seminary formation for priests) and the popular preacher St Jean Eudes.[52] Another major figure in this movement was St Louis Grignion de Montfort, whose spirituality centered on devotion to Mary. The latter two figures brought something of the baroque and devotional style to their work which made them far more popular and accessible and a lot less puritan.

Significantly, the French school is characterized by what William M. Thompson calls a "Christified" Neoplatonism:

> Berulle and his collaborators employ the Dionysian, Neoplatonic schema: We have come from God (*exitus*) and we find our being's fulfilment in returning to our origin (*reditus*). But the French school has thoroughly "Christianized" or "Christified" this pattern: Our emanation reflects Christ, our wounding through sin deepens our need for Christ, and our return to God is through the mediation of Christ.[53]

This spirituality generated a strong missionary movement in rural parishes as it attempted to "Christianize" the French (and later the Italian) countryside.

Recent historians have argued that the medieval and pre-Christian religious tradition continued to dominate the European peasantry right through into the eighteenth century, when the effects of this French spiritual reform began to be felt in the countryside. Parish and rural missions, originating within and generated by the French school, were aimed at imposing a reformed Catholicism on the rural population. In France this movement was reasonably successful. In contrast, in Ireland there is good evidence that the rural population was not fully "Christianized" until the church reforms that began in the 1830s.

Therefore, Sheldrake is right in stressing the continuing influence of popular notions of the earth mother and the sacredness of nature among the rural masses of Europe. But he misses the importance of the influence of the theological and clerical elite in the later Middle Ages and on into the eighteenth century, which held to the pessimistic Augustinian view that humankind was born into the world of sin, evil, and death and that salvation was to be found not in this natural world—which was the dwelling place of the demonic—but in the world to come. So it is very difficult to generalize about seventeenth- and eighteenth-century Catholicism. At least two major influences were at work. While the Italian and Latin baroque leaned much more toward natural symbols and the sensual, the theological and reformed Catholicism of France was more sparse and puritan in tendency, even though French popular devotion was profoundly incarnational. It is the French influence which has predominated in the English-speaking world.

Early modern developments in science and philosophy

The sixteenth-century Renaissance and the scientific revolution of the seventeenth and eighteenth centuries also gradually brought about a change of attitude. During the Renaissance, the idea of nature as God's book which human beings could read was still popular. Francis Bacon, for instance, saw the book of nature elucidating and clarifying the Bible. While the early modern scientists such as Copernicus and Kepler still saw the world as an interactive cosmic organism, a radical change came with the Jesuit-educated philosopher Rene Descartes (1596–1650).

Nature, which had been viewed in the Middle Ages as fundamentally sacred, was secularized—or perhaps more accurately, mechanized—by Descartes. It was Descartes who set the pattern for the relationship between science and religion that has predominated right up until our own time. He saw the natural world as a vast machine; all of its interactions could be explained by the laws of mechanics. He repudiated the medieval view that animals had souls; as soulless beings, their reactions are merely mechanical. Descartes saw human beings as minds (or souls) at work in machines. His philosophy was essentially a restatement of Platonism, evolved within the context of the early development of modern science. For Descartes, nature was seen as governed by laws which could be understood and predicted.

> The universe of Descartes was a vast mathematical system of matter in motion ... Everything in the material universe worked entirely mechanically according to mathematical necessities ... Although the details of his system were soon superseded by the Newtonian universe of atomic matter moving in a void, [Descartes] laid the foundation for the mechanistic world view in both physics and biology.[54]

Isaac Newton took both Cartesian mechanism and natural theology seriously. As an anti-trinitarian monotheist, he argued that God was more concerned with creation than with personal salvation. As Alexander Pope wrote, the Deists "looked through nature to nature's Creator." By discovering the laws of nature, Newton hoped to give glory to God. While there is a real sense in which Newton applied Cartesian notions to describe the mechanics of the natural world, he himself never lost his interest in alchemy and esoteric science. These seem to have expressed the flip side of his personality, and he was never a mechanist in the crude sense that was later to become the norm.

This mechanistic view of nature has achieved a great deal for science and it still predominates in contemporary scientific thinking. But the mechanistic approach sees nature as a vast, inanimate storehouse of useable "resources" that are there to be exploited for the short-term advantage of humankind. It is this attitude that has brought us to the tragic and disastrous environmental impasse that we face today.

Descartes' entire output was placed on the *Index of Forbidden Books*, and Catholic theology over the last few centuries has, in one sense, been at daggers drawn with the mechanistic view of cosmology and the world. Yet paradoxically, at the same time it has integrated much of the Cartesian view of reality. Up until the latter part of the nineteenth century, when the revival of the philosophy of Aquinas was mandated for the training of priests by the Vatican, it was largely the philosophy of Descartes that was taught to student priests in European seminaries. Theology easily embraced the Cartesian notion of the mind in the machine because for so long the Christian tradition had been subverted by Neo-Platonic dualism. Descartes was simply the tag end of Platonism.

Questioning the mechanistic view

Today the mechanistic view of nature is finally starting to be seriously and widely questioned by scientists themselves. Writers such as Sheldrake, Fritjof Capra (*The Tao of Physics*), Stephen Hawking (*A Brief History of Time*), and Paul Davies (*God and the New Physics*) are among the best known. At last a real possibility exists for science and theology to begin to speak to each other.

Actually, there seems to be more optimism and creative thinking on the side of the scientists than on the side of religionists. With the exception of thinkers like the process theologian Charles Birch and the Anglican John Polkinghorne, there is not a great deal of serious response from most theologians to the shift that is occurring among scientists.[55] A popular theological contribution to the discussion that attempts to take science seriously is that of Denis Edwards, whose *Jesus and the Cosmos* sketches out the beginnings of a dialogue with modern science. Edwards draws on the thought of Karl Rahner in this process.[56] This lack of enthusiasm is partly due to the fact that theologians are inherently conservative and tend to avoid issues that lead them to a major questioning of traditional cosmological ways of understanding reality. It may also be due to the fact that mainstream theologians tend be more aware of the serious epistemological problems lurking in this dialogue between science and religion. Theology, of its very nature, is analogical and poetic and deals with realities that are beyond empirical confirmation. This is not to say that theology has abandoned reason; the Catholic tradition has always emphasized that faith must be based in reason. But it is *"fides* quaerens intellectum"— *faith* seeking understanding. In other words, theology seeks to deal with what is by definition transcendent in a way that is consonant with human reason.

Contemporary science has claimed that it tests its theories empirically. However, as we shall see in the next chapter, the newer generation of scientists go much further than this. They argue that there is a purposive power at work in the world. For them nature is alive; the earth and the universe itself are developing organisms. Paul Davies, for instance, argues that self-organizing principles are at work in nature. Rupert Sheldrake says that the universe is guided by what he calls "morphic resonance" (or "M Fields"), which are structures that guide the development of an organism. They act in a manner analogous to a magnetic field. He argues that the laws of nature are more like habits or memories that evolve according to experience and through which new behaviors can be learned. Sheldrake goes even further in *The Rebirth of Nature*, where he actually argues for the radical resacralization of the world.

Parallel to these developments is what deep ecology has called the "Gaia hypothesis." In Greek mythology, Gaia was the nurturant earth goddess. In the mid-1970s the English atmospheric chemist James Lovelock secularized the goddess, and posited the notion that the earth has developed and continues to maintain a self-regulating environment that sustains life and is itself alive. Thus the idea of "Gaia" emerges—the earth as a super-being that is endowed with ethical rights because it experiences consciousness and has the ability to feel pain and to respond to the brutality which we humans inflict upon it. In the Gaia context, the many different parts of the whole only make sense in terms of the whole. Thus Lovelock argues that humanity derives its meaning solely from the earth itself and that human needs and aspirations must be subsumed to the needs of the earth.[57] Theodore Roszak has spoken of "the personhood of the earth," and the concept of Gaia has led to a whole discussion of the ethical rights of the world itself and of the self-regulating capacity of the earth to rid itself of disruptive poisonous elements—such as human beings—as it seeks equilibrium. Clearly the Gaia hypothesis is a secularized version of the ancient religious notion of "Mother Nature."

Most Christian theologians seem quite unconscious of these issues, which clearly have a profound and on-going influence among many different groups of scientists and thinking people in the contemporary world. Seemingly, it is scientists who are making all the running and building the bridges toward a more philosophical understanding of the cosmos. There still seems to be a real timidity among environmentally sympathetic theologians in responding to these issues. And when they do, their focus seems to be inward toward the Christian scriptures and tradition. An exception to this is Jürgen Moltmann, whose *God in Creation* is a seminal work.[58] The works of Charles Birch also reach across the bridge between science and religion.

However, the only contemporary religious thinker to provide theology with a broad theoretical basis upon which to begin a genuine interaction with the radical implications of modern scientific ecology is Thomas Berry. So it is to his views and those of other theologians and thinkers who have responded to environmentalism and ecology that I will now turn.

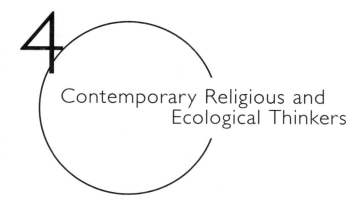

4
Contemporary Religious and Ecological Thinkers

Over the last decade there has been a large increase in the number of books about the environment from both the Protestant and Catholic communities. Among many Protestants, the long term source of this interest has been the philosophy of the Anglo-American mathematician, metaphysician, and polymath A.N. Whitehead and the process theology of Charles Hartshorne and John Cobb, both of whom are inspired by Whitehead's thought. Another important source for some Christian environmental thinkers has been the revival in biblical studies which began in the Protestant churches in the nineteenth century and in Catholicism from the 1940s onwards.

Many of these writers, both Protestant and Catholic, have also been influenced, at least indirectly, by the French Jesuit paleontologist, poet, and thinker Pierre Teilhard de Chardin. While most readers will have heard of Teilhard de Chardin and many of Whitehead, there is a third source for modern religious environmentalism: Henri Bergson.

Henri Bergson

Henri Bergson (1859–1941) was an important French philosopher who is rarely mentioned today in the context of the dialogue between science, religion, and the environment, but who was extremely well-known in the 1920s and 1930s. With Benedetto Croce and Emile Durkheim, Bergson was one of the most influential Continental thinkers during the first decades of the twentieth century. He has been described as "one of the pioneers for the new spirit of our age."[1] For the first decades of this century Bergson was the most famous of all European philosophers and won the Nobel Prize for Literature in 1927. The reason for his influence in his own time is that he gave expression to the neo-Romanticism (or Modernism) that was characteristic of so much of the European cultural milieu from the 1890s to the 1930s. Part of his appeal was the beauty of his language and the fact that he was able to develop a philosophy that met the needs of his time.

Bergson was a key figure in the French philosophical tradition of Spiritualism. Spiritualism is the title given to the movement that recognizes an underlying level in human existence that transcends the empirical and superficially experiential. It is the meta-reality that underlies all reality. Because interest in psychology has become so dominant in our culture, especially through the influence of Freud and Jung, metaphysics and the specifically philosophical effort to penetrate the deepest aspects of human existence has been crowded out. Indeed, there is a sense in which, in the Anglo-American world, psychology has replaced metaphysics. Many people today say they are interested in what they call "spirituality" as an approach to the underlying structures of existence, but they are seemingly only prepared to search for that profound reality at the more superficial, psychological level. Bergson's spiritualism takes us beyond psychology and superficial spirituality to the underlying metaphysical level. His most important book was *L'Evolution creatrice* (1907), which was translated into English in 1911.[2] Despite the clarity of his style, Frederick Copleston speaks correctly of "a certain lack of precision in his thought," and it is this which makes his philosophy difficult to pin down exactly.[3]

Bergson—like a number of French philosophers of his time— was dissatisfied with the materialism of nineteenth century science, but he did not want to lose the insights that came from empiricism, especially from the theory of evolution. His aim was to place science within a broader context than the merely material. He was influenced by the philosophical subjectivism of Immanuel Kant, but Bergson's particular genius lay in his ability to hold together the findings of evolutionary science with a metaphysical and almost theological search for an understanding of the inner core of reality itself.

Bergson's starting point is the way in which the human mind comprehends time. In fact, his philosophy has been summed up as an "intuition of duration." He distinguishes chronological, clock, and date time (what we might call "timed time") from what he says is real time. His aim is to obtain an intuition of pure duration, a penetration into continuity itself without the intervention of mere chronological time. In English this notion is difficult to grasp because of the limitations of the language, but in French Bergson is referring to the slightly clearer distinction between *le temps* (clock/date time) and *la durée* (the real time of consciousness). For Bergson, *la durée* is the sense of time beyond time. Cassell's *French Dictionary* translates *la durée* simply as "duration" or "continuance." Bergson says that the real meaning of *la durée* (there really is no exact equivalent in English) can only be perceived and brought to consciousness through the actuation of memory. This involves not just the memory of past events, but the intuition of a living, on-going consciousness that underlies all particularities. Once we understand "pure duration" we can then perceive that reality is not something permanent, fixed, and static, but that it is essentially a process of "becoming." For Bergson, permanency is an illusion; there are no lasting realities, only on-going action.

But by the word "action" he does not refer to particular activities in the external world which are the products of causes or willed decisions; by "action" he means the meta-dynamic underlying all particular thought and decision. It is the underlying, living force that produces and sustains all thought and will. Again, we discover this reality through careful reflection on the process that permeates all our personal thoughts and willed actions. Here Bergson is not referring to the unconscious as articulated by the psychologists Freud and Jung, although his concept does bear some relationship to Jung's notion of the collective unconscious. Bergson is actually referring to a reality that is beyond the intrapsychic and individual; it is a broader, less personalized concept. He is really attempting to articulate the living force that underlies everything. He is certain that we can discover this within ourselves and bring it to consciousness. This is not exactly what traditional philosophy would call "being" (for Bergson's living force is highly active), but it is very close to it.

This meta-dynamic expresses itself through what he calls an *élan vital* (a vital impulse), a profound life drive which is motivated by the needs of each individual being for survival and welfare. However, this impulse does not constitute the internal purpose that is inherent in each particular organism; in other words, it is not what constitutes our individuality. Instead, it is the undifferentiated life force which underlies everything and impels evolution onward. This life force "is a continuous process in which the original drive divides itself into a growing variety of forms, but retains a basic direction."[4]

Bergson is often difficult to understand precisely. However, he claims that each philosopher has only one basic insight: his was to assert a form of intentionality in the evolutionary process, a direction, however vague, in the on-going emergence of the underlying life force. There is a sense of purposive continuance, of movement forward, of a dynamic vitalism in his notion of evolution which is simply not there in mechanistic or materialist notions of reality. His thought created an ambience that opened evolutionary theory to a more transcendent dimension that unfortunately has been largely forgotten today. In fact, Bergson laid a profound philosophical foundation upon which a very dynamic notion of the natural world can be constructed. Bergson's sense of the profound unity of all cosmic reality and his emphasis on the superficiality of specific differentiation and individuality have a very contemporary ring. Today echoes of Bergson's *élan vital* can be perceived in the Gaia hypothesis of James Lovelock and in the thought of physicists such as Paul Davies. We will look at these contemporary thinkers a little later.

The link between Bergson's views of evolution and religion are complex and difficult. He deals with both realities in *Les Deux Sources de la Morale et de la Religion* (1932).[5] Here he argues that religion and morality are intimately intertwined. He distinguishes between what he calls static, closed religion and open, dynamic religion. Here he is probably distinguishing between what today we would call reactionary, fundamentalist religion and a creative, prophetic approach to belief. According to Bergson, this open, prophetic approach reaches its highest form in Christian mysticism. He says that the mystic loves humanity with a divine love that comes through the power and virtue of God. He seems to be arguing that the mystic is the one who, at the deepest level, perceives the inner, meta-dynamic, underlying meaning of existence itself. The true mystic is the one who perceives, in the deepest sense, something of the life force that impels evolution onward.

Bergson was never an irrationalist. His entire philosophical endeavor was to bring to consciousness the deep, underlying life force. His notion of intuition was close to what today we would call insight. He was born a French Jew, but near the end of his life he was very close to Catholicism. Interestingly, Bergson's Catholic contemporary, Maurice Blondel (1861–1949), tried to use a similar concept to the *élan vital* to construct a Christian philosophy in his book *L'Action* (1893).[6] Similar ideas can be found in the work of the Belgian Jesuit, Joseph Marechal (1878–1944), who tried to relate the thought of Aquinas to modern philosophy. Marechal exercised a profound influence on Karl Rahner, probably the greatest Catholic theologian this century. No school formed itself around Bergson, but he influenced a number of Catholic thinkers, of whom the most important were Edouard Le Roy (1870–1954) and Pierre Teilhard de Chardin.

Pierre Teilhard de Chardin

It is significant that Pierre Teilhard de Chardin (1881–1955) was a near contemporary of both Bergson and Blondel. Teilhard had a lot in common with them, although his thought moved towards the poetic and theological rather than toward the strictly philosophical. He was also a traditional scientist, deeply interested in the origins of the world around him. It was his scientific knowledge of geology, paleontology, and evolution that led him to theorize about an all-encompassing dynamic which embraced the whole of world history. In this process he reintegrated those realities that were most separate in the dualistic world view—matter and spirit.[7]

Teilhard's major contribution to environmental theology is his notion that matter itself is impregnated with a purposive energy that constantly evolves toward ever-greater complexity. (In this he is very much the scientist who deals with real, material things, whereas Bergson is the abstract metaphysician who ignores particular objects in his attempt to discover the underlying force or *élan*). For Teilhard, matter is not merely an inert mass; it is the indispensable pre-condition for spirit. It is the basic living block of life. But, as a living reality, matter is not static; it is in constant evolution.

There are several critical stages through which matter passes on its journey toward ever-greater complexity. The first of these was in the remote past when inorganic matter began its progressive evolutionary growth. The second stage was the emergence of life which, in its turn, evolved into the many living beings which have inhabited the universe. The third stage was the emergence of mind, the critical shift from the dominance of instinct to the dominance of consciousness. It was with the evolution of humankind that consciousness emerged.

> Man is not a fortuitous or accidental phenomenon, but one obviously prepared and, in a sense, willed—evolution's growing success. Far from being an anomalous aberration, he is the key,

the head, the growing point of the universe ... 'evolution become reflexively conscious of itself' ... the noosphere is grafted once and for all on the biosphere.[8]

In Teilhardian rhetoric, consciousness was referred to as the "noosphere." "Man is the only being, within the limits of our experience, who not only knows, but knows that he knows."[9] For Teilhard it is only in humankind that evolution becomes truly personal.

Teilhard says that contemporary human beings are still in the process of evolution toward a higher consciousness. The ultimate development of this is the achievement of the spiritual convergence of individuality, personal freedom, and inter-communion on a cosmic scale, achieving what Teilhard calls "Omega Point." For him, like Bergson, the ultimate focus of evolution is mystical. Rideau calls it "the final transcendent centre on which history converges and in which the universe culminates."[10] Omega Point is usually understood as the point at which everything is brought into union with God. Certainly, it is the point at which the whole of evolution is summed up in Christ. Teilhard writes: "But instead of a vague centre of convergence envisaged as the ultimate end of this process of evolution [we have] the personal and defined reality of the word Incarnate."[11]

The paradox of Teilhard's thought is the sense that matter already contains within itself the potential for spirituality. In his essay "My Fundamental Vision," Teilhard moves from what he calls physics through metaphysics to mysticism.[12] In another poetic and extraordinarily dream-like essay, "The Spiritual Power of Matter," he suggests that in order to perceive the spirituality of matter, an individual must undergo a real conversion.[13]

Never say, then, as some say: "The kingdom of matter is worn out, matter is dead": till the end of time matter will always remain young, exuberant, sparkling, new-born for those who are willing. Never say "Matter is accursed, matter is evil" ... Son of man, bathe yourself in the ocean of matter; plunge into it where it is deepest and most violent; struggle with its currents and drink of its waters. For it cradled you long ago in your pre-conscious existence; and it is the ocean that will raise you up to God.[14]

This is the absolute antithesis of the dualistic understanding of reality. It is much more integrated than the traditional theology and more open to the scientific view of the world which so dominates our contemporary consciousness.

Teilhard's influence on modern theology is enormous, if somewhat undifferentiated. It certainly formed part of the theological ambience of the Second Vatican Council and of subsequent Catholic (and Protestant) thought. The writings that best represent his spiritual vision are *The Divine Milieu* (published in French in 1957)[15] and *The Hymn of the Universe* (1961). By seeing the world as a "divine milieu" (and in this context "milieu" is best translated as "environment"), Teilhard refocuses theology on the temporal processes, however long range, of this world. He shifts our attention from eternity to time, from heaven to earth. He makes it possible for us to think about reality in a different way.

This is not to pretend that there are no difficulties in Teilhard's vision. For me the greatest difficulty lies in the integration of his ideas about christology. For Teilhard, all of reality is ultimately summed up in the cosmic Christ. But just how the "cosmic Christ" is related to the progressive evolution of matter is not clear to me. There is a sense in which his views reflect, as Thomas Berry says, the conventional spirituality and piety of bourgeois French Catholicism.

But this is not to take away from his achievement: his pervasive influence on contemporary Catholicism, modern theology, and religious thought in general is widespread and profound. He is one of the most influential thinkers of the twentieth century.

Alfred North Whitehead (1861–1947)

The contribution of Alfred North Whitehead (1861–1947) to the development of a philosophical basis for environmental theology is very different to that of the Frenchmen Bergson and Teilhard. This is probably because Whitehead emerged from the Anglo-Saxon philosophical tradition and culture. Yet his importance, especially among Protestant thinkers, is considerable. Charles Birch says that he was "probably the greatest polymath of this century."[16] He was primarily a mathematician, first at Cambridge, then at London University. He spent the latter part of his life (from 1924 until his death in 1947) in the chair of Philosophy at Harvard University.

His period in North America was the most philosophically creative part of his life. This can be attributed in part to the way in which Harvard stressed a collegiate atmosphere so that the scientific and philosophical disciplines were brought together in an interactive way. The British academic emphasis on specialization had created a real divide between science and philosophy.[17] However, North American universities like Harvard had, and still have, a more integrated and inter-disciplinary approach to teaching and research. Whitehead's key philosophical book is *Process and Reality: An Essay in Cosmology*; the book was first delivered as Gifford Lectures at the University of Edinburgh in 1927 and 1928 and is very difficult.[18] I have found Whitehead's Lowell Institute Lectures for 1926, *Religion in the Making*, more helpful for his views on religion and metaphysics.[19]

Like Teilhard, Whitehead begins with the stuff of reality itself. He says that reality is not composed of static, separate, mechanistic objects, but that everything is essentially interactive and social. Reality is an interlocking and interconnected continuum in which everything is in ultimate interdependence on the other. The universe is not composed of inert matter, but is a continuous series of events and interactions. Even the most basic entities, such as atoms and molecules, have a real subjectivity and are therefore responsive to other realities. It is Whitehead's emphasis on the inter-subjectivity of all reality which has the most significance for environmental thinking. In his scheme, nothing exists in isolation. Each component part of reality interacts with all of the rest.

For the theologian, the most radical element of Whitehead's metaphysics is his understanding of the nature of God. His key discussion of God is in the final chapter of *Process and Reality*. Unlike conventional materialists, who reject any notion of a God, Whitehead argues that the cosmic process actually requires God. But the God of Whitehead is not the detached, almighty, impersonal, unmoved mover of Aristotelian philosophy. In *Religion in the Making* he identifies this approach essentially with what he calls the "Semitic" notion of God. In this image God is a world emperor, unfeeling and detached from the cosmos. "The fashioning of God in the image of the Egyptian, Persian and Roman imperial rulers ... [meant that] the Church gave unto God the attributes which belonged exclusively to Caesar."[20] He says that the attribution of omnipotence means that God is responsible for everything that happens in the world and is therefore responsible for evil. Whitehead says that this Semitic concept of God demands

> a definite personal individual entity, whose existence is the one ultimate metaphysical fact, absolute and underivative, and who decreed and ordered the derivative existence which we call the actual world. This Semitic concept is the rationalisation of the tribal gods of the earlier communal religion. It expresses the extreme doctrine of transcendence.[21]

Whether Whitehead's description of this "Semitic God" reflects the biblical God is a debatable issue.

Whitehead strongly rejects this "Semitic" concept of God. He asserts that, on the contrary, God is in no way separate from the cosmic process. Whitehead's God is not independent, unchanging, and unsuffering. God is dependent, mutable, and involved in the evolution of everything cosmic. He argues that the analogy of being demands this. He says that God must, in some sense, be like creation. A God who is not like his creatures is simply unknowable. "Any proof which commences with the consideration of the character of the actual world cannot rise above the actuality of this world."[22] Here he seems to be mirroring the argument of Immanuel Kant that it is impossible to argue to an infinite, transcendent God from finite causes. Whitehead's God, in contrast, is sympathetic to and involved in the cosmic process. Here is a God who can find a real place in an environmental theology.

One of the most quoted sayings of Whitehead is that "the safest general characterisation of the European tradition is that it consists of a series of footnotes to Plato."[23] In fact, Whitehead's own philosophy has been called a modern restatement of Platonism.[24] This is particularly helpful in understanding Whitehead's idea of both God and the cosmos, and of God's role in creating the cosmic order.

According to Whitehead, the fundamental principles of intelligibility in the world are what he calls "eternal objects." These are the forms of everything and the patterns of relationship between everything that has existed, exists now, or has the potential to exist. These forms exist independently of ingression into or expression through actual entities. "They are what they are, whether conceived or not, whether instanciated or not, a form of that particular definiteness and no other."[25] By saying that they are eternal, Whitehead means that they are not the product of the actual process of existence. They sound peculiarly like Plato's forms. Eternal objects are really the actual and potential intelligible organizing principles of existence. However, in Whitehead's philosophy these forms are far less important than actual entities. It is the interaction of these actual entities which constitutes the stuff of reality.

The entire stuff of reality, says Whitehead, is made up of actual entities. These are the processes, the interrelationships, the continuities and discontinuities, the matter and the things of which the real world is made. They are complex and interdependent and exist in dynamic, creative, and constant interaction with each other. In fact, the essence of actual reality is *becoming*. "Every actual thing is in its essence, reception, transformation and transmission of energy and information from its total past environment to its total future environment."[26] The correlation with Bergson's thought here is hard to miss.

However, Whitehead argues that the cosmos needs a further element: an everlasting, non-perishable, actual entity—God. God is the link between the eternal objects and actual entities. It is God who provides a foundation for the eternal objects and creates the ambience for their ingression into the process of becoming. It is God that provides the basis for cosmic order.

> It is the Divine envisagement of "eternal objects" with a feeling for the ingression or inclusion of some rather than others which explains the order in the universe ... Apart from the Divine envisagement of eternal objects there would not be a Cosmos or Universe: just completely chaotic, totally un-coordinated, low level happenings completely unknowable.[27]

Unlike other entities, however, God is everlasting and does not perish. God is the necessary Principle for the creation of order in the cosmos. Again, this sounds remarkably like the Platonic Demiurge. So there is a sense in which God is unique, but there is also a sense in which God is very much like other entities— dependent, changing, and caught up in the temporal process. Whitehead argues that unless we hang onto the analogy of being—that God is in some sense like creatures—we have to abandon entirely any search for God. God would simply be unknowable. We are back at the Kantian dilemma between finite reality and the projection of an infinite cause.

But Whitehead goes further than this. He argues that God is bi-polar. From one perspective, God is the principle of order and adjustment among the eternal objects. On the other hand, it is God who has the "feeling" for the inclusion of some rather than others in the actual process of reality. Whitehead argues that it is God's sense of beauty which inclines the divine toward the inclusion of this rather than that. This is what he calls God's primordial nature. But at the same time, God, as an actual entity, is caught up in the process of the world.

By reason of the relativity of all things, there is a reaction of the world on God. The completion of God's nature into a fullness of physical feeling is derived from the objectification of the world in God. He shares with every new creation its actual world; and the concrescent creature is objectified in God as a novel element in God's objectification of that actual world.[28]

What he seems to be saying here is that creation is achieved by an interaction between both God and each actual entity of creation. In fact, Whitehead thinks that God was more of a "savior" of the world than its creator. God's relationship to the world is persuasive rather than coercive.

Whitehead's metaphysics are both contorted and difficult, but his panentheism has had a wide influence upon a large group of theologians who have developed his thought in a quite specific direction. Whitehead's panentheism describes God's intimate interdependence with the world. It clearly avoids the identification of the world with God—which is pantheism—but it does not create such a disjunction as to divorce the world and God entirely. It sets the stage for the possibility of the development of a genuine environmental theology. And this is precisely what process theology has achieved.

Charles Hartshorne and John Cobb

Charles Hartshorne was a student of Whitehead at Harvard, and it was he who first developed a natural theology on the basis of Whitehead's metaphysics. Hartshorne believed that the traditional notion of a separate, supernatural God was no longer tenable. He said bluntly: "We have ... become aware that to worship Being—or the infinite, immutable, absolute or independent—may be to worship not God, but an idol."[29] Hartshorne developed Whitehead's notion of panentheism and the interdependence of God and the world. While God is the supreme giver, God is also a receiver. Hartshorne points out that love is not a one way process; it involves both a giving and a receiving. If God loves, then God not only wants to give love, but also to receive it. This understanding of a God of desire is alien to traditional theism, which thinks of God as omnipotent and self-contained. However, it certainly seems to agree with the understanding of divine love of many of the great mystics (both Christian and otherwise). There is also something profoundly biblical in this notion of a vulnerable God.

Hartshorne argued that perceptive religious people have always felt that humankind could contribute something to God. Indeed, if we can do nothing for God, if God can gain nothing from us, "then the whole point of religion is destroyed."[30] The consequence of this view for environmental theology is obvious: God and the world are interdependent. If the world suffers, so does God. In Hartshorne's view, Jesus is deeply symbolic of God's involvement in the world. "Jesus appears to be the supreme symbol furnished to us by history of the notion of a God genuinely and literally sympathetic (incomparably more literally than any man ever is), receiving into his experience the suffering as well as the joys of the world."[31]

John B. Cobb is a student of Hartshorne, having studied under him in Chicago. He is now Professor at Claremont College, California. Cobb's thought is also rooted in the process philosophy of Whitehead and the evolutionary theology of Teilhard. Both of these thinkers laid the philosophical foundations for an assertion of the radical value of matter. Matter is not an inert substance that can be used at the whim of humans but has an inwardness and a potentiality for spirituality that can be used to provide the basis for an environmental ethic. Cobb is also a panentheist who sees God as deeply involved with the world in a sympathetic, interactive way. He built on Whitehead's notion that the cosmos is not composed of matter in a blandly materialistic sense, but that it is a complex series of interrelationships or events. The world is a process that has a purpose. It is not only human relationships that have value; the interrelatedness of *all* reality is part of the intention of God. Everything created has a value for God. This endows the non-human world with rights.

Fundamentally, these rights center on the possibility of each specific being achieving its purpose. Once we enter the sphere of values that are bestowed by God's creativity, we enter the sphere of ethics.

Cobb has reflected much on the interrelationship of humankind with the non-human world. "Man will in fact care for the sub-human world sufficient to heal it and adjust himself to its needs only if he views it as having some claim upon him, some intrinsic right to exist and prosper."[32] Because humankind is the only life-form capable of love, human beings have a special co-responsibility with God to care for the cosmos. But this human responsibility is rooted in the intrinsic rights of creation and not in some form of self-interest. Cobb speaks of the non-human world's "intrinsic right to exist and prosper." He is critical of traditional Christian attitudes, which he sees as inadequate to confront the massive environmental problems of today. The solution is to expand Christian belief to include the recognition of the rights of nature.

In *The Liberation of Life*, which Cobb co-authored in 1981 with Charles Birch, the argument is made that all forms of life have a true potential for experience that must be respected by us.[33] On this basis they argue strongly for animal rights. All matter, from sub-atomic particles to human beings, has value: "If there is intrinsic value anywhere, there is intrinsic value everywhere."[34] Another interesting recent book in the process tradition which integrates a range of approaches to environmental theology is Jay B. McDaniel's *Earth, Sky, Gods and Mortals*.[35]

Charles Birch

The Australian biologist and environmental thinker Charles Birch had his considerable contribution to the development of an ecological theology recognized when he received the Templeton Prize for Progress in Religion in 1989. Birch is an Anglican with an evangelical background. He says that it was the Student Christian Movement at Adelaide University that helped him see that "there were alternative interpretations of Christianity to fundamentalism."[36] He trained as a biologist in Melbourne and Adelaide and eventually retired as Challis Professor of Biology at the University of Sydney. He has been closely associated with the attempt by the World Council of Churches to develop an environmental theology and ethics.

Birch's work reflects his biological training and background, but he integrates his scientific knowledge with a profound and wide-ranging theological approach. His thought is very much in the process tradition. Among his many books, the two most recent are *On Purpose* and *Regaining Compassion: For Humanity and Nature*.[37] Birch is a panentheist who holds that God is profoundly present in nature. He believes that reality is not merely mechanistic but alive and purposive. He is not arguing here for the eighteenth-century deistic notion of a purpose imposed externally on the world by an "all-powerful deity who left nothing to chance." He also rejects the notion of atheist evolutionists like Jacques Monod that chance is "the only principle in nature."[38]

Birch's position is that all sentient creatures are, to a greater or lesser extent, able to choose.

> Richness of life depends upon the purposes we freely choose. That which animates human life animates alike the rest of the entities of creation. The evidence of science leads to a view of the universe as purposive in the sense that its entities exist by virtue of a degree of freedom which allows them a degree of self-determination ... the whole of the universe and its entities look more like life than like matter.[39]

He argues that our human experience is simply the highest and most intense level of the continuum of life; in other words, all sentient, living things share life experience at varying levels of intensity. Because of this, Birch admits that there are different degrees of intrinsic value among living things; this is based on their different capacity for sentience. He consequently argues that a life-centered ethical approach will place upon us an obligation to work to maximize the well-being of all life-forms. He refers to this as a "biocentric ethic":

> A Christian biocentric ethic takes the neighbour to be all that participates in life. The needs of neighbour stretch beyond human needs, as does the reach of love.[40]

It is on the basis of this biocentric ethic that he is deeply committed to the care and liberation of animals. An ethical approach to ecology will also involve working through the practical consequences of the different degrees of value of various life-forms. But the underlying motif will be that of compassion which alone helps us make sense of our world.

> Compassion is to be extended to all creatures who share the earth with us ... We should respect other creatures because of their intrinsic value and not simply because they are useful to us ... The gradation of intrinsic value implies a diversity of rights. The greater the richness of the experience of the subject the greater the rights ... We need to develop a non-anthropocentric, biocentric ethic, which extends the concept of rights and justice to all living creatures.[41]

Birch's work is a fine example of the way in which theology and science can be integrated to create a strong ecological ethic. This finds its fullest expression in the compassion which is God's most fundamental characteristic, a compassion which extends to all creatures, not just to humans. The challenge for the Christian, he says, is to mirror that deep and wide-ranging compassion.

Birch was intimately involved in the development of an ecological theology in preparation for the Seventh General Assembly of the World Council of Churches (WCC) held in Canberra in 1991. The theme of the Assembly was "Come Holy Spirit, Renew the Whole Creation." It is instructive to examine the actual fate of the WCC's environmental report at this most recent General Assembly.

In the Christian communities such issues are usually swept aside by seemingly more pressing anthropocentric issues, such as social justice and the liberation and development of the third world. This is exactly what happened at the Assembly at Canberra. The Assembly occurred during the course of the Gulf War and understandably this became the major political issue. At the same time, there were strong moves by the third world churches for more influence in the WCC; the Council was seen as too Eurocentric. Muscle-flexing by churches from developing countries led to a highlighting of the centrality of human liberation that largely pushed ecological theology into the background. Ecology also became confused with the issue of "syncretism" when the Eastern Orthodox, as well as more conservative evangelical Protestants, became concerned with the theology of several speakers who were accused of abandoning the exclusivity of Christianity by integrating indigenous religious traditions into their expression of Christianity. The excellent paper "Liberating Life: A Report to the World Council of Churches" (prepared in September 1988) was largely lost in a plethora of other matters.[42]

I mention the fate of ecology at the WCC Assembly because it is typical of the way the churches deal with this topic. It is good as window dressing, but it is not really taken seriously. The seemingly incurable anthropocentrism of the churches means that the call to protect nature is soon swamped by the pressing reality of human needs. Human development quickly takes over from ecological conservation.

Sallie McFague

Sallie McFague is a fascinating contemporary Protestant and feminist theologian at Vanderbilt Divinity School in Nashville, Tennessee. Her essay and book on the idea of the world as God's body is an original piece of theology.[43] She is generally in the process tradition. What she sets out to do is to construct a new theology of nature and of God which connects God with the human process rather than distances God from creation.

McFague approaches theology through the images and models that we use to describe God. She asks the basic question: "How would we act differently if we imagined the world to be the body of God rather than ... the realm of the Almighty King?"[44] She sees the fundamental task of theology to be a creative and imaginative interpretation of reality rather than a discursive explanation of biblical, credal, and doctrinal texts. In a footnote she refers to an essay by Dennis Nineham who says that it is "at the level of the *imagination* that contemporary Christianity is most weak." He goes on to argue that people today

> ... find it hard to believe in God because they do not have available to them any lively imaginative picture of the way God and the world as they know it are related. What they need most is a story, a picture, a myth, that will capture their imagination, while meshing in with the rest of their sensibility in the way that messianic terms linked with the sensibility of first century Jews, or Nicene symbolism meshed with the sensibility of philosophically minded fourth century Greeks.[45]

I will return in detail to this question of the development of the Christian imagination.

McFague's theology is, in an interesting way, a provocative restatement of the Catholic theology of tradition. "Tradition," in this sense, refers to the reality that all theology is always in the process of development, that belief is never static as the human mind explores and teases out the consequences of a religious mystery that is not exhausted by any theological or religious formulae, no matter how sacrosanct. McFague also restates the fact that all theology is metaphorical, in the sense that it is an image of a reality that is, in itself, transcendent and thus, by definition, defies definition. When a theological metaphor becomes a model—such as the image of God as "father"—we have a metaphor with staying power. But the question has to be asked whether such models have outstayed their usefulness. McFague says that models of God "are not definitions of God but likely accounts of experiences of relating to God with the help of relationships we know and understand."[46] Given that our accounts of experience often change, we need to ask whether our religious models need to change also.

McFague says that at the core of the whole theological process is a sensitivity and receptivity to prevailing contemporary mythic imagery. "One cannot hope to interpret Christian faith for one's time if one remains indifferent to the basic images that are the life blood of interpretation and greatly influence people's perceptions and behaviour."[47] McFague, like Thomas Berry, holds that the scientific approach to life is the prevailing myth or metaphorical model in our contemporary world. In the light of this, she lays down four criteria for developing a modern theology of the relationship of God to nature and humankind. Firstly, such a theological cosmology must be informed by science. Secondly, it must emphasize the interrelatedness of human beings with the whole of nature. Thirdly, it must be creation-centered rather than redemption-centered. Fourthly, it must recognize the interconnectedness of peace, justice, and ecology. McFague then proceeds to construct a theology within these parameters.

She points out that the prevailing image of God in Jewish, medieval, and Reformation thought is the monarchical view of God—the idea of God as reigning sovereign. Because this is still the prevailing model that we use to describe God, we do not notice that it has had clear historical interrelationships with the political models of the world from which it emerged, such as kingship in ancient Israel or the medieval notion of the anointed kingly figure. One might add that it was also the prevailing model used by the absolute monarchs who controlled Europe in the seventeenth and eighteenth centuries before the French Revolution, and by western European countries in the colonial period before World War II. The Sri Lankan priest Tissa Balasuriya has pointed out that the monarchical model of God was very useful for the colonial powers in Africa and Asia as they projected themselves as God's vice-regents deputed by the divine sovereign to keep the "natives" in their place.[48] It was, and continues to be, a very useful model for the absolutist papacy of the period after 1870 and the First Vatican Council in its attempts to stifle a more collegial model in the Catholic Church.

McFague asks: will this sovereign-monarchical model continue to work for our age? Or is it dysfunctional for those of us who live in a very different type of society? And how does the notion of "Christ the King" (a Catholic feast introduced as recently as 1925 by Pope Pius XI) make sense in the modern world? McFague quotes that Harvard theologian Gordon Kaufman, who argues that this monarchical model of God leads to an "asymmetrical dualism" whereby God is viewed as totally distant from the world and the rest of the cosmos.[49] In this monarchical view, our cosmic home here on earth is not God's primary residence. God resides elsewhere. This deeply hierarchical theology is destructive of both the cosmos and us, for if God lives in heaven (wherever or whatever that might be) our earthly home has no real value. Ultimately, this view is also destructive of the image of God itself, for God is seen as irrelevant to what happens here on earth.

Paradoxically, this monarchical view encourages a very anthropocentric perspective on our place in the cosmos. For if God is largely absent, we are his vassals who assume his power and sovereignty in relationship to the non-human world, which we see as ours to dominate and exploit. It is in this context that Genesis 1:26–28 becomes a normative text for the pro-development lobby. Thus McFague concludes:

> No matter how ancient a metaphorical tradition may be and regardless of its credentials in scripture, liturgy and credal statements, it still must be discarded if it threatens the continuation of life itself. If the heart of the Christian gospel is the salvific power of God, triumphalist metaphors cannot express that reality in our time, whatever their appropriateness might have been in the past.[50]

McFague argues that theology must begin the development of an appropriate contemporary metaphor for God which can replace the kingly notion. This new metaphor must be informed by science and be creation-centered, it must be concerned with justice and ecology, and it must relate human beings with nature. McFague has a radical new image to suggest: the world as a bodily expression of God.

According to McFague, the world is the incarnation of God's very being and presence, in the same sense that Christ's body is an incarnation of God's presence. McFague reminds us that the central doctrines of Christianity are dominated by body language: the incarnation of Christ in human flesh, the resurrection of Christ's body, the body and blood of Christ in the eucharist, the church as the body of Christ, the sacramental symbol of the bodily union of the spouses in Christian marriage, and the doctrine of the final resurrection of the body. As theology progressively abandons the pagan Platonist and Aristotelian dualism that so permeates the Christian tradition, the possibility of imagining the cosmos as God's body becomes more plausible. God is envisaged as the life-giver who enlivens the entire world-body. "The universe is 'in' God and is God's visible self expression."[51] McFague makes an interesting comparison: our bodies are essential to our existence, but we are not reducible to them. We are inspirited flesh. So, she argues, the world is essential to God, but God is not reducible to the world. Like Charles Birch, McFague is not a pantheist but a panentheist.

> In the metaphor of the universe as the self-expression of God—God's incarnation—the notions of vulnerability, shared responsibility and risk are inevitable. This is a markedly different understanding of the God-world relationship than in the monarch-realm metaphor, for it emphasizes God's willingness to suffer for and with the world, even to the point of personal risk. The world as God's body, then, may be seen as a way to remythologize the inclusive, suffering love of the cross of Jesus of Nazareth. In both instances God is at risk in human hands. Just as once ... human beings killed their God in the body of a man, so we once again have that power ... we [could] kill our God in the body of the world.[52]

In this passage McFague seems to succeed in maintaining a christological context for her theology of God.

Clearly the notion of the world as God's body is a very different way of seeing the reality of God's relationship with the cosmos than the monarch-realm model. In the older, transcendent model, God knows the cosmos externally and acts toward it and all of its creatures in a fatherly, loving, and benevolent manner. But in the notion of the world as God's body, God suffers when the world suffers. God's relationship is internal and emphatic, intimate and sympathetic.

> If the entire universe, all that is and has been, is God's body, then God acts in and through the incredibly complex physical and historical-cultural evolutionary process that began eons ago. This does not mean that God is reduced to the evolutionary process, for God remains as the agent, the self, whose intentions are expressed in the universe.[53]

The notion that God loves bodies and the world is actually more in keeping with the biblical tradition and with basic Christian doctrine. It turns away from the anti-matter bias of so much of Christian history. A God involved with the world means that God is at risk. This notion also posits an important ethical foundation: if the world is God's body, then to destroy part of the world is actually to destroy part of the body of God. Such an act would be totally immoral.

An interesting aspect of McFague's argument is her emphasis on the importance of space. In *The Body of God* she points out that bodies have both a temporal and spatial reality; that is, they exist in a specific place that is contextualized by a specific history and events in a real time context.[54] She says that today "space should become the primary category for thinking about ourselves and other life forms." This would lead us to a sense of identification with a specific place in the world, to a land with which we truly identify. However, for a people of a European cast of mind this is especially difficult. The cultural emphasis over the last few hundred years has been on time. We are fixated on the notion that we must produce more, know more, do more than the generations before us. McFague points out that space is a "democratic notion": everything needs space. But we are "ruining space," and we may only have a few hundred years left if we continue to degrade the world at the rate we are polluting it now:

> When this occurs, justice issues emerge centrally and painfully. When good space ... becomes scarce, turf wars are inevitable. Wars have usually ... been fought over land, for land is the bottom line.[55]

Furthermore, the earth is our home, our place. This is where we belong. But religious people especially have difficulty with this: "Christians have often not been allowed to feel at home on earth, convinced after centuries of emphasis on other-worldliness that they belong somewhere else—in heaven."[56] With a developed sense of place this false other-worldliness can be left behind.

This same theme of space has been taken up recently by two other Protestant theologians. Geoffrey R. Lilbourne is an Australian who has been teaching for many years in the United States at the United Theological Seminary in Dayton, Ohio.[57] Drawing on both Aboriginal and biblical notions of land and place, he shows how these notions have been marginalized by the urbanized and secularized theology that still dominates Christianity. Cavan Brown, a Baptist pastor with a lot of experience in the Western Australian outback, draws on culture, history, and religious experience to examine the role of the desert journey in theology and faith.[58]

But to return to McFague: this new image of the world as the body of God is not without difficulties. One of the most problematic is that the metaphor of the immanence of God in the world implies that God is actually involved with evil. This identification does not arise in the monarch-realm model, for the external God is over and against evil; God is in conflict with and victorious over the evil powers, or, as suffering servant, frees his subjects from evil through suffering. Despite this, what McFague is doing is challenging us to imagine God's relationship to reality in a different way. This involves leaving behind old symbols in order to preserve the very process of symbolization itself. God is not to be found by looking upward to heaven, but out into the world. There "we meet the world as a Thou, as the body of God where God is present to us always and in all times and in all places."[59]

Jürgen Moltmann

The other important contemporary Protestant theologian who has written widely on the environment is Jürgen Moltmann. He is certainly not in the process tradition, but his Gifford Lectures for 1984–1985, *God in Creation: An Ecological Doctrine of Creation*, are especially significant for the development of a Protestant environmental theology.[60] He does not mince matters regarding the importance of the ecological crisis:

> What we call the environmental crisis is not merely a crisis in the natural environment of human beings. It is nothing less than a crisis in human beings themselves. It is a crisis of life on this planet, a crisis so comprehensive and so irreversible that it can not unjustly be described as apocalyptic ... it is the beginning of a life and death struggle for life on this earth.[61]

Coming from the most influential contemporary German Protestant theologian, that is very strong language indeed!

Moltmann's books reflect the organic nature of his theological development. He first came to prominence in 1964 with his *Theology of Hope*.[62] He is of that generation of Germans who have been most profoundly dislocated by Nazism and the Second World War. He himself says that he had become deeply pessimistic, but that then he came under the influence of the Marxist thinker Ernst Bloch's philosophy of hope. As a result, in *Theology of Hope* Moltmann developed a sense of optimism about the future and identified God as the transforming "power" that invades contemporary life.

But in 1973 came a very different book, *The Crucified God*.[63] Answering those critics who argued that he had retreated from an optimistic religiosity to a negative one, Moltmann said:

> This book [*The Crucified God*], then, cannot be regarded as a step back. *Theology of Hope* began with the resurrection of the crucified Christ, and now I am turning to look at the cross of the risen Christ ... The theme then was that of *anticipations* of the future of God in the form of promises and hopes; here it is the understanding of the *incarnation* of that future, by way of the sufferings of Christ, in the world's suffering.[64]

It is significant that in as early a book as *The Crucified God* he identified the sufferings of Christ with the world's suffering. He had already begun his journey toward a theology of ecology.

In the late 1970s, Moltmann—in the best German tradition— began a systematic treatment of theology. This commenced with trinitarian theology. *The Trinity and the Kingdom of God* (German edition 1980) took the identification of the suffering of Christ and the suffering of the world further, and the book revealed subtle hints of Moltmann's panentheism as he emphasized the immanence of God in both human history and nature.[65] Many of his evangelical Protestant readers became increasingly disturbed by his views. But it was his systematic treatment of the doctrine of creation in *God in Creation* that affirmed the relationship of interpenetration, fellowship, and mutual need between God and the world. This was taken further again in his 1989 christology *The Way of Jesus Christ*.[66] Here he argued that the process of God's incarnation, which began in Jesus Christ, will only be completed in the future deification of the cosmos.

Moltmann's development toward an ecological theology is characterized by the consistency typical of a German scholar. But given his status as an evangelical Protestant, his stand on ecology is a very important one. For the evangelical tradition emphasizes the absolute centrality of the Bible, and for a theologian of his standing among Protestants to place ecological theology as such a central theme is crucially important.

With the exception of Teilhard, all of the thinkers I have considered so far have generally been from the Protestant end of the spectrum. We must now turn to the contemporary Catholic thinkers in the area of ecological theology.

Thomas Berry

The most important contemporary Catholic thinker in ecological theology is Thomas Berry. Because of his increasing influence he could be justly called the "Teilhard de Chardin of our time." He is a cultural historian and anthropologist of vast erudition and vision. He is a polymath in the truest sense. His thought does not span mere centuries but millennia and eons. Probably because of the range of his knowledge and speculation he has only gradually become known outside a small coterie of readers and thinkers in the United States. "Through the late 1970s and 1980s Berry's ideas simmered at the edges of Catholic thought," but nowadays they are increasingly permeating the mainstream of environmental activism and theology.[67]

Much of Berry's early writing is to be found in the far-sighted, lay-run Catholic periodical *Cross Currents*.[68] He has also informally published a series of *Riverdale Papers* on a range of topics. His first books (*Religions of India* and *Buddhism*) were published in the late 1960s and have recently been reprinted.[69] His first major work on ecology was *The Dream of the Earth*, published in 1988.[70] In 1992 Berry published (with Brian Swimme) *The Universe Story*.[71]

Thomas Berry was born into a Catholic family of thirteen in 1914 in Greensboro, North Carolina, where his father worked on the railways.[72] Berry says that the great determining element of his early life was his experience of the natural world. He says that he had, from early childhood, an antagonistic attitude toward modern and mechanistic views of existence. He joined the then rather strict and semi-enclosed Passionist order at the age of twenty, where as a student he began to read the Chinese, Hindu, and Buddhist classics. Eventually he was able to read classical Chinese and Sanskrit, and this broad reading in the seminary gave him a background for his later studies.

He was ordained a priest in 1942 but never did much ministerial work. After concluding a doctorate in the late 1940s on the eighteenth-century philosopher of history Giambattista Vico, he went to China as a missionary but had to leave after a year with the advent of the Communist regime. He worked as a military chaplain with NATO in Europe during the Korean War then taught at the Institute for Asian Studies at Seton Hall University in Orange, New Jersey, and the Center for Asian Studies at New York's Saint John's University.

Berry had known the thought of Teilhard de Chardin since his student days and it was Teilhard's approach that showed him that Christians need not be alienated from the natural world. He says that the publication in 1962 of Rachel Carson's *Silent Spring* "touched something deep in my thinking." It focused for him the degradation of the environment by chemicals. In 1966 Berry began to run the doctoral program in History of Religions at Fordham University in the Bronx. During his Fordham years he became increasingly concerned about the natural world, a concern which reconnected him with his childhood love of nature. The fuel crisis and the escalating devastation of the world meant that ecological issues were aggravated in the late 1960s and early 1970s, with the growing awareness "that the earth was troubled deeply in its very structure." Over the last three decades it is the natural world itself that has become the primary focus of all of his thought, and in 1979 he retired from Fordham to head up his own Center for Religious Research in Riverdale, New York.

Berry's study and reading have given him an extraordinary historical and cultural context for understanding what is happening in and to the modern world. This is how Berry describes himself:

I started off as a student of cultural history. I am primarily an historian. What I have to say are the probings of an historian into human affairs in a somewhat comprehensive context. During my university studies I sought to understand the unity and differentiation of human cultures and the dynamism that shaped their sense of reality and value ... I wished to get beyond the classical civilisations, back into the earlier shamanic period of the human community. The more I gave to the study of the human venture, the more clearly I saw the need to go back to the dynamics of life itself. I was progressively led back to what I call the study of the earth community, including its geological and biological as well as its human components. I call myself a geologian.[73]

Here Berry describes himself in terms that could be applied to another Catholic cultural historian, Christopher Dawson. Dawson's emphasis was very much on the role of religion in the formation of culture, especially European culture.[74] Berry is influenced by Dawson, but he thinks that Dawson is too narrow in his focus. Berry goes back further than European culture to the wisdom tradition of native peoples and then places that wisdom within the context of the biological and geological history of the world. In fact, *The Universe Story* is really a brief history of the cosmos akin to Stephen Hawking's *A Brief History of Time*.

Berry says the key role of religion is to provide us with an interpretative pattern, a way of making sense of ourselves, our world, and all that happens. However, he believes that contemporary religion—and specifically modern Catholicism—has largely failed us. He says that there are three central elements that make up twentieth century history: the devastation of the earth, the incompetence of religion and cultural traditions to deal with this devastation, and the rise of a new ecological vision of the universe. He says bluntly: "The greatest failure of Christianity in the total course of its history is its inability to deal with the devastation of the planet." He points out that Christians have a sensitivity to suicide, homicide, and genocide, "but we commit biocide [the killing of the life systems of the planet] and geocide [the killing of the planet itself] and we have no morality to deal with it." This is because "religion is absorbed with the pathos of the human."

Berry maintains that anthropocentrism is the dark side of biblical religion. Until the sixteenth century the church recognized that there were actually two revelatory manifestations of the divine: the primary one was the natural world (which was seen as the "first scripture") and the second was the church and the biblical tradition (which presupposed the natural world). But this balance has been lost over the last four hundred years because "there is an inherent tendency in biblical religion toward alienation from the natural world." He says that even the creed itself is unbalanced: it mentions the Creator-God right at the beginning but then goes on to focus almost exclusively on Christ, redemption, and the church.

Berry maintains that our theological view of God is incomplete if we do not take seriously the fact that it was God who made the world and that therefore God is profoundly related to it. This has a very serious result: "If we lose the splendor of the natural world, we lose our true sense of the divine." The only solution is to shift Christian faith out of its sin-redemption myopia into a broader historical and ecological context. He considers that contemporary secularism and modern science have also failed to help us interpret the significance of the natural world. Just at the moment when we have learned so much from science and modern knowledge, we have lost our ability to interpret the meaning of the world.

> The supreme irony is that just at this moment when such expansive horizons of past, present and future have opened up, mankind is suddenly precipitated into an inner anxiety and even into a foreboding about himself/herself and the meaning of it all. Unable to bear such awesome meaning, men reject themselves as part of the world around them, the past as well as the future. While primitive people ... had a sense of the magnitude of human existence ... we are beset by a sense of

confusion and alienation ... Contemporary men have no spiritual vision adequate for these new magnitudes of existence ... To create such a skill, to teach such a discipline, are the primary tasks of contemporary spirituality.[75]

It is significant that Berry says that the key task is spiritual. But his understanding of the meaning of spirituality far transcends the superficial, psychologized religiosity that characterizes so much contemporary spiritual discourse. His understanding of spirituality begins with the world itself, and he says that everything must be judged in the light of our relationship with it. In this way he shifts the focus of modern spirituality outward and away from its anthropocentric, unhealthy, and intense preoccupation with the human and the psychological. He says: "All human institutions, professions, programs, and activities must now be judged primarily by the extent to which they inhibit, ignore, or foster a mutually enhancing human-earth relationship." Again, he stresses that if we lose our sense of a rapport with the world, we lose our sense of the divine. For it is the cosmos which stimulates and nourishes our imagination, and any diminishment of our sense of the natural world stifles our imaginative faculty. Without imagination our whole inner world would be shriveled up, and without an inner world we simply could not relate to the divine. The close interconnection of imagination with spirituality is further enhanced by Berry's poetic definition of religion:

Religion is poetry, or it is nothing. How can a person be religious without being poetic? Certainly God is a poet—it is God who made rainbows and butterflies and flowers. It is the most absurd thing in the world to think of dealing with religion in any other way than poetry and music ... Take John of the Cross—all the great mystics have been poets. You cannot do it any other way.

Critics of Berry have said that his views are too optimistic and do not take into account the pain, suffering, and awful oppression that are part and parcel of the earth process. For most species, existence "has been a story of struggle, loss, and early death."[76] Feminists and those concerned with social justice ask if Berry's views can be integrated with a concern for equality. Others are critical because he is insufficiently christological, or even claim that his views are post-Christian, despite the fact that he says that genuine religion requires what he calls the "Christ presence."

What does he mean by this? His answer would not satisfy adherents of fundamentalist forms of theology or those who want to emphasize Christian exclusivity. Typically, he contextualizes the Christian teaching on Christ by situating the origin of the notion of the presence of Christ in the broader history of religion. He points out that most ancient peoples have recognized the need for a trans-earthly presence which has been focused in the notion of the shaman. Among American Indians, for instance, the shaman goes into the spirit world to bring back guidance, healing, power, and energy. He thus points up the shamanic aspects of the Christ presence: Christ is a guiding, healing, and empowering presence that comes to us from the transcendent world in human form. Berry argues that historically all peoples have had the idea of savior personalities who bear the divine presence. In the Bible, this presence is borne by the historical personality of Jesus. Berry emphasizes that historical realism is very important in the Christian and western tradition. In other words, he says that for Christianity it is important that the man Jesus, who became the Christ presence, was a real, living, historical personage.

Another element at the core of Berry's thought is the need for the development of a *new cosmology*. By "cosmology" he means the way in which we understand the world and the position of human beings within it and our relationship to it. He says that in developing a new cosmology, Christian theology must begin by taking the world seriously; secondly, theology needs a larger concept of time; thirdly, religion must recognize that life is an interactive biological continuum; fourthly, we need a new creation myth.

Berry begins by saying that we must take the world seriously. This means that human beings have to see themselves in perspective: human history is minuscule in comparison with geological and biological history. The processes of the cosmos are fifteen billion years old, those of our earth have been developing for four billion years, while homo sapiens has been on earth for only 60,000 to 100,000 years. For Berry, the starting point of theology must therefore be the cosmos and the world which has been here for so long. In this context, the usual points of departure and authority for theology—the church, the Bible, doctrine, the papacy—are very relative and circumscribed in focus. We must face up to our insignificant point on the total temporal spectrum.

> We now experience ourselves as the latest arrivals, after some 15 billion years of universe history and after some 4.5 billion years of earth history. Here we are, born yesterday.[77]

The temporal insignificance of humankind becomes very clear in *The Universe Story*.

So Christian theology is a late arrival. But Christianity is a profoundly historical religion, for it teaches that God intervenes in and through the persons and events of history. Biblical history has a beginning (creation) and an end (the *parousia*). This gives the western cultural tradition a markedly progressive rather than a cyclic notion of history, as is characteristic of most of the other great religions. Yet Christian thinking suffers from a paradoxical historical amnesia. It lacks a sense of a broader cosmic history and the extraordinary age of the world. The borders of the Christian imagination are limited by the constraints of biblical history. Berry argues that as a result of this historical amnesia, those of us who live in the western "biblical-classical tradition" find it very difficult to adopt a non-domineering relationship with the planet. This has had very destructive consequences.

Throughout the entire course of [Christian] tradition, the autism has deepened with our mechanism, our political nationalism, our economic industrialism ... [We need] a new interpretation of the western historical process ... The only suitable interpretation of western history seems to be the ironic interpretation. This irony is best expressed, perhaps, by the observation that our supposed progress toward an ever-improving human situation is bringing us to wasteworld rather than wonderworld.[78]

Secondly, Berry moves away from the traditional interpretation of the biblical (and western) concept of time in which God begins the process through the direct creation of the world and ends it at the eschatological "day of the Lord." In this interpretation, historical time is circumscribed by a beginning and an end, and the delimited nature of the temporal process makes it manageable. Biblical history claims to demonstrate that God intervenes at specific times and in specific ways to guide the process of salvation and that the peak moment of this is the life of Jesus Christ.

Up until very recently, this historically limited approach was taken literally by the mainstream church. Paul Hazard has shown in his book on the eighteenth-century Enlightenment, *The European Mind 1680–1715*, that it was Bishop Jacques Benigne Bossuet in the late seventeenth century, in his *Discourse on Universal History*, who popularized the idea that we are able to calculate the age of the world exactly through the use of the biblical text.[79] From biblical evidence Bossuet estimated that the world was created in the year 4004 BC. By tightly delimiting the historical context, this approach allowed God to stand outside the world in eternity (which was defined as time omnipresent to itself) and to supervise the whole business of history and intervene where and when necessary.

For us today, historical earth-time equals at least four billion years and cosmos-time equals fifteen billion years. Thus, in our contemporary context, time is expanded to the extent that it seems limitless. As a result, our modern historical context has been so extended that it is hard for us to conceive of a God who stands statically outside of this enormous temporal range in some form of "eternity." Furthermore, the cosmos today is viewed as an on-going energy event rather than a sudden creation at a specific point in time. It is a dynamic, self-explanatory process that is caught up in its own inner development. The challenge for theology is to move toward discovering God in the cosmic process rather than over and above it. In this approach, God's creativity is shown through the geological history of the cosmos and through the evolution of biological processes, rather than through miraculous interventions from outside, however spectacular.

Thirdly, Berry's new cosmology demands that theology take biology and geology seriously. In this he is very Teilhardian. Berry sees life as an interactive continuum from the most primitive forms to the most highly evolved and complex—us! Human beings are not separate creatures whose lives and value somehow stand over and against the rest of creation. Berry stresses that all life is profoundly related genetically. It is the genes that pass on the ever-increasing complexity of life. For Berry these genetic relationships constitute a profound oneness. He insists that we must rediscover our genetic coding which will lead us back to our rootedness in the processes of organic life. Humankind is not separate and over-against all other reality. It is a constituent part of it.

> Our bonding with the larger dimensions of the universe comes about primarily through our genetic coding. It is the determining factor. It provides constant guidance in the organic functioning that takes place in all our sense functions; in our capacity for transforming food into energy; in our thought, imagination and emotional life. Our genetic coding enables us to experience joy and sorrow ... It provides the ability to think, speak and create. It establishes the context of our relationship with the divine.[80]

The realization of our genetic relatedness with everything will mean that, unless we are prepared to destroy something of ourselves, we will have to work to preserve the common thread of our ecological life rather than destroy it by "developing" it. Thus Berry confronts theology with the need to take seriously the genetic coding which defines both our humanity and our individuality, as well as constituting our relationship to the rest of reality.

Fourthly, the new cosmology demands a new myth—or, as Berry increasingly calls it, a new "story." He says that creation myths (stories of the origin of the cosmos and humankind) are a fundamental substratum for all culture. These stories provide all societies with basic information: they tell us where we came from and where we are going and define the nature of our relationship to the transcendent. For instance, the Genesis account of creation provides the Jewish and Christian cultures with a basic notion of God, humankind, and humankind's relationship to God and to nature. Genesis also explains the origin of sin and evil and the ambivalent attitude of human beings to their earthly lot; basically we "want to be like gods" by breaking our ties to the earth.

Creation myths are important because they define cultures—and in the process divide cultures from each other. As long as religious traditions insist on their own myths, they will emphasize their differences. However, Berry says that a new situation has arisen in the contemporary world. For the first time we have a shared, common myth of origins. This is because the scientific myth of creation has taken over from the biblical myth in the western world as the predominant way of structuring meaning. He argues that science gives contemporary culture a common story of origins and a creation myth that is universal and roots us in the totality of the living universe. A story that begins with the primal atoms and moves through the whole evolution of life is one that can unite us. We need this form of myth, especially as we face environmental problems that are not just local but worldwide.

In *The Universe Story* Berry and Swimme attempt the ambitious task of sketching out the story of the contemporary myth of creation. Berry argues that we are now at the end of the Cenozoic period—the period covering the evolution of the earth over the last sixty-five million years.[81] Berry calls this the "lyric period of the evolutionary process, the period of the flowers, the birds and the mammals."[82] We are now at the terminal phase of the Cenozoic period as our pollution and industrial economy close down more and more of the world's living systems. We are plundering the earth and "an overlay of mechanistic patterns has been imposed on the biological functioning of the living world," although most people are only dimly aware of the terrible things that are happening to the planet.[83] Berry uses the word "autistic" to describe the contemporary human condition.

However, what Berry and Swimme call the "ecozoic period" is now beginning to emerge. What are its characteristics? It will be a time when human beings realize their profound unity with the whole of creation, when we abandon the attitude that the whole of reality is here for us to use, and when we realize that the individual subjectivity of all living things must be protected. "That the universe is a communion of subjects rather than a collection of objects is the central commitment of the Ecozoic."[84] As a result, all species must be protected and their habitats and environments guarded. Human beings simply cannot continue to impose mechanistic patterns on the life structures of the universe.

Critics have argued that Berry's notion of "story," despite his avoidance of all transcendent references, is both biblical and deeply Christian. Berry certainly seems to assume a progressive understanding of history and he appears to see the natural world as simply part of an historical process. By contrast, Buddhist ecologists are less historically oriented and much more concerned with individual living realities.

Berry and Swimme argue that in order to bring about the ecozoic period we need to develop an integrated vision that will draw the whole of reality together. The problem is that the wide diversity and specialization of scientific knowledge results in a very fragmented conception of reality. In order to draw the story together, an imaginative understanding is needed that has overtones of a shamanic vision. "The next phase of scientific development will require above all the insight of shamanic powers, for only with these powers can the story of the universe be told in the true depth of its meaning."[85] Here the shaman is the wise one who not only sees the whole picture, but is also capable of expressing the underlying meaning pattern that helps us make sense of reality, the spirit at the core of the vision.

> Both a competence and a willingness to engage in the immense effort needed to tell the story is what is now needed, especially if this story is to become what it should be: the comprehensive context of our human understanding of ourselves. This is a task that requires imaginative power as well as intellectual understanding. It also requires that we return to the mythic origins of the scientific venture.[86]

It is clear that Berry and Swimme intend *The Universe Story* to be an attempt to construct something of this shamanic vision by telling the all-embracing myth of the story of the universe. (It is important to note that Berry clearly distinguishes the shaman from the prophet—and he also makes it clear that it is shamans that we need today, not prophets!)

Berry has a deeply passionate, personal commitment to the world: "It is the degradation of the earth that hurts me." But his vision is not only theoretical; it is also practical. He points out that in our contemporary culture the earth economy pays an enormous price to support the human economy. The absurdity is that the gross domestic product increases while the gross earth product declines. He argues that economic ethics demand that the real cost to the earth be built into the cost of production. Often we could not buy things if we had to pay for the real environmental cost.

Education also has to move away from dichotomized knowledge toward an integrated understanding of the story of the cosmos. Young people must learn that all things have subjective, individual value; they are not simply objects to support human consumption. The destructive myth of development must be replaced by the overarching myth of the story of the world.

Berry has often spoken of "bioregions." By this means regions that have biological and ecological interdependence. Australia is a good example of a bioregion where the peculiar conditions of the island continent have led to the development of unique flora and fauna. Within the wider bioregion are smaller, interdependent bio-ecological entities. An example of this is the Hudson River Valley, where Berry himself lives. Both levels must be protected. Governments need to move toward the development of constitutional protection not just for human beings but for entire bioregional communities. Both law and morality must recognize biocide and geocide, as well as suicide, homicide, and genocide. Those who break the law and commit the sin of destroying the earth and its living forms must be held both morally and legally responsible. Moral theology must come to recognize that it is a sin to destroy the earth.

There is also the need to develop a new "earth-centered" language. Just as feminists such as Mary Daly have realized that patriarchical language is a means of oppression and needs to be changed, so Berry says that we need to become increasingly sensitive "to the non-human languages of the surrounding world." It is becoming increasingly clear that animals are able to communicate at times in the most complex ways. But Berry takes this further:

> We are learning the mountain language, river language, tree language, the languages of the birds and all the animals and insects, as well as the language of the stars in the heavens. This capacity for understanding and communicating through these languages, until now enjoyed only by our poets and mystics, is of immense significance since so much of life is lived in association with the other beings of the universe.[87]

All of this points to the need for us to move from a human-centered to an earth-centered language. Berry says that this will involve the need to shift from the use of scientific, literal, objective language "to a multivalent language much richer in its symbolic and poetic qualities."

Finally, Berry emphasizes that the creativity of the earth only exists because of a delicate balance of forces. He says that it is the delicate curvature of space-time that assures the energy of the universe.

> The universe is shaped in its larger dimensions from its earliest instance of emergence. The expansive original energy keeps the universe from collapsing, while the gravitational attraction holds the component parts together and enables the universe to blossom. Thus the curvature of the universe is sufficiently closed to maintain a coherence of its various components and sufficiently open to allow for a continued creativity.[88]

This balance of forces gives the earth its special qualities. It is as a result of these forces that life has been able to emerge. The industrial age has profoundly upset and endangered this balance. The ecozoic era will have to be the time when human activities on the earth are brought into alignment so that a creative balance can be achieved on the planet.

While Berry does not explicitly reflect upon the consequences if we fail to bring our behavior back into alignment with the creative balance of the earth, it is quite clear from all that has been said that he thinks that if things do not change radically it will be the end of humankind as we know it today. Without the image of God in the world, true religion and spirituality and the search for God will become almost impossible. For if the beauty of the world is distorted or destroyed, our possibility of discovering the fundamental revelation of God is swept away. If we can find no image of God in the cosmos, we will never be able to discover it in ourselves.

Berry has influenced several significant contemporary Catholic thinkers, and it is to these that I will now turn. Two of the most important are Matthew Fox and Sean McDonagh.

Matthew Fox

Timothy James Fox was born in 1940 and grew up in Madison, Wisconsin—among, as he says, "the farmlands and lakes." He joined the Dominican friars at the age of nineteen, took the religious name of Matthew, and studied for the priesthood at Aquinas Institute in the Chicago suburb of River Forest. After ordination, he went to the Institut Catholique in Paris to study for a doctorate in spirituality. There he came under the influence of the Dominican historian of medieval theology, Father M.D. Chenu, who helped Fox articulate the notion of creation spirituality, an idea which has become basic to his thought. Fox also cites the medieval Dominicans Meister Eckhart (1260–1327), Thomas Aquinas (1225–1274), Hildegarde of Bingen (1098–1179), and Mechtilde of Magdeburg (1207–1282/98) as the major mystical and theological influences on him.

He returned to the United States in the early 1970s and published his first book in 1972, *On Becoming a Musical, Mystical Bear: Spirituality American Style*. He followed it in 1976 with *Whee! We, Wee All the Way Home: A Guide to a Sensual, Prophetic Spirituality*.[89] He taught firstly at Barat College in Lake Forest, Illinois, and then at the archdiocesan seminary, Munderlein College in Chicago. There his Institute in Culture and Creation Spirituality began in 1977. In 1983 he brought the ICCS to Holy Names College in Oakland, overlooking San Francisco Bay. He felt that in California the Institute could be more committed to "deep ecumenism," and he has gradually assembled a faculty that includes a Sufi, a Yoruba priestess, a Zen master, a Lakota medicine man, and the controversial Starhawk, a Wiccan witch. The most important of Fox's subsequent books are *Original Blessing* (1983) and *The Coming of the Cosmic Christ* (1988).[90] In 1992, in the middle of his dispute with the Dominican order, he published *Sheer Joy: Conversations with Thomas Aquinas on Creation Spirituality*.

At the heart of Fox's theology is the notion of creation spirituality.[91] He claims that this is the most ancient religious tradition to be found in the Bible, but that it also goes back beyond biblical times to the aboriginal religions of the world. Creation spirituality celebrates goodness in the totality of life and the struggle of humanity to be compassionate and to find its meaning joyfully within the rest of nature and with a sense of justice. To achieve this, Fox says that we are challenged to give expression to the mystic and artistic in ourselves. For the divine is inherent in the cosmos and especially in the human species, and it always seeks expression through the beauty of art and mysticism. Because everyone is at heart an artist and mystic and can give expression to this, Fox maintains that creation spirituality is non-elitist, optimistic, and feminist.

Central to Fox's thought is his notion of original blessing, which obviously stands in contrast to traditional Christian theology's emphasis on original sin. Fox argues that the cosmos has been blessing humankind since its formation in the original fireball billions of years ago.

> It has made decisions on our behalf, decisions about the rate of expansion of the fireball and decisions about the temperature of the fireball, decisions about supernova explosions that gave birth to the elements of our body, decisions that allowed the sun, the earth, the rocks and the water to evolve. When we look back on it as scientists are doing today, we realize the universe has intended us and this is a blessing.

If original blessing is so ancient, the notion of original sin is, in contrast, very recent; it goes back to the fourth century AD and to the theology of Augustine. Fox maintains that the notion of sin is very anthropocentric and is only as old as the human race. The theology of original sin, an idea which he contends is not found in the Bible, feeds on the human fears which lead to the introspective conscience and to a deep concern about personal salvation. The theology of original sin supports dualism and the patriarchal church's control of personal life and morality.

In contrast, in Fox's creation theology, Jesus is a prophet of compassion. Fox quotes the beatitude "Be compassionate as the

Creator in heaven is compassionate" (Luke 6:36). He argues that in the gospels Jesus is not a theologian but a cosmological story-teller and a prophet who spoke the truth and tried to liberate others. And he paid the price of all who confront the religious and secular authorities. Jesus also broke the taboos towards women in his culture. Thus Fox sees him as a feminist: "I think this had a lot to do with his crucifixion." He also notes that the New Testament, early Christianity, and the early Eastern church's theological tradition never thought of Christ in terms of personal salvation. "They celebrate what they call 'theosis', the divinizing of the universe, and they don't get stuck on the introspective conscience of the human." Their focus is on the cosmic Christ.

Fox is particularly scathing on contemporary fundamentalism—both Catholic and Protestant—which he sees as a crude off-shoot of Augustinian theology. He says that fundamentalism's "Jesusolatory" is so extreme as to be anti-trinitarian and thus heretical. The excessive focus on the man Jesus means that many people have lost the sense of God as Creator. This is why fundamentalists are so indifferent to the destruction of the environment—what Fox calls "the travail of Mother Earth." They have also lost a sense of the role of the Holy Spirit of Christ "which is the spirit of the Cosmic Christ." In contrast to fundamentalism and conventional church theology, what Fox has attempted to do is to articulate a broad cosmic spirituality that will give a context to contemporary environmentalism. While Fox's own spiritual foundations are in the medieval Christian mystical tradition, he stresses that "deep ecumenism" demands that all of the mystical traditions of the world must be brought to bear on the salvation of the cosmos.

Sadly, in March 1993, Matthew Fox was expelled from the Dominican order with the obvious approval of the Vatican. Fox has never adopted the cautious and respectful approach toward church authority that characterizes most theologians, and his theology certainly upsets conservative and fundamentalist Catholics. But it was his enormous popularity in the English-speaking world with a wide range of people from both within and especially outside

Catholicism, and his apparent espousal of some new age ideas and approaches, that probably tipped the scales against him in Rome. He did not win too many friends in high ecclesiastical places in August 1988 with his essay "Is the Catholic Church Today a Dysfunctional Family? A Pastoral Letter to Cardinal Ratzinger and the Whole Church".[92] Cardinal Josef Ratzinger is the Prefect of the Congregation of the Doctrine of the Faith. In the "Pastoral Letter" Fox describes the Catholic church as a maladjusted, addictive family led by an authoritarian, sadomasochistic, sick, and deeply psychologically disturbed hierarchy. The Vatican, he argues, is a dysfunctional, fascist, and self-deluded organization that projects all its problems outward onto others with whom it never deals directly. And what are the results?

> The church's failure to share the great wisdom of our western mystical tradition constitutes a grave sin of omission which results in patriarchal cynicism and the loss of hope. It feeds a kind of collective hysteria that arouses the christofascists of our day, those who, in the name of Christ or Jesus, terrorize us.

Fox's confrontational tactics horrified many cautious (and fearful) theologians and Catholics, but personally I could not agree more with his diagnosis!

Disputes with the Vatican had come to a head in 1987 when Ratzinger demanded that the witch Starhawk be dismissed from the ICCS faculty. Fox refused. A year of Vatican-imposed silence followed in December 1988. The Vatican then put pressure on the Dominican order to either deal with or silence Fox permanently. The actual dismissal was apparently the last act of the Irish international head of the Dominicans, Father Damien Byrne, before he left office. Byrne had protected other Dominican theologians under Roman scrutiny, such as Schillebeeckx, but the pressure on him in Fox's case was considerable. A very unfortunate dispute also seems to have developed between Fox and his regional superior in Chicago, Father Donald Goergen. Goergen, himself a theologian, was the author of *The Sexual*

Celibate, a path-finding book that raised both eyebrows and laughter in church circles when it was first published in 1974. Goergen claimed that Fox had refused to return to a Dominican house in Chicago, and Goergen apparently instituted procedures for expulsion on the grounds of disobedience. Such grounds are, of course, very tenuous nowadays, when many members of religious orders (including many Dominicans in Fox's own province) live with impunity outside established houses of their provinces. The result has been the formal expulsion of Fox from the Dominican order, ironically just after he had published the book *Sheer Joy* on the greatest Dominican of all, Thomas Aquinas. In May 1994, Fox was received into the priesthood of the Episcopalian church.

On the face of it, the Dominican order's action can only be described as unfortunate. However, the final responsibility for this nasty and narrow-minded attitude lies with Ratzinger and John Paul II. Between them they have created an atmosphere of totalitarian inquisition in the contemporary Catholic Church, the results of which are the expulsion from religious life of highly intelligent mavericks like Fox. Sadly, this comes at a time when the Catholic Church most needs creative thinkers, especially in environmental theology.

Sean McDonagh

A very different approach to the development of a theology of ecology is taken by Sean McDonagh, an Irish Columban priest who spent twenty years in the Philippines. He is the author of three influential books, *To Care for the Earth: A Call to a New Theology*, *The Greening of the Church* and *Passion for the Earth*.[93]

McDonagh spent most of his time in the Philippines as a missionary among the T'boli people in southern Mindanao. His approach to environmental theology is practical. The T'boli are a tribal people who lived for centuries in forested hills, and their entire life and culture are centered on the forest. McDonagh describes what has happened to these people:

I do not need weighty tomes to convince me of the seriousness of the problem facing the human community and the earth. I can see the trail of death opening out here before my eyes as I look at what was once an extraordinarily fruitful and colourful land. Until relatively recently, almost all of the Philippines was covered by dense, tropical rainforest. But over the past forty years the forests have almost disappeared. Lumber companies have attacked them with a vengeance in order to supply an insatiable appetite for tropical hardwoods in Japan, Europe, Australia and the United States. Landless farmers have followed the logger ... The scale of destruction is horrendous.[94]

McDonagh points out that the destruction of the forest has led to the disintegration of the T'boli people and their culture.

This devastation has also led to the erosion of the rich topsoils which in turn have blocked estuaries and caused flooding in coastal cities and towns. There is now evidence that the sea and coral reefs around the Philippines are being polluted and destroyed by the murky water which results from the erosion run-off. Worst of all, the destruction of the forest produces "the most despair-filled aspect of the ecological crisis"—the irreversible destruction of species.[95] This situation, which has been obvious for a number of years in the Philippines, led to the Catholic bishops issuing a Pastoral Letter in January 1988, What is Happening to Our Beautiful Land? The Letter is clearly influenced by the thought of McDonagh and spells out the consequences of what has happened in the Philippines:

We often use the word progress to describe what has taken place over the past few decades. There is no denying that in some areas our roads have improved and that electricity is more readily available. But can we say that there is any real progress? *Who has benefited most and who has borne the real costs?* The poor are as disadvantaged as ever and the natural world has been grievously wounded. We have stripped it bare, silenced its sounds and banished other creatures from the community of the living.

> Through our thoughtlessness and greed we have sinned against
> God and his creation [emphasis added].

In a real way, the question "Who has benefited most and who
has borne the real costs?" lies at the core of McDonagh's thought.
While much of his ecological approach is parallel to that of
Thomas Berry, his great contribution is to link social justice issues
in a very practical way with ecology. For him the questions of
culture, justice, and ecology are intimately connected.[96] This
clearly springs from his experience of working with the T'boli.
He argues that the environment and the third world poor have
borne the real costs of so-called development and that the rich
have simply become richer. This is especially the result of the debt
crisis which today affects almost every third world country. Both
the environment and the poor are sacrificed to pay off debts that
were run up in the 1970s to finance often failed or
environmentally destructive "development projects." He argues
that there are good biblical precedents simply to wipe off these
third world debts.

McDonagh also says that in order to deal with these issues a
new moral and systematic theology needs to be developed. He
points out that the Catholic Church has been very slow to do this.
There are too few papal statements on ecology and the
environmental crisis. There are two reasons for this: the church's
deep-seated anthropocentrism, and the lack of a broad Christian
theological framework through which the sheer enormity of the
ecological crisis can be grasped. Christianity has been so
myopically buried in its own self-understanding and traditional
myth that it has simply lacked the broad vision necessary to grasp
the size of the problems facing us.

In the next chapter I want to suggest ways in which something
of that broad theological framework can be sketched out. In doing
this, I will clearly be drawing on much of the thought that I have
outlined in this chapter.

5

God's Earth
Human responsibility for environmental destruction

I will begin this chapter, which attempts to develop an ecological theology, with some environmental facts about which there is general agreement. Nowadays there is a genuine consensus about responsibility for the present parlous situation of the earth. This consensus can be summed up in three statements.

Firstly, there is almost total agreement that our planet is facing serious, even disastrous problems. There is less consensus over the cause, but many would argue that a fundamental element is our contemporary technological culture. Human beings are responsible for the use of technology. As a consequence, human beings are also directly responsible for the destruction of our earthly home. It is above all our impact on the planet, especially since the end of the Second World War, which has seriously upset its balance and destroyed its harmony, beauty, and productiveness. This technological assault on the world has been reinforced by the enormous growth in the human population since about 1750 in Europe and Asia, since 1850 in the Americas, and after 1900 in Africa.[1] The world now faces a catastrophic growth in human population which we increasingly recognize as unsustainable. The problem of population leads directly to the next issue.

At the core of the present ecological crisis is the profoundly manipulative attitude of human beings. We seemingly cannot leave things alone. We see nature as an object to exploit, control, and above all "develop." We are apparently unable to let reality be. We seem determined to rearrange the natural world to suit our needs. It is this apparently compulsive human manipulation that leads directly to environmental destruction.

Thirdly, we seem to be an incurably anthropocentric species. While all species are, of course, self-centered, human beings manifest a peculiar "autism" that often blinds us to the full effects of our actions. This autism is our most destructive vice. We constantly upset the balance of nature by our need to focus on and exploit natural realities for our own benefit. The balance and the interactive integration of the natural systems of the world have been lost as a result of this anthropocentrism. Yet, paradoxically, we are the only species with the power of self-reflection, with the ability to stand back and see what we are doing. Despite this, our autism seems to be deepening, and the evolution of environmental self-reflection has a long way to go before it really affects the way we live.

The modern mania with development, environmental exploitation, and the destruction of the earth's balance confronts us with a moral and ethical problem of great magnitude. For we human beings have to accept the entire blame for the present disastrous state of the world; it emerges from our attitudes, actions, and behavior. There is no other explanation; as ecologists argue, the natural world is not inherently self-destructive but constantly strives for balance and harmony. We humans cannot sidestep our appalling ethical and moral responsibility for what is happening to the earth. So what are we going to do?

The need for conversion

We are going to have to change quickly and profoundly—or, to use the appropriate religious terminology, to experience "conversion"—if we are going to develop a more nurturant and caring attitude toward the natural world. What is called for is the ecological equivalent of deep spiritual change, and this is always a very difficult and painful process. The additional problem that we face is that this will have to happen soon or else there will be too little of the earth left to save.

Most normal people in developed countries nowadays are quite supportive of mild expressions of environmentalism. They are happy to cooperate with the recycling of paper, plastics, and glass and to compost other rubbish when it is easy and convenient and when local government assists them. They are concerned about endangered species, especially the more attractive ones such as the pandas of China and the koalas of Australia, and they want to help preserve the beauty of the world. With the advent and popularity of four-wheel drive cars, a small group of people in those developed countries that still have some wilderness territory (Australia and North America, for example) have actually been able to experience something of genuine wilderness.

But ecology is simply not a central and immediate element in the world-view of most people in developed countries. They see environmentalism as theoretically important; it consistently rates very high in the hierarchy of public issues, and most people even think of it as the most important of the long-term issues. But usually it remains in the realm of the theoretical. It does not really impact immediately on people's lives. Insofar as they articulate any contemporary world-view or environmental attitude to life, most people hope that some compromise between ecology and development, brokered by government, can be reached without any appreciable affect on their own living standards. But the fundamental truth is that their *real* priorities are elsewhere. Ecology is a luxury that, when the economic chips are down, people will theoretically support, but in practice will have to afford to do without.

Just as we must undergo a conversion and a change of life if we are to be persons of genuine spiritual conviction and religious faith, so to become ecologically aware we must pass through a real conversion process to come to an existential consciousness of our human relationship to the world. It is only when we pass through this process that we realize that spirituality and ecology are not mutually exclusive but actually belong together. Indeed, they increasingly need the support of each other. This is not to say that a genuinely secular person cannot undergo ecological conversion, but it is to assert the deep compatibility between spirituality and ecology. For someone to get to this point of ecological commitment requires a profound change of attitude to the natural world. A real cosmological "conversion" has to occur. This will involve a deep interior change and the consequent making of a personal commitment. The result of this will be a strong sense of biological and existential identification with other living things and ultimately with the land and the earth itself.

The process whereby we open up to the possibility of this type of identification varies from individual to individual. But as in the case of religious faith, there are some common elements. It originates in one of two ways: either in an identifiable, specific event or experience through which a whole new attitude to the world dawns; or through a drawn-out process whereby a person gradually becomes aware of a profound permeation of their whole being with the sense that, as human beings, we originated on this earth, that we belong here, and that this is our only home and there is nowhere else to go. The two processes can be combined: the transformative experience can gradually unfold its significance through a process of conversion to a new attitude toward the earth.

These moments of conscious realization are usually tied to a specific place or event. They can be special experiences of natural beauty, or of the fragility of nature, or even of the appalling pollution that can result from human activity. For instance, a visit to the polluted coalfield region of Silesia in southern Poland around Katowice, or to parts of the Czech and Slovak Republics or other parts of eastern Europe, would certainly convert anyone whose sensitivities were not completely blunted by industrialism or greed to a strong pro-ecological stance. The unique beauty of a place can also have a transformative effect: I will never forget a visit to one of the most beautiful places in the world—Tasmania's original and unique Lake Pedder—just before it was drowned by the state Hydro-Electricity Commission. The Tasmanian Commission was—and still is—dominated by a compulsive and myopic "technologism" that is expressed in the need to build dams. In the decision to dam Lake Pedder it was supported by the then Labor state government. For me, that visit to Lake Pedder involved the experience of an exquisitely beautiful place that was destined for destruction by a human and political decision that, in retrospect, can only be described as of little or no practical value and utterly environmentally benighted—a form of ecological vandalism unequalled in the world. It is only to be hoped that the Tasmanian government makes reparation to the world by taking seriously the recent suggestions of ecologists that the dammed lake be released and that an attempt be made to restore the beauty of Lake Pedder. However, it must be admitted that there are experts who think this is unlikely to succeed. So we are confronted again with the awful truth that once something is lost, it is lost *forever*.

This process of bringing to consciousness our sense of oneness with the earth manifests itself through the release of a deep feeling of sympathy and unity with the specific place in which we are—and more generally with the land, the animals, the trees, the plants, and the natural world—as profoundly and personally connected with oneself. We feel in our own bodies the suffering, joy, and beauty of the world around us. Just as it is difficult for a normal sensitive person to read about or see the injuries and sufferings of our fellow human beings, especially when these are deliberately brought about by other human beings, so a parallel sensitivity needs to develop regarding all living things. It is difficult and painful to read the *Annual Report* of Amnesty International about the on-going world-wide torture and traumatization of political and religious prisoners of conscience. It is the same for the person who is ecologically sensitive. It is deeply painful for them to read about or see the destruction of native, old-growth forests by the wood-chip industry, or to view the slaughter by cars and especially trucks of small animals on our roads, or to hear about or see on television the destruction of sea life by Japanese, Taiwanese, or Norwegian fishing activities. Coterminous with this experience is the determination to do something active and specific about human destructiveness toward the environment.

Ecological conversion involves the sacrifice of the extreme elements of our modern sense of individuality as we begin to recognize our commonality with and interdependence upon all other species. This sense of our rootedness in the whole of reality works unconsciously at a level parallel to religious belief; and, like belief, it needs to be articulated and brought regularly to consciousness. It is an expression of what Thomas Berry has called our "biological connectedness" with the whole of reality.

Just as with religious belief, ecological conversion requires a *post-factum* reflexive, intellectual understanding. St Anselm said in 1097 that "fides quaerens intellectum"—"faith seeks understanding." A latter-day ecological Anselm would realize that a rediscovery of our rootedness in the natural world would also require *post-factum* intellectual and scientific reflection. We need to understand how the environment actually works, how dynamic interactions impact on each other, and what our human relationship is to it all. Ecological commitment must be underpinned by study, knowledge, and understanding.

A sense of connectedness

The way in which this process of ecological conversion becomes real for a person through a sense of relationship with a specific place, or individual or group of living things, is illustrated by the native people of the Eastern North American woodlands. These people use specific words to connote this reality, words which take us to the heart of North American religion and its intersection with nature. Depending on their language group, Native Americans use the words "orenda," "manitou," or "wakanda."

In North American religion there is no dichotomy between nature and the supernatural. If anything, there is no concept of "nature" as a religiously neutral reality, as there is in western scientific thought. Instead, these words connote the power of personal and spiritual presence in the various aspects of the natural world. They point to the belief that there are other-than-human-persons. These other-than-human-persons act with human beings as causative agents in the world. As A. Irving Hallowell says:

All other "persons"—human or other than human—are structured the same as I am. There is a vital part which is enduring and an outward appearance that may be transformed under certain conditions. All other "persons" too have such attributes as self-awareness and understanding. I can talk with them ... they have personal identity, autonomy, and volition.[2]

As a result, the natural world takes on a whole wealth of personal meanings and presences that westerners simply do not experience. Thomas Berry puts it this way:

These experiences are extraordinarily deep manifestations of spiritual presence throughout the universe. They convey the notion of the mystique of the land and vegetation, what might be called a mystique of the cosmological order.[3]

It is only when we concretize environmental awareness through a deep existential and spiritual connection with this or that being, presence, or specific place that we begin to make a genuine and lasting environmental commitment.

This closely resembles what the Australian Aborigines and most other indigenous people feel in relationship to particular places in their own land. The anthropologists R.M. and C.H. Berndt, in their book *The World of the First Australians*, sum up the Aboriginal attitude to land in four assertions:

(a) *Everywhere* in Aboriginal Australia land was/is god-given; it was/is sacred land highlighted by especially significant sites of spiritual importance.

(b) The land was/is inalienable and its charter was/is that of the Dreaming.

(c) Aboriginal man had/has an incontrovertible right of possession.

(d) A spiritual linkage existed/exists between a person and a specific site or part of the country by virtue of his [her] birth. This is more than an association with a piece of land ... the land *is* him [her], in spiritual terms. It cannot be removed from him [her]—not even by death.[4]

It is the fourth assertion which is most important in the context of this discussion. For the Aborigine, the link with a specific site is an unbreakable bond between the person who has come to religious awareness and a specific place in the landscape.

Given the extraordinary mobility of contemporary society and our lack of a sense of connectedness with one place, the white person probably initiates their ecological awareness by a sense of union with the whole of a landscape. It begins when we first see the color of the land, and when we begin to advert to the animals and birds that inhabit it. In Australia, for instance, it begins with a sense of connection with the whole flora and fauna of the continent. But this eventually needs to be narrowed down to a specific type of place (such as the mountains, or desert, or tropical country), or even to a particular spot.

One of the great drawbacks of migrant societies is that the land is generally not construed by the new arrivals as of value in itself. Instead it is seen as a place of opportunity for familial, personal, and material development for the on-going flow of arrivals. This is why migrants are often so destructive to a place. The environmental concerns of the land are usually (though not always) of little or no concern to them. The new country is seen merely as a place to settle and to attempt to establish a new life-style to compensate for the opportunities that the old country did not provide. For the first generation the new country usually remains remote and alien. Most of the migrants who have come to Australia since 1947 have remained in the larger cities. The same can be said for the United States. The Australian landscape still seemingly remains foreign to them. The appalling degradation and ruthless exploitation of the Australian landscape by the Anglo-Celtic settlers of the nineteenth and early twentieth centuries is a testimony to the profound sense of alienation experienced by most Europeans on arrival in a place that was totally different to anything they had experienced before. Part of the tragedy of the Aboriginal people of Australia is that they had to stand by and see their land, which was part of the essence of their being, occupied, stripped of its tree cover, and given over to destructive animals such as sheep and cattle. Much the same pattern occurred in the United States, and again the conquered indigenous people were forced to stand aside as so much that they valued in their environment was destroyed.

A developmental ideology underpins migration. In post-Second World War Australia, migrants have been used by governments and economists to support the myth of "taming the land", the creation of larger domestic markets, and ever-greater and on-going development. William J. Lines has pointed out in *Taming the Great South Land* that these European migrants to Australia were used as a labor force for the large scale developments that characterized Australian social and economic thinking in the 1950s and 1960s.[5] The most obvious example of the development mentality was the Snowy Mountains Hydro-Electricity Scheme in south-eastern Australia.

This was also the period of the beginning of the mining "boom" in Australia. Lines tellingly quotes the blunt words of the then Victorian premier, Henry Bolte: "We can make this country into a quarry to serve the whole world."[6] The developmental mania of that period treated much of Australia as if it were a kind of ecological *terra nullius* (a territory belonging to nobody) that was to be opened up for mineral exploitation. Another extreme example of developmental mania, as already noted, was the Tasmanian Hydro-Electricity Commission, which saw the state of Tasmania not as one of the most beautiful natural places in the world but as a set of "problems" created by nature awaiting their technical solutions.[7] Lines sums up the post-Second World War attitude accurately:

> In the 1960s politicians abandoned all pretence to some higher goal. Development became a necessary good in and of itself; development required no further justification. The means had become the ends. Human life on the Australian continent aimed at nothing beyond economic development. Conquest lost any immediate rationale and became an end in itself.[8]

Similar large-scale developments occurred in the United States and Canada during the same period.

But back to post-war migration. With increasing population and the on-going degradation of the ecological systems of the receiving country, it becomes harder and harder for the new settler to be able to bring to consciousness and articulate a sense of identification and a spiritual connection with the new land. The crass materialism that characterizes many migrants blocks out spiritual awareness and the ability to relate to the new land in any profound sense. Their spiritual and cultural lives still dwell in the old country, and their emotional sustenance is still drawn from the culture they left behind. Multiculturalism is all very well, but it has its negative side! Leaving the old country and the traditional values behind usually occurs particularly slowly. Identification with the new country, especially with the ecological and spiritual aspects of that country, takes time—even generations. In the meantime, more and more pressure is being put on the receiving environment. This may not be true of all migrants, but it is certainly true of the majority. The protection of the environment is a good and ethical reason to stem the flow of migrants to receiving countries.

The process of conversion

When I say that this experience of connection with other living species and with a particular place normally only happens as a result of conversion, I am using the word "conversion" in the proper sense. For non-religious people this will not necessarily express itself in religious terms, but for those for whom spirituality and religion are important issues, the event will have generalized but clearly religious overtones. In other words, conversions occur within the epistemological frameworks that help us make sense of our lives and through which we give expression to our most important experiences. This conversion (whether secular or spiritual) can be, but need not necessarily be, a sudden event; some people can actually trace it to a specific moment. It can also happen over a period as our attitudes change gradually but profoundly and a real interior shift occurs at an unconscious level which only slowly rises to consciousness.

The Bible, of course, knows all about the psychological dynamics of repentance, change, and conversion. It is also very realistic about how the process actually happens. Conversion normally occurs at a time of personal or communal crisis, at a point when basic and far-reaching decisions can no longer be avoided. In the Hebrew scriptures it is usually the prophets who challenge people to turn from their hard-heartedness and blockheadedness to God. In the gospels Jesus also introduces a note of crisis, a time of decision, when a commitment for or against God's reign has to be made. Today we face a monumental ecological crisis, a time of choice for or against the very life of the earth itself. So crisis, which is the primary circumstance for the act of conversion, is already present in our world. It is a time of *kairos*, a time for decisions to be made.

The second element in the conversion process is repentance, or the ability to see oneself in perspective. It is only when we can break out of the narrow confines of our self-made world that we realize how stubbornly we have followed what the prophet Jeremiah calls "our own heart" (Jeremiah 9:13–16). The net result of hardness of heart, human stubbornness, and a failure to see ourselves as others see us is a terrible blindness. Today some of us have to begin to see ourselves from the perspective of the rest of creation. We realize that we are not the ultimate fulfillment of the cosmic process but, as Thomas Berry says, "the affliction of the world, its demonic presence."[9] When this really dawns on us, it is an appalling and frightening moment of self-realization.

Self-realization—seeing ourselves from the perspective of others—is the most significant moment in the conversion process. This is because it generates a genuine vulnerability and admits the possibility of each of us being permeated at a profound level by a new vision. This actual existential moment of conversion ushers in the possibility of a new way of seeing things, a new attitude, a fresh approach to life. Central to the ecological conversion process is the realization that, as human beings, we are genetically and biologically rooted in the earth and totally dependent upon it. We are not angels, separate beings who are said to exist in isolation from the material process. As the priest said in the old Ash Wednesday Catholic ritual as he put the ashes on the recipient's forehead: "Memento, homo, quia pulvis es, et in pulverem reverteris"—"Remember that you are dust and unto dust you will return." This prayer clearly says that we have come from the earth, that we live in dependence upon it, and that ultimately we will be re-absorbed by it. The core of anthropocentric self-righteousness is the presumption that we are somehow above this world when in fact we are totally dependent upon it for our very existence. Yet our anthropocentric myths continue to shield us from these truths about ourselves, just as pious self-righteousness protects so many who are afraid of a genuine religious encounter with God. This moment of perspective, of seeing ourselves as the rest of the cosmos sees us, is a real spiritual, psychological, and philosophical breakthrough, a painful moment of vision that leads to freedom and a whole new attitude.

Ecological conversion demands a third movement: the discovery of and commitment to a completely new way of seeing the whole of reality. It demands a new perspective on life. We are only at the edge of developing what this might mean in practice. A theology intersected by ecology and an ecology shaped by theology will demand not only a whole new ethical attitude to the world and to all reality in it; it will actually revolutionize all of our approaches to the ultimate questions of meaning and purpose. What I will try to do now is to tease out some of the implications of this new way of seeing reality.

Is it true that "only a god can save us"?

The ethical question about conversion to a biocentric ethic leads us straight to the central theological question that is embedded in environmental degradation. If the world upon which we depend for our existence is dying all around us as a direct result of our own action, the question has to be asked: where is God in all of this? Will God stand by and allow the world to be destroyed? What connection is there between the apparent absence of God from the world and the results of environmental destruction?

This question is very similar to the one raised by the Nazi holocaust. Where was God at Auschwitz and all the other camps? Where was the God who purportedly freed the Jewish slaves from ancient Egypt as the trains unloaded their human cargo at Dachau, Birkenau, Sobibor, Treblinka, and Majdanek? Where was God when nearly six million Jewish people were killed? Indeed, one historian of the holocaust, Martin Gilbert, says that the estimate of six million is "a minimum."[10] How do you explain the absence of God in the face of such insane but efficient human destruction?

The same question can be asked as more species slip over the edge into extinction and an environmental holocaust surrounds us. Where is God? Will God intervene and, if so, how? Does the natural world have no significance for its Creator? And have we so secularized the world that the only value it has for us is as a storehouse of useable materials to support human life and development? Has it no ultimate meaning and purpose in itself? What is God doing as the number of humans increases to the extent that the entire world will soon be polluted beyond redemption by the sheer overwhelming size of the human population? Should the world be turned into a feedlot to support ever-growing numbers of humans with every other species sacrificed?

The thought of the German existentialist philosopher Martin Heidegger (1889–1976) seems a rather strange place to begin a discussion of these ultimate questions that revolve around the relationship between the theology of God and ecology—especially in view of my reference to the holocaust and Heidegger's well-known anti-semitism. However, one of the key issues in Heidegger's philosophy is the problem of modern technology. He argues that the forces let loose in our world by technocratic attitudes and the environmental destruction that result from technological processes are so powerful and pervasive that it will only be through the intervention of a "god" that we can be saved. His statement on this issue appeared in a well-known interview published in *Der Spiegel* in 1978, just after his death. In the article he discussed, among other things, his controversial relationship with National Socialism, and his remarks were seen as something of an apologia for his behavior during the 1933–1945 period. In the interview he also makes the following extraordinary statement:

> Philosophy will not be able to effect an immediate transformation in the present condition of the world. This is not only true of philosophy, but of all merely human thought and endeavour. *Only a god can save us.* The sole possibility that is left for us is to prepare for a sort of readiness, through thinking and poetising, for the appearance of the god or the absence of the god in the time of foundering, for in the face of god who is absent, we founder.[11]

Heidegger argues that we have already entered the period of "foundering," for the effects of the on-going environmental destruction of the world are now upon us. "Only a god can save us" because we are unable to do anything ourselves to control modern technology and its destructive effects. Technology has so dominated western culture and philosophy for the last four hundred years that we are unable to reverse this dominance merely through our own efforts. There is a sense in which Heidegger was an environmentalist long before the word became popular, and ecologists are increasingly recognizing him as a foundational thinker upon whose philosophy a coherent approach to the world might be built.

This statement about a savior "god" is, at first sight, unusual for a German philosopher who, while he was born a Catholic and spent a brief time in a Jesuit novitiate (less than a month) and a period as a theological student at Freiburg University, usually described the Judeo-Christian God as an "alien power." While Heidegger was not an atheist in the proper sense, he certainly considered, like Nietzsche, that the Judeo-Christian God was dead in terms of any influence in the contemporary world. Although Heidegger's professional reputation has been badly scarred by his support for the Nazi Party and his failure to make any response to the holocaust[12] his thought actually went through several stages of development, and the English theologian John Macquarrie argues that Heidegger had in fact moved in a more mystical direction at the end of his life.[13]

So what does the statement about "god" mean in the wider context of Heidegger's life and thought? Is it a dying man's pious wish as he retreats back to the traditional notion of providence from his young Catholic manhood? Who or what is this "god" to which he refers, and in what way is this "god" meant to save us?

In fact, the Der Spiegel comments are not all that unusual in the light of Heidegger's whole approach to philosophy. His thought centers around the concept of being (Sein) and for him Sein has no being at all except being-in-the-world. In other words, the absolute starting point of his thought is that which exists in the world. George Steiner (ironically himself an English Jew), in his fine book Heidegger, explains it like this:

> Dasein is "to be there" (da-sein), and "there" is the world: the concrete, literal, actual, daily world. To be human is to be immersed, implanted, rooted in the earth, in the quotidian

matter-of-factness of the world ("human" has in it *humus*, the
Latin for "earth"). The world *is* ... it is here and now and
everywhere around us. We are in it. Totally. To express this
radical immanence, this embeddedness, Heidegger uses the
composite *In-der-welt-sein* (a "being-in-the-world", a "to-be-in-
the-world").[14]

At heart, Heidegger's philosophy centers on the question: why
do individual things exist? Why is there anything in the world at
all, rather than nothing? For Heidegger the absolute "thisness" of
things, their sheer quiddity, is deeply important. He had a
profoundly concrete sense of the world. His thought has strong
overtones of the philosophy of the medieval Franciscan, John
Duns Scotus, on whom Heidegger did his "Habilitation" degree at
Freiburg. One is reminded here also of the English Jesuit poet,
Gerard Manley Hopkins, and his interest in Scotus. Hopkins also
focused closely on the individual reality of specific things.

Heidegger became convinced that the entire intellectualist
development of western philosophy since Plato has masked rather
than revealed *Sein* (being). He argues that Plato, Aristotle, and
Descartes are fundamentally responsible for a rationalistic-
technocratic approach to life which Heidegger identifies with
nihilism. He says that the net result of this western Platonized
philosophical tradition is the destructive technology of the
contemporary world. George Steiner puts it this way:

> Creation *should be* custody; a human construction *should be* the
> elicitation and housing of the great springs of being. But we
> know that reality is otherwise. Technology has ravaged the earth
> and degraded natural forms to mere utility. Man has laboured
> and thought not with but against the grain of things. He has not
> given lodging to the forces and creatures of the natural world
> but made them homeless. Today penitential ecology and
> attempts at reparation, probably futile, are a mounting element
> in social sensibility and the politics of disgust. But Heidegger
> came much earlier. His advocacy of the sanctity of the

environment ... is grounded ... in the rootedness of existence
in the actual contours of the ground.[15]

The context of the discussion in *Der Spiegel* was Heidegger's
notion of Technology (with a capital "T"). His view was that we
needed a "god" to save us from the destructive consequences of
technology precisely because it is such an all-pervasive power in
our lives and in western culture. His view is that particular
technological applications not only already determine every detail
of contemporary existence, but that technology itself is actually a
mode of being. It has an existence and a dynamic independent of
its particular realizations. His view is that technology is more than
a way of thinking about and acting in reality. Technology vitiates
our relationship with the world because it enframes and, at the
same time, masks the actual being of the world. By "enframes" he
means that technology creates the prism through which we view
being. When we harness nature to technology we turn things-in-
the-world, which have internal values in themselves, into mere
objects for our use, and in the process we distort their very
essence.

Thus, for Heidegger, technology is not just the process of
particular technological applications that can be studied and
measured historically. Nor is it just an intra-psychic mental
phenomenon, a way of looking at reality. At the deepest level,
technology actually has being and exists *in itself*. Heidegger admits
that this phenomenon is very difficult to articulate because it is
concealed behind a multitude of "beings" which express
themselves as particular technological entities. He holds that,
especially since the eighteenth-century Enlightenment, we have
been involved, in the words of Christopher Manes in his book
Green Rage, in "another episode in the 'forgetting' of Being in all
its limitless possibilities."[16] Manes continues:

> By trying to fix beings in a utilitarian mode, technological
> society is converting the world into a standing reserve of
> fungible goods. Things are no longer allowed to present

themselves even as objects but are reduced to interchangeable parts in a network of use. This "unworld", as Heidegger calls it, eventually diminishes the humanity it purports to serve as humans themselves are converted into "human resources", with significance only to the degree that they are useful to the imperatives of technology.

Manes expresses Heidegger's view of technology well when he says that "Technology totalises existence along one axis, the axis of utility, and all other rich, poetic, wild ways in which a human being is able to encounter the world are excluded." [17]

The German word *Gestell*, which means both "frame" and "mask," is a key word for Heidegger. He says that technology is actually a frame of being through which particular technological manifestations express themselves. *Gestell* also means that technology masks or hides reality. To use an English idiom, we are lost because we cannot see the wood for the trees. We have focused so much on technology and its particular applications and we have become so involved with it that we have lost our sense of the reality of the world that lies behind it. Our concentration on technology is so complete that we can no longer recognize or get in touch with real being-in-the-world.

Thus the ecological crisis that has resulted from technology is metaphysical rather than merely ethical. We simply cannot decide *by mere willpower* to turn away from the worst aspects of technology and resolve to live in harmony with nature, because our involvement with technology is not the result of personal or communal initiative or decision. This is seemingly why he says that "only a god can save us," for a "god" exists in the realm of metaphysical being and it is at this level that the real change has to occur. Heidegger has apparently despaired of the possibility of philosophy offering a solution and has turned the issue into what can only be described as theological. Heidegger is clearly arguing the pessimistic position that we are caught in a destructive process that is largely beyond our control. Jan Van der Veken sums up his view: "Technology is something which dominates us far more than we dominate it." Heidegger is not alone in his pessimism about technology: the Protestant thinker Jacques Ellul, the Marxist philosopher Herbert Marcuse, and the sociologists Theodore Roszak and Lewis Mumford all share Heidegger's despair with technology and concede that it will be extraordinarily difficult to change modern attitudes. What he seems to be articulating is the sense of fear that one finds among many ecologists that it is already too late, that we will be unable to turn the attack on nature around in time to save what is left. He suggests that technology is a totally impersonal, destructive force that has so possessed modern humankind that we will inevitably destroy our earthly home. The technological process has been going on, in its modern form, since the sixteenth century and the invention of modern mechanism by Rene Descartes. It expresses itself in the attitude that nature is nothing more than a "giant gasoline station":

> This radical revolution in outlook has come about in modern philosophy. From this arises a completely new relation of man to the world and his place in it. The world now appears as an object open to the attack of calculative thought, attacks that nothing is believed able any longer to resist. Nature has become a giant gasoline station, an energy source for modern technology and industry.[18]

So where does Heidegger's "god" come into all of this, and how does his "god" help us? This is linked to the question: what are we to do in the face of the horrendous environmental destruction that confronts us?

Heidegger argues that we can prepare ourselves for the coming of this "god" by what he calls "thinking" and "poetising." By these words he seems to be indicating that we ought to begin to conceive of reality in a different way—that we should try to get ourselves to imagine new and different possibilities. By "thinking" we will come to understand our metaphysical predicament and by "poetising" we will develop our imaginations so that we will be able to perceive the actual presence of "god," the saving being. (I think it is appropriate to indicate some type of identification between Heidegger's "god" and the Christian notion of God— although he might have questioned this.) Heidegger is arguing that if we understand the power that technology has over us, we will not just try to wish it away. We will come to understand that the task that faces us is not *just* ethical but is metaphysical, involving the evolution of a new *Gestell* (frame) through the prism of which we will begin to encounter nature and reality from a different, non-technological perspective. This frame is explicitly theological, and George Steiner and John Macquarrie both correctly argue that Heidegger's thought has strong theological elements in it.[19]

In developing this new theological perspective, the ability to "poetize" will be just as important as the ability to think. We will need to be able to imagine other options besides technology as a way of dealing with reality and the natural world. Imagination will also be a key element in ecological theology, for it is only through imagination that we will be able to perceive the God who is sacramentally and symbolically present in all of the realities of the natural world.

So it seems to me that Heidegger points to the theological direction in which we need to move. But the questions remain. What will this God be like, and what will happen to our traditional notions of God as a theology of ecology develops? If, as the great historical religions have consistently argued, the cosmos is somehow the product of God's creative action, will God stand by and allow the natural world to be progressively destroyed? Or will God intervene—and in what way? Is there a limit to human freedom to manipulate and destroy the world and have we reached that limit? If not now, when will we reach it? What is God's relationship to the world which has produced such diversity, when one species—humankind—seems so set on destroying so many other species, as well as the very basis of life on earth itself?

All of this adds up to a fundamental question of absolute and central importance not just for the future of the human species, but for the future of the world itself. I think that Heidegger has correctly posed the question. I am not certain that he has answered it.

At the core of all serious religious endeavor is a set of basic questions about God. Who or what is God? And what is the nature of God's relationship with the natural world? In what sense is God transcendent and in what way is God present to the natural world? Can we safely refer to God any longer as a "creator"? Is God accessible to us? Can we even experience the transcendent? How, and in what way, is this achieved? And what images of God as "savior" are there on offer in the contemporary world?

Will the God that saves us be the God of the modern physicists?

These questions about God, the nature of the transcendent, and the relationship of it all to the environment have become even more acute in our contemporary world. One reason for this is environmental degradation. Another is the consensus that has been developing among physicists and astronomers in recent times about the origin of the universe and its early development. Both contemporary ecology and modern theories about the big bang and cosmic origins confront us with a set of profound and ultimate questions about God, creation, and the relationship of the transcendent to the evolution of the world and our part in the world process. How is God related to the world, and in what sense can God be called "creator"? What does theology have to say to modern cosmological theories?

This series of interrelated questions embedded in modern physics, astronomy, cosmology, and issues about the origin of the universe have brought us to the edge of a "black hole" that takes us beyond science to theology and even mysticism. It is the scientists who have brought us to this point, and it is mainly the scientists who have tried to set out the speculative issues implicit in this "black hole." Most theologians have preferred to stay in their church-bound ivory towers rather than deal with these difficult contemporary issues. Yet these questions about ecology and science are of central importance for any discussion of environmental theology. They stand at the core of contemporary cosmology and determine how we think about the origins of the universe, the nature of its early development, and whether the earth as a habitable place has any future at all. The way in which we think about these questions shapes how we image both God and the world. Is God to be seen as part of the creative process, or as largely (or even entirely) absent from it? For cosmology is the major factor in determining how we think of the divine and how we imagine God's relationship to the world. So, as well as questions about ecological destruction, a theology that takes environment and science seriously must also confront issues about the origin and history of the universe. In the last few decades, this question of origins has moved from the realm of theoretical physics and astronomy to popular science writing. This in turn has generated a very considerable interest in the wider community in what are questions of theological importance.

At the core of the discussion about the relationship between science and religion is the question of creation. Christian theology has always maintained that there are two elements in God's creative activity. Firstly, God is seen as the creative *cause* and *source* of all that has come to be. Modern religious thinkers have not tried to determine the way in which God's creative work has been achieved. Most would now lean toward the notion of a process somehow initiated by God which then developed according to the laws of physics and the norms of geological and biological evolution. Secondly, God is also seen as the one who *sustains* in existence all that was, is, and will be. Reality continues to exist because God wills it so. However, both of these elements of God's creativity are now being challenged by the notions of some contemporary theoretical physicists and cosmologists.

Central to modern theorizing about the origins of the universe is the big bang theory. At present most researchers agree that this model makes the best sense of contemporary scientific observation; the theory also appeals because of its consistency, form, and beauty. Stephen Hawking, for instance, is quite clear about the attractiveness of models that are mathematically "aesthetic" and which are put forward basically for "metaphysical reasons."[20] The big bang theory was first suggested by Edwin Hubble in 1929. It posits a time "when the universe was infinitesimally small and infinitely dense."[21] About fifteen billion years ago this dense mass of matter exploded, releasing enormous energy, and it is in this fireball that all reality ultimately finds its origin.

The theory of the big bang has been systematically developed by a series of scientists. Two of the most creative and accessible of contemporary scientific thinkers about the big bang are Stephen Hawking and Paul Davies.[22] Despite the complexity of the material they discuss, both are lucid writers.

Hawking's ultimate aim is to enunciate a complete description of everything in the universe in a single theory. He is actually trying to achieve for contemporary science something similar to what Thomas Aquinas attempted to do for theology and human knowledge in the thirteenth century. In order to achieve this, Hawking sets out to describe the initial conditions at the time of the early evolution of the universe, bringing together the two basic concepts of modern physics: general relativity (which describes the physics of gravity) and quantum theory (which describes matter and energy at the atomic level). Hawking actually posits a world that has no real boundary in space-time and therefore has no need for a creator God. Carl Sagan says that Hawking describes "a universe with no edge in space, no beginning or end in time, and nothing for a Creator to do."[23] Time is swallowed up by space which itself does not have a boundary. The result: a quantum theory of gravity. Hawking argues that the event that brought about the big bang did not itself have a cause.

Ironically, Hawking says that he first outlined his theory of a universe without a boundary at a scientific conference in the Vatican in 1981. Apparently he seems to have misunderstood what Pope John Paul II said to this conference and took it as another attempt by the church to muzzle science. Hawking says the pope "told us that it was all right to study the evolution of the universe after the big bang itself because that was the moment of Creation and therefore the work of God."[24] In fact, that was not what the pope said at all; John Paul set no limits to scientific inquiry but argued that science was not able to answer the question of *why* the universe actually exists at all. He was not trying to turn Hawking into a modern Galileo!

Despite this, Hawking's theory of quantum gravity does have important consequences for a theology of creation. In *A Brief History of Time* he says:

> The idea that space and time may form a closed surface without boundary also has profound implications for the role of God in the affairs of the universe ... So long as the universe had a beginning we could suppose it had a creator. But if the universe is really completely self-contained, having no boundary or edge, it would have neither beginning nor end: it would simply be. What place, then, for a creator?[25]

This process seems to close off neatly the need for a God to begin the whole cosmic process causally, or to maintain it in existence, for the cosmos is a self-enclosed entity. Hawking's universe has a finite past (he agrees that the big bang occurred fifteen billion years ago), but he says that we can never reach time zero, for time fades before we can get to the singular point of beginning. In Hawking's argument time has actually become a dimension of space. It should be noted that he is not saying that the universe *always* existed; it is just that his theory apparently excludes the need for some creative force to initiate the big bang. In other words, his universe is self-referent and needs no creative cause to begin, nor to maintain, its process. It simply is.

Paul Davies attempts to take up where Hawking leaves off. He accepts that "given the laws of physics, the universe can create itself." But he pushes the question beyond the unbounded cosmos to the laws of physics themselves. These are the principles that underpin reality and according to which the universe acts. It is these laws that are the source of quantum gravity and which explain the existence of the cosmos. Davies asks: is God somehow to be identified with these laws or normative forms?

> Now that physicists and cosmologists have made rapid progress toward finding what they regard as the "ultimate" laws of the universe, many old questions have resurfaced. Why do the laws have the form they do? Might they have been otherwise? Where do the laws come from? Do they exist independently of the physical universe?[26]

Davies, with what seems to me to be a neat epistemological side-step, then attributes what in the past would have been called divine attributes to the laws of nature: they are universal, absolute, eternal, all-powerful, and "in a loose sense, omniscient." He says quite clearly that "the laws have been invested with many of the qualities that were formerly attributed to God from which they were once supposed to have come."[27]

Davies goes on to identify these laws with Plato's "perfect Forms which acted as blueprints for the construction of the fleeting-shadow world of our perceptions."[28] In fact, his whole notion of ultimate reality, as expressed through the laws of physics, seems very Platonic. He appears to describe a mathematical God who (or should I say "which"?) is absent from the world, but who is the source of the physical laws which govern reality and is strikingly like Plato's Demiurge or the Enlightenment's "Great Architect of the Universe." The feeling that Davies conveys is that this absent God is remarkably like a modern physicist. Our gods are usually in the image of ourselves!

Sustaining the Platonic connection, Davies also says that time only came into existence at the commencement of the universe. With a slightly patronizing air, he concedes that "one Augustine of Hippo, a Christian saint who lived in the fifth century" realized that "the physical world ... was made with time, not in time"[29] Having rejected the idea of an eternal world, Augustine, following

Plato and Plotinus, distinguished time and eternity as two different orders. Eternity for Augustine was simply timelessness; it was a sense of the present totally present to itself. God, by living in eternity, was totally present to God's-Own-Self. In God there was no "before" and "after." The world, as a created reality, brings time into being. Augustine is clear on this:

> If we are right in finding the distinction between eternity and time in the fact that without motion and change there is no time, while in eternity there is no change, who can fail to see that there would have been no time, if there had been no creation to bring in movement and change, and that time depends on this movement and change?[30]

So Davies is right to draw on Augustine to support his view "that the Big Bang must coincide with the beginning of time, and any discussion about what happened before the Big Bang, or what caused it (in the usual sense of that word) is simply meaningless."[31] For it is impossible for us to conceive what an eternity in which "there is no time" might be like.

However, Davies is honest enough to admit that these notions leave us feeling uneasy. The reason for this uneasiness is clear to the philosopher: lurking within this scientific discussion of God and the beginning of the cosmos and time is an epistemological problem of considerable magnitude. Epistemology is that important branch of philosophy that deals with the process of how we know and the limits of that knowledge. Davies—and Hawking to a lesser extent—seem to me to move back and forth between scientific knowledge and theological speculation as though the two were perfectly compatible and there were no real difficulties in juxtaposing them. This is simply not true. Science operates within its sphere of knowledge; theology has its own epistemology.

For all its vast unified theories and speculation, modern science still tries to base itself in empirical and verifiable reality. Hawking is quite clear about this:

I'd like to emphasize that this idea that time and space should be finite without boundary is just a *proposal* [his emphasis]: it cannot be deduced from some other principle. Like any other scientific theory, it may initially be put forward for aesthetic or metaphysical reasons, but *the real test is whether it makes predictions that agree with observation* [my emphasis].[32]

Clearly empiricism is still the dominant scientific epistemology. But, as Augustine understood so well, the theological way of knowing, in contrast to the scientific epistemology, is analogical, poetic, symbolic, and sacramental. Despite the assertions of Christian fundamentalists, theology and faith are neither literal nor empirical. Both point beyond themselves to the mysterious, inexpressible transcendent that stands both partially within and yet ultimately wholly beyond theology's limited and circumscribed words and images. (This does not mean that theology is excused from trying to work it out, for faith in its healthiest forms, to quote Anselm again, always seeks understanding.

Certainly, it has to be admitted that much scientific discourse these days (especially that of Hawking and Davies) approaches the analogical and poetic. I never cease to marvel at the assured way scientists discuss the intimate, first instant of the big bang. Hawking, for instance, says, "We are therefore fairly confident that we have the right picture, at least to about one second after the big bang."[33] Despite the apparent accumulation of physical evidence and the elegance of the theory, such references seem to me much more like poetry than empirical science. This is not to say that such statements are not true; it is simply to point out their essentially symbolic and analogical nature. Scientific discourse sometimes sounds like the discourse of theology. But this does not mean that the two can be glibly equated as Davies, especially, tends to do. Also, there is very considerable debate within the scientific community about Hawking's views. To his credit he himself has never endowed his theories with "infallible" status. What he is actually saying is that *if* there was a unified, all-embracing theory, it would look something like quantum gravity.

Among Hawking's critics is Owen Gingerich of the Harvard-Smithsonian Center for Astrophysics. Gingerich argues that the non-boundary condition of the universe is actually achieved by a scientific "sleight of hand"; Hawking has simply replaced the classical starting-point with quantum singularity.[34] Thus, despite Hawking's "non-boundary" theory, both he and Davies do assume that there was something before the big bang; at least the laws of physics themselves are "eternal." If this is the case, there must have been a "before" the non-boundary universe, for these laws are assumed to have governed the process of the evolution of the big bang. Without abandoning our epistemology and logic entirely, it is hard not to join Gingerich in asking the question: surely there was something before the non-boundary universe? Examining this question, H.R. Pagels makes the interesting observation:

> The nothingness before the creation of the universe is the most complete void that we can imagine—no space or time or matter existed. It is a world without place, without duration or eternity, without number—it is what the mathematicians call 'the empty set'. Yet this unthinkable void converts itself into a plenum of existence—a necessary consequence of physical laws. Where are these laws written into that void? What tells the void that it is pregnant with a possible universe? It would seem that even the void is subject to a law, a logic that exists prior to time and space.[35]

Biologist Rupert Sheldrake is also critical of Hawking and Davies' "attempts to create a mathematical Theory of Everything."[36] Sheldrake emphasizes that Hawking's attempt to integrate all reality is actually built on "gigantic assumptions." He makes several pertinent criticisms. Firstly, he accuses Hawking of a reductionist assumption that everything can be explained in terms of particle physics. In other words, there is a sense in which it is the mathematician and not God who is omniscient. Secondly, if nature itself evolves (and remember, Sheldrake is a biologist, not a physicist), why should the laws of nature not evolve as well? Why are the laws of physics assumed to be fixed and eternal? And who set them in place?

Sheldrake goes on to argue that the laws and regularities of physics do not come from the will of God, nor from a kind of platonic eternity, but from what he calls "habits."[37]

> The habits of most kinds of physical, chemical and biological systems have been established for millions or even billions of years. Hence most of the systems that physicists, chemists and biologists study are running in such deep grooves of habit that they are effectively changeless. The systems behave *as if* they are governed by eternal laws, because the habits are so well established. The idea that they are governed by eternal laws is an idealisation or abstraction that approximates to the facts, but it is not a metaphysical truth.

While not accepting Sheldrake's theory of "morphic resonance," I agree with his notion of nature as involved in an organic process and acting more according to habit than to law. Elegant and even beautiful as numeric constructs might be, there is something far too cerebral and abstract about mathematical physics for it to be necessarily a description of the real world.

Clearly there are some genuine problems with the God of the physical scientists. Their God is certainly unattractive in any human sense, and an abstract, mathematicized, Neo-Platonic Demiurge could hardly be said to care about the natural world, let alone inspire any radical ethical change in humankind. In fact, Heidegger would argue it was exactly this Platonized intellectualism that is the source of destructive western technology in the first place. Steiner puts it clearly: "Heidegger ... [says] that it is the continued authority of the metaphysical-scientific way of looking at the world, a way almost definitional of the West, that has brought on, has, in fact, made unavoidable the alienated, unhoused, recurrently barbaric estate of modern technological and mass-consumption man."[38] The God that we seek is clearly not the God of the physicists.

Will the God that saves us be the Protestant God of Karl Barth?

Theology is primarily focused on the interface between the transcendent and the human experience of earthly reality. So it could be reasonably expected that religious thinkers would move to meet this modern scientific interest in ultimate questions half way. But such has not been the case. The mainstream theological response to contemporary science is characterized either by an exaggeratedly biblical approach to the new cosmology or, on the part of some, by the revival of elements of the thought of the very influential twentieth-century Protestant theologian Karl Barth. Generally, most religious thinkers seem reticent, even fearful, of what might be implied in the new scientific and cosmological approaches that are emerging. Some of the theologians who do tackle the scientists tend to approach them with an uncritical awe that seemingly assumes they are necessarily right. As a result theology has offered very little in response to modern scientific and ecological theory. This is worrying in view of the importance and influence of modern scientific theories.

As I have noted, the central and constant question that confronts all theology is: who or what is "God"? Different ages and cultures have given a range of answers. Eastern Orthodox Christians generally lean toward an idea of a God who is sacramentally and symbolically close to the world, a God whose image and presence can be discerned in creation. In contrast, there is a strong element in a whole tradition of contemporary Protestant theology that leans in a Calvinist-Barthian direction toward the notion of a God who is other-worldly, distant from and radically different to the cosmos and to us. This theology argues that it is only through Christ that humankind can truly encounter God.

The Catholic end of the theological spectrum stands somewhere in between. Like Orthodoxy, Catholicism is more sacramental in its vision of God and can therefore discern the divine presence in both creation and people. This is especially true of the Catholicism of Latin countries, the more baroque cultures, and the emerging local churches of Africa, Asia, and the Pacific. But in northern Europe and throughout the English-speaking world, where the influence of Protestantism has been strong, Catholicism generally leans toward a notion of God as separate and other. However, universal Catholicism has a strong sense of Christ as the human image of God and, in a tradition that has only recently been neglected, Catholics have tended to see the Blessed Virgin Mary—the "Queen of Heaven"—as almost the living feminine representation of God.

However, in the English-speaking and European worlds, the old theological and church divisions are increasingly breaking down. Our expanding scientific notions of an almost infinite universe seemingly demand that God be profoundly involved in cosmic existence. There is less and less room for a God "out there." This is not to say that the notion of God as transcendent is wrong. It is just that it is less relevant for our time. In fact, the notion of God as utterly Other and divorced from cosmic reality will become decreasingly tenable as Christian theology and an ecological world-view conjoin.

I think that a similar fate is overtaking Karl Barth's early theology of God, especially as outlined in his commentary on Paul's *Epistle to the Romans*.[39] I emphasize Barth's theology because his influence is still very strong among many Evangelical Christians and ironically he is an almost exact contemporary of Heidegger.

The thought of Karl Barth (1886–1968) focuses on the absolute demands of religion and its independence of all other forms of knowing and perceiving. Barth was reacting to the extremes of nineteenth- and early twentieth-century liberal Protestantism which had effectively psychologized, sentimentalized, and domesticated God by emphasizing the primacy of personal religious experience. Barth, in contrast, insisted on the "godness" of God, and highlighted the notion that God's word is a *pure* gift to humankind and that we cannot know God except through Christ, the Holy Spirit, and the inspired word of the Bible. As George Steiner points out, Barth's God "is Judge of the *Nichsein* (the non-being, the being-nothing) of the world."[40] In 1936 Barth began his large, multi-volume *Church Dogmatics* which attempted to free Christian theology totally from any experiential or philosophical basis by a complete dependence on the Bible and patristic theology as its sole sources. Barth does not say that nature and humanity are "bad," for they are the creation of the good God. But for Barth natural theology "exists in direct opposition to a theology based on the Word of God, leading to a 'knowledge' of God, the world and man which is different from what ... they really are, and thus to error and falsehood."[41]

It is probably just as well that Barth was dead well before the notion of "ecological theology" was invented, for even the processes of traditional natural theology (the attempt to perceive God through natural, unaided human reason) were anathema to him. He holds that there is no point of contact between God's revelation in Christ and the Bible, and our natural knowledge and experience of the holy. His theology is based on the notion of the absolute sovereignty of God and the total need for biblical revelation. He says that the world itself tells us nothing of God. He consistently denies any form of symbolic or sacramental status to the world. Barth argues that God is so totally and utterly other that there is no way in which natural reality could possibly point beyond itself to the transcendent. He is particularly scathing about the medieval, Thomistic notion of the *analogia entis* (the notion of analogy of being between God, the world, and us); he comments: "I regard the 'analogia entis' as the invention of Antichrist and I think that because of it one cannot become a Catholic."[42] In his later life Barth modified this extreme stance a little.

While a dose of Barthian neo-orthodoxy might not go astray with the charismatics and fundamentalists who have domesticated and trivialized God, the future development of the doctrine of God in an ecological world-view certainly does not lie in a neo-

Barthian direction. His thought has driven a wedge between a sovereign God on the one hand and the natural world on the other, and the influence of his views has prevented the development among many Protestants of a much-needed contemporary theological approach which would strive to find some common ground upon which science, ecology, and religion might begin to talk to each other in a meaningful way.

This is not to say that we ought not be cautioned by neo-Barthian views on analogy and natural theology. There are real limitations built into both of these approaches. But, in my view, the answer to the question about the kind of God that will save us does not lie in the revival of a neo-Barthian God who is so absolutely other as to be completely divorced from the created universe.

Will the God that saves us be the God of the argument from design?

At the heart of all of natural theology is the argument from design. This argument posits the notion that the beauty, order, purpose, and benign environment of the world for living beings points toward a Creator who is wise, powerful, and good. There are obvious problems, of course, with this argument; the natural world is clearly not always a benign place and gentle to all living things. Nature is often a very destructive force to many forms of life, including humankind. However, this does not invalidate the persuasive strength of the argument from design.

The origins of the argument are found among Greek thinkers such as Xenophon and the Stoics.[43] The idea was adopted from Greek thought by early Christian apologists and has been used throughout church history as a way of underpinning the existing faith of believers. In the thirteenth century it was used as one of Aquinas' *viae* ("ways") to God. But in the eighteenth century Enlightenment its popularity waned among orthodox believers, and natural theology was transmuted by the Deists into a form of natural religion.

The weaknesses of the argument have subsequently been exposed by modern science. Darwin's evolutionary theory demonstrated that the elements of the argument that were attributed to the design of God could actually be explained by random mutation and natural selection. Many modern thinkers have argued that the evolution of even the most complex aspects of biological life are not actually driven by any sense of divine purpose, or by design at all, but simply by instinctual need. Arguing along these lines, the zoologist Richard Dawkins in *The Blind Watchmaker* rejects the whole notion of evolution following a prepared scenario.[44] His book is pointedly subtitled "Why the evidence of evolution reveals a universe without design." And there is always the argument that the cosmos results from pure evolutionary chance, the most well-known modern proponent of this argument being the French biologist, Jacques Monod.[45] It is significant that Dawkins is a zoologist and Monod a Darwinian evolutionist.

In contrast to their approach, a restatement of the argument from design has emerged over the last few decades, mainly from physicists and astronomers. It seems that physicists tend to have more sympathy with philosophical and theological approaches. Biologists, in contrast, are, as physicist John Polkinghorne has argued, "much more critical of religious belief and feel much less inclined towards it."[46] (There are exceptions to this, of course— Rupert Sheldrake, for instance.) Polkinghorne writes:

> Biology at the end of the twentieth century is more or less similar to what physics succeeded in doing in the eighteenth century, with the Newtonian theory of the solar system ... Two hundred years later physics has become wiser, and found that the world is something more interesting than that.[47]

As a consequence physicists and astronomers tend to be inclined toward more comprehensive views of the cosmos. Paul Davies is one obvious example.

Physicists with a Christian background and commitment, such as Owen Gingerich of Harvard and John Polkinghorne of

Cambridge (who is now an Anglican priest), have argued that the extraordinary facts of cosmic evolution cannot be sufficiently explained by either instinct, random evolutionary events, or pure chance.[48] Gingerich and Polkinghorne both contend that the intimate details of the development of the big bang, the nuclear resonance of carbon and oxygen, the process of stellar evolution, and the survival of biological life are all too finely and perfectly balanced to argue for anything other than, as Fred Hoyle says, the guidance of a super-intelligent mind.

But it must be said that none of this is a "demonstration" or, even less, a "proof" of the existence or providence of God. Natural theology is more about hints and observable coherences; it is about persuasive arguments rather than compulsive proofs. Aquinas always modestly referred to what others have called his five "proofs" as nothing more than *viae*—"ways"—for those who are *already* believers. The purpose of his "ways" was to deepen the faith and understanding of such people. As Polkinghorne has said:

> Creation speaks of there being a Mind and Purpose behind cosmic history ... The laws of nature are not sufficiently intellectually satisfying to be treated as a given brute fact. They evoke metaquestions which go beyond science's power to answer.

Natural theology remains within the context of human knowledge and simply points toward theology, properly speaking.

Natural theology has developed a specific epistemological explanation of the relationship between God and the natural world. It is best expressed in what the great medieval thinkers Aquinas and Bonaventure called "analogy." Aquinas says that our comprehension of God is derived from our experience of the perfections that we can see in our fellow humans beings and in the creatures and the world around us. For instance, we know that God is beautiful because we can see beauty in the natural world; we know that God is good because we can see goodness in the creatures around us; we know that God is wise because we experience human and natural wisdom. However, *our* experience of beauty, goodness, and wisdom is not the same as beauty, goodness, and wisdom in God. So God's reality and our knowledge are not univocal. But neither, according to Aquinas, is it true that divine reality and human knowledge are equivocal; that is, that there is *no* correspondence at all between our perception and the reality of God. Aquinas held firmly that God is knowable through the use of natural reason. Therefore, our experience of God has to sit on a spectrum somewhere between univocal and equivocal knowledge. The word that he uses for this form of knowledge is "analogy."

> Now we know God only by way of creatures ... So the words we use of God all express (imperfectly) one and the same thing in God, but do so by way of many different conceptions in us, and are not synonymous ... That is why such words are not used univocally (i.e. in exactly the same sense) of God and of creatures ... Now such words are not pure equivocation either, for then all talk of God would be invalidated by logical fallacy. Such words apply to God and creatures neither univocally nor equivocally but by what I call analogy (or proportion) ... Whatever we say of God and of creatures we say in virtue of the relation creatures bear to God as to the source and cause in which all their creaturely perfections pre-exist in a more excellent way.[49]

In other words, Aquinas says that we are able to experience a natural apprehension of God from our perception of the world around us and through our interaction with that world and all living creatures in it. This makes the world fundamentally important in the business of our apprehension of God. Without the natural world, our analogous knowledge of God would be limited or even non-existent.

St Bonaventure (1221–1274) approaches analogy more poetically than Aquinas. (Bonaventure was, of course, Franciscan Master General and, in the last year of his life, Cardinal Bishop of

Albano, and he would have inherited the cosmic outlook of Francis of Assisi.) He says that every creature is a *vestigium Dei*; the word *vestigium* here literally means a footstep, a track, a footmark. So every creature contains a trace of the divine and a trajectory toward God. In the case of human persons, Bonaventure takes this further when he says that we are the *imago Dei*, the image of God, for humankind alone possesses the spiritual powers which allow us to be ever more conformed to God. Philosophy, however, is merely the starting point for contemplation and the beginning of the *Itinerary of the Mind Into God* (as he called his major spiritual work). The historian Georges Duby comments that with Bonaventure medieval Catholic theology "deliberately set its course toward mysticism."[50]

There are both strengths and weaknesses in this analogical approach to God. Its strengths are that it clearly recognizes that the whole world is a sign or symbol of God, and it grounds this recognition in a coherent philosophical argument. Yet within this very rationalism lie its weakness and limitation: it can truncate the imagination by objectifying the symbol and, in the process, lose the overtones and undertones that a more naturally receptive approach would begin to perceive. However, if analogy is used in a more broadly symbolic way whereby the world and all that is in it is seen as pointing beyond itself, and the symbol is not turned into an object through which its sacramental connotations are lost, then the notion of analogy can coalesce with experience and yet retain the elements of philosophical argument. At least it posits the foundation for a natural theology that takes the world seriously as a symbol of the transcendent. It has moved beyond the dualism of so much theology and the disjunctive extremes of neo-Barthianism.

Nature as the symbol of the mysterious presence of God

With the insights of the analogical approach to God we have at last begun the process of answering the question: what type of God will save us? God is essentially indefinable and inexpressible. It is when we try to define and delimit who or what God is, when we try to frame a concept of God or to capture or constrain God by our thought, that we become most foolish and idolatrous.

Some, especially those of us who are professionally religious, have often been through a "messianic" stage in our spiritual maturation when we thought that we knew who or what "God" was or is. It is usually not expressed in such direct language and we would certainly never claim openly to anyone that we "knew" God. Instead, it is expressed through an almost unconscious assumption that our immature "knowledge" of God is reliable and even definitive. The tendency is to talk knowingly of "God" and in the very process run away from the experience of God. But religious development soon teaches us that we know little or nothing of the *mysterium tremendum* that we call "God," and that all even the most spiritually mature person can say is that they can perceive traces of the infinite in their experience. These traces of transcendent mystery are often actuated by an encounter with nature. They can also arise through profound contact with another person; through deep intellectual, scientific, or intuitive insights; through art, literature, and especially music; or through any of the other transforming things that occasionally happen to us.

I am speaking here of profound and metaphysical realizations rather than the self-actualized "peak experiences" referred to by the psychologist Abraham Maslow. By this term Maslow is referring generically to the most wonderful, transforming experiences of a person's life. In Maslow's view, people who have had "peak experiences" feel more integrated and perceptive, more at one with the world, less aware of space and time.[51] Maslow says that such experiences need not be religious; they can be quite secular in both origin and context. Certainly, he confines his own discussion of peak experiences to a purely psychological context. But he does tend to conflate the religious and secular experiences as though the two were perfectly compatible.

I would seriously question this identification. In my view there is a species of peak experience that contains within it a clear trajectory toward a sense of the transcendent. I agree that sometimes such experiences may begin in the way described by Maslow, and I would certainly not want to limit them solely to explicitly religious people. But the experiences about which I am speaking go much further than Maslow suggests. Instead of allowing a person simply to dwell in the good feelings evoked by the experience, they actually point the recipient beyond the self. They open up a window into a broader context of meaning. This type of experience is not so much a form of self-possession as an opening-out toward possession by a presence that is greater and deeper than the individual. Such experiences dwell more in the spiritual and transcendent realm than in the psychological. Because every person has the possibility of perceiving transcendent presence, everyone has the potential to encounter such experiences. But for a fuller interpretation of such experiences we should draw on theology rather than psychology.

So my argument is that we find the divine in the midst of the world, and even, as Paul Tillich has said, in the midst of the secular. For there is a vector toward the sacred right at the core of ordinary life. But to be able to perceive this vector one must leave behind purely or even partly psychologized interpretations of experience and shift the focus of intuitive perception toward the deeper, more abstract plain of metaphysics and spirituality—or even, as Henri Bergson would say, mysticism. Thus the task that confronts us today is to gain an insight into what we see and experience as human beings, so that we can pass beyond the human symbol and its psychological interpretation to perceive the transcendent reality that stands behind it.

But our age is so immersed in the psychological interpretation of experience that we have seemingly lost the ability to discover the actual meaning of our most significant experiences. There is a sense in which modern psychology, especially in its more superficial "pop" forms, is the tag end of the secularized anthropocentrism of the last few centuries: all meaning in the world has been invested in *human* subjectivity and it is human experience, both negative and positive, that has become the sole norm of all that is significant to us. Our focus is almost completely on ourselves. The advantage of an ecologized theology is that it shifts us away from human subjectivity as the sole focus of all conscious, ethical, and religious endeavor: it points outward toward the wider world of the cosmos and challenges us to broaden our perspective as we try to interpret the meaning of reality for ourselves and sort out our relationship to it. The deep shift that is occurring in our time is that it is increasingly in the natural world that we will discover genuine traces of the transcendent, rather than in ourselves and in our relationships with each other. The predominance of psychology as the interpreter of all our experience is coming to an end. It is by looking outward to the natural world that we will discover not only the context and meaning of our existence, but also the clearest contemporary traces of the transcendent. And it is here that we will experience the possibility of genuine mysticism.

Many people argue that nowadays God is *the* problem. Where is this God and how does the divine impinge on us? Paradoxically, it was not only modern science that progressively drove God out of the world. The older style of theology, both Protestant and Catholic, also drove God out of nature and the world. This theology retained its regard for the ultimate inexpressibility of the divine, but in the process of protecting this, drove God out of the cosmos and defined transcendence in a most unworldly way. We have seen something of the origin of this in the Platonized theology that entered the Christian tradition in the period of the early church. But the active expulsion of God from the cosmos really occurred in the period from the seventeenth century to the present. Nature was mechanized by Newtonian physics and came to be viewed solely as a repository of natural resources to be exploited by humankind. Christian theology simply accepted this mechanized cosmology; no coherent critique was offered of the Cartesian philosophy that underpinned modern science. Theology allowed God to be driven out of nature, not so much intentionally but as a byproduct of the mechanistic view of the world. The secularization of nature drained it of all its sacramental and iconographic significance. An increasingly unworldly God was created. The so-called "God of the gaps" was merely an intermediary stage in the progressive mechanization of the world as the divine was called in to plug the holes in scientific understanding. But God was finally driven out of nature in the twentieth century and the "death of God" theories and the secularized theology of the 1960s and early 1970s was a clear theological signal of God's final banishment from the cosmos.

The ecological movement of our time has created a unique opportunity for the rediscovery of the temporarily departed God. With the development of a less mechanized and more integrated notion of nature, it is now possible to rediscover the iconographic value of the cosmos. So the task that faces theology today is to try to retain a sense of God's mystery while maintaining a perception of God's presence in and through the cosmos and the interactive life-forms that ecological science is coming to understand. In order to be able to rediscover God in the world, we need to develop the ability to see God in a new way that paradoxically draws on some very traditional Christian notions. I have said that God is the *mysterium tremendum*. What we need to do now is to explore what this term "mystery" means. And behind the *mysterium* is the extraordinary presence about which the great mystics speak. Also, in order to make sense out of the mystery of God's presence, we will need to develop what David Tracy has called the "analogical imagination," a notion I will explore later in this chapter.

God and nature as mystery

I have already talked about Aquinas' doctrine of analogy—the idea that the world and nature reveal something about God to the perceptive person. A more contemporary way of explaining analogy is through the broad sweep of religious experience. Peoples of pre-technocratic culture, such as the Australian Aborigines or the Native North Americans, live out their religious lives in a natural world of symbols. Their thought and experience emphasize the sacramental, symbolic nature of reality rather than the superficially rational explanation of it. Specific times, places, and ceremonies draw them beyond the obvious, banal, everyday world into another more transcendent realm of inner experience and meaning. Their interior lives are lived in relationship to quite specific places and to a temporal cycle of ceremonies which constitutes their religious expression and gives a sense of purpose and direction to their lives. Their sense of time is cyclic and repetitive rather than chronological and purposive.

It is difficult, if not impossible, for those of us who live in contemporary western technocratic society to reinvent for ourselves the religious world of indigenous people. Our sense of time and history as a consistent movement forward toward an ultimate goal psychologically precludes us from entering the cyclic world of indigenous people. But we do have a desperate need to rediscover, through a more sacramental and iconographic approach to reality, the sense of the presence of the transcendent in the natural world itself. This is actually quite possible for a religiously and environmentally attuned modern person, and in the process we do not have to abandon our sense of time and history. In fact, as long as wilderness lasts, we will still have the potential to enter into what the historian of religion, Rudolf Otto, has called the experience of the "holy" or the "numinous."[52] We are able to experience both the numinous and the sheer sanctity of specific parts of a given landscape and to apprehend, by analogy, a transcendent presence that stands both within and yet paradoxically beyond the mysterious place. But to be able to do this we have to be able to find such places. As more and more wilderness and places of natural beauty give way to exploitation, commercialism, and space for an ever-growing human population, our potential ability to be able to experience the holy becomes ever more limited.

But it is not just the disappearance of wilderness and the natural world that is the problem. There is also a barrier to the apprehension of the sacred built into our attitude to life itself. We are both pragmatic and phlegmatic in our approach to virtually everything, and our minds are so highly developed analytically that it has become almost impossible for us to apprehend the presence of the transcendent in the world around us. Our mental perceptions are simply not attuned to this way of thinking. That is why we can destroy nature and beauty so easily. We have divided up every aspect of the natural world and analyzed its component parts and estimated its economic value. In the process we have simply lost the ability to see nature as an interlocking whole. We are entirely focused on the economic value of specific segments of the environment. We have expelled from our mental horizon any sense of iconographic mystery in the natural world. For instance, woodchippers, along with the governments, industries, and trade unions that support them, have no perception at all of the mysterious beauty of an old-growth forest, nor of its value as an ecological micro-environment. Their crude pragmatism focuses entirely on however many tons of "product" they can gain. Their sin—and what they do is *profoundly* sinful—is to so narrow their focus that all they see is economic exploitation and profit. It is a prime example of the autism that characterizes our society and so-called "rational" economics.

The fact that we can analyze how things work and that we know a lot about the natural world does not mean that we have exhausted the question of the meaning of that world. Nor does it show that we actually understand the real significance of what we analyze. The natural world still retains its mystery, its ability to point beyond itself and remind us of a mysterious presence that stands behind and beyond it. I am not suggesting that modern analysis is bad, or that we should surrender to the pseudo-intellectual mushiness and puffed-up self-importance of many of the so-called "new age" religious movements. However, I am saying that we are probably at the end of rationalism's usefulness as the uniquely *dominant* mode of thought. But it is hard for us to come to grips with this because our modern western minds are so developed analytically that we have atrophied our ability to comprehend the broader meaning of the natural realities that surround us.

Antonio Salieri, in Peter Shaffer's play *Amadeus*, talks about a north Italian image of God with "trader's eyes." At the crudest level, modern western culture sees everything with "trader's eyes"; we break everything down into a cost-benefit analysis whereby reality is judged only by its economic value. A forest or landscape is assessed almost exclusively in monetary terms. Can we sell the timber? Will it be economically viable if we "develop" it? What can we *do* with it? Can we bring in "tourists" to add value to the dollar? We seemingly can never let anything simply "be."

There is another modern way of seeing reality which derives from our analytical attitude, but it is a way which can work either for or against environmentalism. It is seeing everything with "scientist's eyes." This is the tendency to analyze everything in order to understand how it works. It is not as crude a view as that of the "traders," for science is a far more elevated approach to nature than the crassness of economics, but both remain within the analytical spectrum. Nowadays, some aspects of science are beginning to change: ecology is commencing the process of discovering the profound inter-relationships between things and it is moving the analytic approach to nature in a more integrated direction. Again, this is not to argue that analysis is bad. I have never supported the view of the irrationalists who want to do away with all the advances of European humanism and the Enlightenment. The Enlightenment has brought us too many benefits. I am simply saying that analytical thought needs to be integrated into a wider and more comprehensive approach to reality.

Behind analysis stands the mystery of things. "Mystery" is a poverty-stricken word in English. In our language it means putting the pieces of a puzzle together to solve a problem, like Agatha Christie's Poirot or Sherlock Holmes. In this sense, a mystery is soluble. It is a matter of using the clues to find the solution. But the classical Greek word *mysterion* means much more than this. The origins of the word lie in the Greek mystery religions, but the word has been Christianized and transformed in meaning. It is often used in the theology of Paul. For him the ultimate mystery is God's plan to bring salvation, unity, and fullness to the whole created cosmos. It is significant that he is a genuine universalist and sees the *pleroma*—the fullness of God—permeating all reality. In a colorful image, Paul says that the whole world, as well as humankind, has been "groaning in one great act of giving birth" until both are set free from the bondage of sin and limitation. [53] So the ultimate core of the "mystery" for Paul is to bring the whole natural world and the whole of humankind into unity and into the fullness and totality of life that only God can give.

The Catholic theologian Karl Rahner has described God as the "holy mystery." He uses this term as a way of escaping the circumscribed, limited concept that the word "God" can often conjure up for modern people. He contrasts the notion of the holy mystery with the subjective, limited, and often legalistic and destructive notion that many people have of "God." [54] Thomas Berry says that he also prefers to abandon the use of the word "God" because of the connotations implied in it. It is certainly a loaded word, although I must admit that I still prefer to use it interchangeably with the word "transcendent." Rahner's use of "holy mystery" taps into the long-lasting Christian mystical tradition of the intense desire for the transcendent, which brings the human person face-to-face with the sheer, incomprehensible mystery of God. However, the paradox is that it is the mystery and indescribability of the transcendent that lures many of the most perceptive human beings to undertake the search for God.

Christianity is a dynamic, some might say "restless," religion because it encourages a desire to search for God. The fourth century spiritual theologian Gregory of Nyssa in his *Life of Moses,* expresses this restlessness in terms of a constantly deeper exploration of God:

> This truly is the vision of God: never to be satisfied in the desire to see him. But one must always, by looking at what he can see, rekindle his desire to see more. Thus no limit would interrupt growth in the ascent toward God, since no limit to the Good can

be found, nor is the increasing of the desire for the Good brought to an end because it is satisfied.[55]

In Christian mysticism this search is expressed most often in terms of negation; God is not to be found in expected places or through predictable means. The early Christian theologians often refer to this as the *theologia negativa*. Gregory defines this as "the seeing that consists in not seeing, because that which is sought transcends all knowledge, being separated on all sides by incomprehensibility as by a kind of darkness."[56]

The mystical theology of Gregory of Nyssa was taken up and developed by a fifth-century writer (probably a Syriac monk) whom today we know only as Pseudo-Dionysius. He was a spiritual writer of great and continuing influence, especially after his works were translated into Latin in the Middle Ages.[57] At the core of his theology is the notion that no word can in any way describe the reality of God. God dwells in a super-essential darkness, far beyond the realm of light. We ascend to our primitive glimmerings of the transcendent by following the *via negativa*. The *via negativa* is explained in an important passage in *The Mystical Theology* where Pseudo-Dionysius refers simply to the transcendent as "it" as a way of denying all of the connotations that are loaded into the word "God":

> Again, as we climb higher we say this. It is not soul or mind, nor does it possess imagination, conviction, speech, or understanding ... It cannot be spoken of ... It is not number or order, greatness or smallness, equality or inequality, similarity or dissimilarity. It is not immovable, moving or at rest. It has no power, it is not power, nor is it light. It does not live nor is it life ... It cannot be grasped by the understanding since it is neither knowledge nor truth.[58]

Here is the *via negativa* in its most blunt and arresting form. The point of this type of theology is to stress the absolute mystery of God, the fact that analogous knowledge is no more than an analogy and that we never even remotely begin to understand the transcendent mystery out into which we face. Aquinas stresses that after every effort has been made to discover God through natural reason and revelation, we have to admit that "the ultimate in human knowledge [is] to know that we do not know God."[59]

This notion of the "darkness" and mystery of God has been emphasized by the Eastern church tradition. But the same human experience of darkness is also explored by many of the great western mystics, including the Spanish saint and poet John of the Cross (1542–1591). He describes the driving passion that propels the mystic out into the darkness of incomprehension toward the extraordinary presence that alone will satisfy. Roy Campbell's translation of St John's poem "En una noche oscura" conveys something of the almost restless compulsion to enter into a dark presence that is ultimately transforming:

> Upon that lucky night
> In secrecy, inscrutable to sight,
> I went without discerning
> And with no other light
> Except for that which in my heart was burning.
>
> It lit and led me through
> More certain than the light of noonday clear
> To where One waited near
> Whose presence well I knew,
> There where no other presence might appear.[60]

It is interesting to note that St John had a great love for the natural world and was filled with a desire to be alone in it and experience it to the full. It should also be noted that he refers twice to a "presence" without any further specification. It is this same experience of transforming personal presence that we can discover in the natural world. However, Ross Collings points out the apparent dichotomy in St John's thought between his clear love for nature and his insistence on the terrible naked nothingness of the mystical ascent.[61] This is resolved for St John through the paradoxical situation of experiencing everything by sacrificing everything.

Ironically, the potency and importance of mysticism can be best illustrated through an examination of the dynamics of fundamentalism. The key problem with religious fundamentalism of any kind is that it takes religion far too *literally*. It transforms that which is essentially experienced as poetic and metaphorical and expressed in symbolic language into a crude form of literalism and legalism. It fails to comprehend that religion is a vehicle that conjures up and points toward a reality which, by definition, utterly transcends our everyday knowledge and experience. Religion brings us into the realm of symbols. Symbolic thought has certainly become more difficult in our sanitized, technocratic culture. We are dominated by the superficially rational. And this actually explains the modern growth of fundamentalism in all religious traditions: it is an expression of the atrophy of the imagination, of our alienation from nature and the world which is the original source of the religious quest itself. Fundamentalism is the application to religious experience of the literal and limited use of religious language and a superficial rationalism that is profoundly stultifying. It is a symptom of a deep spiritual alienation and a sickness that can only be cured by the rediscovery of the natural source of human religiosity.

Experiencing the transcendent

How then can this experience of the desire for the mysterious presence of the transcendent be understood? And how can it be applied to the natural world and to ecology?

The natural world is the original human source of religion and spirituality. As I have already noted, most indigenous people have traditionally seen specific places in their landscape as numinous, places where deeper levels of consciousness and spirituality are released, and where, in the terms of Carl Jung, the depths of the personal and collective unconscious can be activated and contacted. Such places take indigenous people away from banal, everyday concerns and insert them into a space that points beyond itself. In this space they experience a genuine vector toward the transcendent. It is significant that the Hebrew people experienced their God in the escape from the quasi-urban environment of ancient Egypt, and especially in the isolated and stark landscape of the desert and mountains. This is not, for one moment, to say that God cannot be experienced in the products of human art and culture—in beautiful sacred art, music, churches, and worship. Nor am I saying that God cannot be experienced in everyday reality. I am simply arguing that the natural world is the *primal* place where human beings experienced the transcendent for many centuries before the advent of Christianity, and that especially in our contemporary world we need to rediscover at least some forms of that primal experience. But rather than undertaking the rigors of religious mysticism (which is really a rare path that only a few can undertake), most people in the contemporary world must find another way to experience the transcendent.

That is why I suggest that it is to the natural world that we must turn if we are to recover some sense of the presence of the transcendent. In this context the reality of religious symbol is often best evoked by personal experience. There are still areas left in countries such as Australia, Canada, and, to a lesser extent, the United States where one can truly be alone in places of great natural beauty and profound mystery. To be in a place like this is to experience a silence that opens one up to an aloneness and an experience of physical and spiritual vulnerability. At the same time, there is a profound sense of the oneness of the self with itself and with the surrounding place. I remember once experiencing this in the natural amphitheatre of Raymond Creek Falls in the Snowy River National Park in far eastern Victoria. I was there alone. The falls are one of those remote, compact and exquisitely beautiful micro-environments that one still finds in the Australian bush, despite the depredation of human settlement. These places are sacred in the truest sense. The sacredness of the place can be highlighted when you discover there something inappropriate and totally out of place. I noticed that someone at Raymond Creek Falls had seemingly deliberately left a beer bottle behind them, right on the bank beside the crystal clear pool beneath the Falls. To discover the bottle was an experience of ultimate crassness, like an act of sacrilege, a deliberate insult to a precious place.

At somewhere like Raymond Creek Falls, the perceptive person can discover that the natural world itself can be the locus and stimulus for genuine mysticism. A sacred place like this is both symbolic and analogical in the sense that the sum total of the natural parts do not explain the mystery of the place; it both creates and conjures up in the consciousness of a receptive and perceptive person a note of the presence of transcendence and beauty that draws one both inward and outward simultaneously. Inward to the profound existential emptiness and loneliness that all of us always have deep within us but which we rarely bring to consciousness and confront. Outward to a transcending presence that both cradles and stands over and against us.

Sacred places in a landscape are sacramental and iconographic in the truest sense. The liturgist Aidan Kavanagh describes the Catholic notion of sacraments as "unsettling encounters between living presences divine and human in the here and now."[62] This is what I experienced at Raymond Creek Falls: an unsettling encounter with a living, transcendent presence. This is what the natural world does for the perceptive person: it can become, in the truest sense, the locus for a profoundly disturbing but always creative encounter between the divine and the human. And, as Kavanagh says, that is exactly what a sacrament is. (In this context it should be noted that the Catholic tradition has far too narrow a definition of the notion of "sacrament." It confines it to seven—baptism, confirmation, eucharist, marriage, orders, reconciliation, and anointing. But there are many other even more personally transforming rites of passage, and these also are sacraments. The greatest of them is the sense of the presence of the transcendent mediated through the external sign of a sacred place in the natural world.)

Such experiences also take a person beyond chronology into the depths of time. While we do not leave the present behind, we do enter into a kind of timelessness that takes us beyond the here and now to connect in a mysterious but real way with the past and the future. This too is the function of a sacrament. The beautiful Australian novel and film *Picnic at Hanging Rock* was about this notion of time beyond time.[63] It is significantly set at Hanging Rock, a rather strange and numinous rocky outcrop not far from Melbourne but still very much part of the Australian bush. The beautiful girls who disappear at Hanging Rock are seen as having slipped from the present of chronological time into a timelessness that is conjured up and suggested by the mysterious landscape.

Those of us who think only in terms of a linear notion of time have great difficulty shifting ourselves into a sense of time that is neither chronological nor cyclic. To experience this notion of a time that stands outside of ordinary time, we have to attain what the theologian John S. Dunne calls "time out of mind": an ability to escape from the present, from the prison of the now, to see ourselves in the context of the totality of our own lives and the totality of all life.[64] Basing himself on Augustine's *Confessions*, Dunne argues that we only actually become ourselves and discover God through a process of recollection and memory that puts us in touch with the time that transcends the present. He says that to encounter God we have to "appropriate" personally all of our experiences and the totality of our whole life story. T.S. Eliot seems to be saying something similar in "Burnt Norton":

> Time present and time past
> Are both perhaps present in time future
> And time future contained in time past ...
> What might have been and what has been
> Point to one end, which is always present.[65]

Certainly, the encounter with a sacred place in the natural world opens us up to this much richer notion of a presence that transcends linear time.

What I have just described is sometimes referred to as "nature mysticism" or "cosmic consciousness," and, as William James has pointed out, this transforming encounter with nature is a common enough human experience.[66] But I want to stress that the mysticism to which I am referring should not be confused with the visions, locutions, levitations, telepathy, and other preternatural paraphernalia normally associated with an hysterical personality or charismatic religion. Genuine mysticism, as we have seen, is characterized by a profound sense of the transcendence of space and time, usually accompanied by an intangible but real sense of personal presence. Sometimes this is quite specific (when the presence of God is invoked), but mostly it is unspecific—there is just a powerful sense of something transforming, yet cradling the individual who experiences it.

Cosmic consciousness and religious mysticism

Up to this point I have talked as though cosmic consciousness was perfectly compatible with the mystical experience that is common to the great religious traditions (and in this context I am referring most specifically to Christian mysticism). However, the comparative religionist R.C. Zaehner seriously questions this compatibility. He asserts that there is an essential difference between the two:

> In strictly religious mysticism, be it Hindu, Christian or Muslim, the whole purpose of the exercise is to concentrate on an ultimate reality to the complete exclusion of all else; and by "all else" is meant the phenomenal world or, as the theists put it, all that is not God. This means a total and absolute detachment from Nature, an isolation of the soul within itself either to realize itself as "God", or to enter into communion with God. The exclusion of all that we normally call Nature is the *sine qua non* of this type of mystical experience.[67]

Zaehner recognizes that both are genuine forms of mysticism but maintains that they are specifically different. He argues that cosmic consciousness is a real, spontaneous, mystical experience characterized by a profound sense of the transcendence of space and time. This sort of thing is not confined to a particular type of person "nor does it appear to be the result of a particular desire to transcend oneself."[68] But he emphasizes that there is no necessary reference to God or to the transcendent in nature mysticism, which can be spontaneously experienced by anyone. On the other hand, religious mysticism, in his view, refers explicitly to God and requires of the participant formation and deep commitment to belief and asceticism over a long period. Above all it requires a profound detachment. It is not called the *theologia negativa* for nothing!

At first sight there is a sense in which Abraham Maslow's "peak experiences" can be related to cosmic consciousness. In fact, such experiences are sometimes interpreted in the same context, but at a more superficial level. Zaehner's description and discussion of the experiences of the French writer Marcel Proust seem to have more in common with Maslow's peak experiences than with cosmic consciousness as such. But Zaehner does not make this connection. For him the key distinction is between religious mysticism and cosmic consciousness. The basic problem with Maslow's peak experiences is that he only sees these experiences on the psychological level, whereas the fundamental meaning of mysticism must be sought at the deeper metaphysical level. A theology of cosmic consciousness is not just about human experience; more importantly it is about the transcendent reality "out there" that creates the possibility of that experience in the first place. Maslow remains exclusively within the sphere of the psychological.

In my view, Zaehner drives too divisive a wedge between religious mysticism and cosmic consciousness. The Jesuit philosopher Joseph Marechal (1876–1944) did not draw so sharp a distinction. In this he is more in agreement with William James—and, incidentally, with the thought of Aquinas and a whole strand of the Christian tradition. Marechal says that the fundamental characteristic of all mysticism is a "feeling of the immediate presence of a Transcendent Being."[69] He argues that an intuition of the divine, or at least of a transcendent presence, characterizes all forms of mysticism and that it can be experienced in all religions and "even apart from all religious belief."[70] Marechal says that both forms of mysticism are experienced through an "intellectual intuition." He explains this intuition as "the empirical feeling of presence, the perception of a spacialized reality." He defines intuition as the "direct assimilation of a knowing faculty with its object."[71]

Later, when discussing genuine religious mysticism, Marechal writes that "mystical contemplation is neither a sense-perception nor an imaginative projection nor a discursive knowledge but … one of those intuitions whose exact type we do not in our ordinary experience possess."[72] In Marechal's view, mystical experience ranges across a spectrum that includes cosmic consciousness, a mysticism inspired by nature, art, or beauty, right through to the transforming and radical events that characterize religious mysticism at its deepest and most extraordinary. Thus his understanding of mysticism is less divisive and more unitive than Zaehner's. All forms are characterized by an intuition of a transforming sense of presence and a feeling of sacredness that all of us can experience at varying depths and as a result of varying stimuli.

This is why, if we are to be religious beings at all who are turned outward toward the transforming presence that pervades the whole cosmos, we desperately need the natural world, the isolated wilderness, the places of beauty and silence where we can be most truly ourselves by looking out beyond our subjectivity beyond the borders of the self, to where the intuition of cosmic consciousness can pervade our being. Since the vast majority of us will not undertake the hard road of religious mysticism, we need the natural world to provide us with the experience of transcendence whereby we can discover the depths of grace that help us to make sense of our human condition. Karl Rahner, in his essay "Nature and Grace," points out that human beings in their very essence have "a natural desire for the beatific vision"—or, to rephrase this in more contemporary parlance, long for that which transcends and completes them through an ecstatic vision of nature and beauty.[73] Rahner's view is that God's grace pervades the entire created cosmos and that all of us, in our inner core, are essentially oriented toward the transcendent. Thus the world becomes, in the literal sense, a sacrament of the presence of God, a "mysterious infinity," where the transcendent is to be discovered.

> Man can try to evade the mysterious infinity which opens up before him ... Out of fear of the mysterious he can take flight to the familiar and the everyday. But the infinity which he experiences himself exposed to also permeates his everyday activities ... Man experiences himself as an infinite possibility.[74]

Certainly the church, through its worship, continues to try to give to humankind an experience of that "mysterious infinity." The cogency and power of the marvelous liturgical symbols of the past—the architectural ambience of a beautiful church or a great cathedral, the plain chant, polyphony, and other sacred musical masterpieces, the beauty and poetry of the church's language—continue to comfort and confront those of us who understand the symbolism and to draw us into an ecclesiastical world of deep spirituality. But these beautiful church symbols have progressively lost their potency for many of our contemporaries and have been increasingly abandoned. They have been largely replaced by the banality and crassness of much modern church music and worship. A boring biblical "evangelicalism" has pervaded the Catholic as well as the Protestant end of the spectrum. There is a real sense in which the churches have failed to provide the symbolic and liturgical super-structure which would assist modern people to enter the transcendent realm.

But the failure of the church has forced our contemporaries—and many of us who are still part of the Catholic tradition—to seek other and new forms of religious expression. The beauty of nature and the wilderness has become vitally important for the spirituality of many people. It is increasingly in the cathedral of the environment that our contemporaries are rediscovering a way into the realm of the transcendent; they are discovering the sacred presence that stands behind the natural world.

It is important to note here that I am not talking about pantheism or some form of nature worship. There is a sense in which the Hebrew and biblical suspicion of the dangers of polytheism and Caananite fertility beliefs has developed into a near paranoia in the Christian tradition about the worship of nature. Any attempt to find God in nature is branded by biblio-centric and fundamentalist Christians as "pantheism" or "new age." In this context, it is significant that the last person burned by the Roman Inquisition—as distinct from other Inquisitions—was the Dominican Giordano Bruno (1548–1600), whose complex mystical views were reduced by his inquisitorial accusers to a crude "pantheism."

There is also no doubt that the survival of paganism in rural Europe right up until the eighteenth century reinforced the fears of many church authorities, both Catholic and Protestant, about nature worship and fertility rites and the danger of the pollution of the Christian faith. The French historian Jean Delumeau has argued a thesis which is certainly well documented for France, that the actual "Christianization" of rural Europe was only really finally achieved in the seventeenth century.[75]

What is happening today in ecological theology is not nature worship, nor is it a modern form of pantheism or "new ageism." It is simply an expression of the modern search for that which transcends individual and societal existence and which contextualizes both the self and society; it is, in the literal sense, an expression of innate human religiosity and spirituality. It is a growing realization of the need for a cosmic consciousness and, as such, is part of the genuine mystical tradition. In this sense it is an historical return to the first source of human religiosity. Increasingly, it is primarily in the experience of the natural world, rather than in the context of the churches, that many modern men and women are rediscovering the transcendent and are encountering anew something of what the great religious traditions have usually called "God."

The analogical imagination

By now you might well be thinking: it is all very well to talk about cosmic consciousness or natural mysticism, but allowing that enough of the natural world survives for some people in the future to be able to reach this level of experience (and that is a questionable presupposition), how do we open ourselves sufficiently to develop the religious faculty that is within all of us? And what is this faculty?

Among earlier theologians such as Aquinas, writing at a time when the vast majority of people were believers, something parallel to the faculty was often referred to as the sensus fidelium (the sense of the faithful). Rahner, writing in the midst of modern skepticism, refers to a similar faculty as the "supernatural existential." The term that I will use is the "analogical imagination."

This phrase is borrowed from David Tracy's book *The Analogical Imagination*.[76] For Tracy it refers basically to the on-going theological and critical interpretation of the Christian revelation, its tradition, and its texts in the light of contemporary culture. Even the greatest theologians have only a limited and partial view of the whole historical sweep of revelation and tradition, but this does not mean that on-going interpretation cannot proceed analogously. Tracy defines analogy as "a language of ordered relationships articulating similarity-in-difference."[77] By this he means that the insights of different theologians into revelation and tradition will vary in emphasis, but this does not mean that they render each other invalid. Instead, they are the different but analogously-related, on-going, and progressive interpretation of the same revelation and its tradition. It is the historical context that provides the stimulus for the development of each of these different theologies. Thus for Tracy the analogical imagination is the insightful ability to perceive the limited but interconnected legitimacy of the historical developments of the original revelation. It is precisely the faculty of analogical imagination that present-day fundamentalists lack. They are hopelessly bogged down in the erroneous notion that their interpretations of the biblical text are not historically and culturally conditioned.

But here I want to use Tracy's notion of the analogical imagination in a slightly different sense. I intend to use it to refer to the inner facility of being able to imagine the analogous connection between the sacredness of the natural world, and particular places and realities in that world, and the perception of the presence of the transcendent. In this interpretation, the analogical imagination is the ability to perceive the transition between the here-and-now individuality of the personal experience of a place or a beautiful reality, and the vector within it toward that which both cradles and transcends it. In simple terms it is the ability to make a connection between an experience of the natural world and the presence of a transcendent reality that stands both within and yet beyond it. It is the activation of an ability to perceive and be conscious of the vector between our human presence in a natural phenomenon or place and a sense of the transcendent presence that contextualizes the event.

The Jesuit poet Gerard Manley Hopkins (1844–1889) expresses one element of what I am trying to get at in his word "inscape." Hopkins has a deep affinity with nature and a profound respect for each individual aspect of the natural world. For Hopkins every single thing is necessarily unique; no one being, even of the same species or genus, is exactly the same as another. Every individual reality in nature "radiates back a meaning" that is unique to the sympathetic and intuitive observer.[78] Inscape is *that* unique meaning. "Inscape ... is the expression of the inner core of individuality, perceived in moments of insight by an onlooker who is in full harmony with the being he is observing."[79]

The notion of inscape is original to Hopkins, but he found a real affinity with the thought of the medieval Franciscan John Duns Scotus, whom we have already seen influenced Heidegger. Scotus has a unique doctrine of individuation: unlike Aquinas, who said that individuation is achieved through the association of a form with matter *signata quantitate* (an obscure phrase which means something like "quantitative determination"), Scotus developed a far more specific and differentiated notion. For Scotus, individuality was the ultimate inner core of each separate being, what he called the *haecceitas*, the "thisness," of the thing. It is that which makes a being this specific being and no other. Scotus is clearly reacting against the generalizing tendency of medieval philosophy which was concerned with the universal forms which gave species their commonality and community. Hopkins found support in Scotus' theory for his own notion of inscape.[80]

There were other elements in Scotus' thought which attracted Hopkins. For instance, Scotus held that the incarnation was necessary because

> God had to be made available to the human senses. This in turn postulated that the material world was a symbol of God, not divorced from Him, a view to which Hopkins wholeheartedly subscribed emotionally, even if he needed the authority of Scotus to feel easy with it.[81]

So what relationship does inscape have with the analogical imagination? Hopkins' notion of inscape is two-sided: it involves our sympathetic and committed gaze at a being, or a place in nature, or a living reality. In response, we receive the communication of the unique individuality of the being that is contemplated. Implicit in that response of individuality is the possibility of discerning a vector toward the transcendent. The analogy that the religiously perceptive person observes is that the very uniqueness of each being implies a transcendent presence that stands behind it.

However, in order to be able to see this connection, the creative imagination of the observer must also be active to perceive the analogy between the unique individuality of the other and the transcendent that creates it and holds it in existence. In this sense, imagination is the ability to be able to see links and connections that are not superficially apparent. Imagination is the faculty of intuition—it is what John Henry Newman called the "illative sense," the ability to make the oblique connections which help to make sense out of apparently unconnected realities.[82] Imagination perceives the deeper, analogous significance in things that at first sight seem obvious and clear. But when someone "inscapes" a reality, a more profound meaning is yielded up; one discovers the transcendent presence in the individual. It is precisely the analogical imagination that we need to develop if we are ever going to discover the presence of the transcendent in the natural world.

What, then, happens to the uniqueness of Christ in a religion like this? And what other connections are there between theology and ecology?

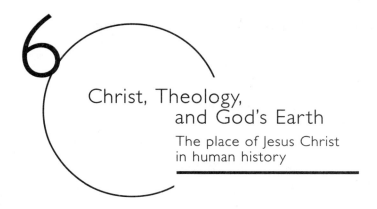

Christ, Theology, and God's Earth

The place of Jesus Christ in human history

To this point I have said little or nothing about Jesus Christ and the role that he might play in ecological theology. The reason for this is clear: once you change your view of the world and its history, you also have to shift all of the key elements in your religious cosmology. We have already seen that an ecological world-view causes us to reconfigure our understanding and image of God. It is inevitable that it will have the same implications for the role of Jesus Christ.

Until the development of critical historical studies and the expansion of our knowledge of the long history of humankind in the eighteenth and nineteenth centuries, it was easy to see the life of Jesus as the centerpiece of history. His central role was easy to maintain within the narrow and circumscribed ambit of biblical history. Nowadays, it is difficult enough to fit Jesus into the broad sweep of the whole of human history, let alone into the immensely larger picture of the story of the cosmos. But as a Christian I cannot avoid the challenge of trying to comprehend the significance of Jesus Christ within this broadest of all contexts. There is no difficulty seeing his place in explicit biblical cosmology and history, but it is precisely this narrow historical focus that is losing its grip on our imagination as we move toward a cosmology which images the world in terms of a big bang fifteen billion years ago, and a human race that is the offspring of a minor sub-section of mammalian evolution—the hominids—that emerged a couple of million years ago. How can Jesus be seen as the focus of history and the definitive mediator between God and humankind, as Christianity argues, when he is such a late arrival on the stage of cosmic and human history? The two thousand year long history of the church is a mere blink in human, let alone cosmic history.

The question of Jesus' position in history is pivotal to this discussion. Both biblical scholars and theologians make a distinction between the Jesus of history and the still-living, glorified, creative Christ of faith, between the historical man Jesus and the Christ, the "anointed one" of God. They argue that the historical Jesus of Nazareth was the man who lived in the Roman imperial province of Judea in the time of the Emperors Augustus and Tiberius, "who was crucified under Pontius Pilate, died and was buried." On the "third day" he was raised up by God and the early Christian community experienced him as alive and as their savior. They then came to believe not only that he was alive but that he also pre-existed—that he was, in fact, the creative reality that had brought the cosmos into existence. It is all marvelously summed up in the famous Pauline hymn:

> Christ Jesus,
> who, though he was in the form of God,
> did not regard equality with God
> as something to be exploited,
> but emptied himself,
> taking the form of a slave,
> being born in human likeness.
> And being found in human form,
> he humbled himself
> and became obedient to the point of death—
> even death on a cross.
>
> Therefore God also highly exalted him
> and gave him the name

that is above every name,
so that at the name of Jesus
every knee should bend,
in heaven and on earth and under the earth,
and every tongue should confess
that Jesus Christ is Lord,
to the glory of God the Father. (Philippians 2:6–11)

In a parallel passage in the Letter to the Colossians Paul images Christ as a divine-human presence as the whole of cosmic reality begins. He focuses on the human image of Christ in the very process of cosmic-coming-to-be:

He is the image of the invisible God, the firstborn of all creation; for in him all things ... were created ... all things have been created through him and for him. He himself is before all things, and in him all things hold together. (Colossians 1:15–17)

Christ is there as a divine-human presence as the cosmos explodes into being. He is created and then in him and through him everything else comes to be. The whole purpose of creation is "for him" and he is the hovering breath of God that holds all things together.

These images are powerful and striking, and Pierre Teilhard de Chardin for one was especially influenced by them. John L. McKenzie, discussing the Pauline authorship of Colossians, comments that in this letter "the cosmological-Christological synthesis, while not unparalleled in earlier writings, is here much more complex."[1] A similar theology of a descending God in Jesus and an ascending and exalted Christ can be found in the New Testament writings attributed to St John.

Christ and ecology—some contemporary views

At first sight this seems to be a theology that fits in nicely with ecological concerns. As the ultimate source of creativity in the world, the glorified Christ could surely be expected to be a dedicated ecologist!

Teilhard de Chardin, Thomas Berry, Matthew Fox, and a number of other ecological thinkers have shown considerable sympathy for the notion of the "cosmic Christ." Matthew Fox's influential book *The Coming of the Cosmic Christ* distinguishes clearly between the post-Enlightenment's preoccupation with the historical Jesus and the more ancient and traditional figure of the cosmic Christ.[2] Fox correctly points out that the cosmic Christ cannot be divorced from the historical Jesus:

> A theology of the Cosmic Christ must be grounded in the historical Jesus, in his words, in his liberating deeds, in his life and orthopraxis. The Cosmic Christ is not a doctrine that is to be believed in and lived out *at the expense of the historical Jesus*.[3]

Fox maintains that a dialectic (he uses the word "dance") is needed between time (which he identifies with the historical Jesus) and space (which he attributes to the cosmic Christ).

Thomas Berry has developed the idea of the cosmic Christ along different lines. His ideas on this issue are comprehensive and he has attempted to integrate the figure of Christ with a range of religious and cosmological ideas from various sources. Berry's thought is rooted in the theology of the Trinity and in the image of Christ as creator as presented in Paul's Letter to the Colossians. Christ is the hovering "breath of God" that holds all things together. For Berry, Christ is the human presence in the actual process of cosmic-coming-to-be. He seems to imply that there is a purposive aspect to creation by saying that everything is ordered to an ultimate human presence. This is, of course, very Teilhardian and also, it seems to me, rather anthropocentric.

In his reflection on the role of Christ, Berry also introduces some interesting concepts from Hindu, Buddhist, and Chinese thought. He shows that in the great religious traditions there are similar forms of savior-personalities whose personal reality pervades everything. He claims that the Hindu notion of *Purusha* suggests something of this. *Purusha* is a complex term that refers to the uncaused spirit that permeates all reality. It is the pure consciousness to which all things aspire and the transcendent spiritual principle which is to be found everywhere.[4]

The notion of a savior-personality emerges more clearly in Buddhism. Berry makes reference to the enormous and continuing influence of the person of the Buddha: "Looked upon as a saviour-personality, he became progressively identified with the transcendent experience of which he spoke so often."[5] Something of the notion of Buddha as a savior-personality is expressed through the term *Tathagata*. Of this Berry says:

> Few terms in the entire range of Buddhist terminology are so difficult to comprehend as this one. It must have existed prior to the time of Buddha to designate a prophetic personality with a salvation mission to all mankind ... Such a person could not be considered as just another one of many great personalities known and praised extensively in one of the traditional societies of mankind. Seen by his followers as a unique saviour-type personality, he was a bringer of salvation, the supreme good sought by man. He was the healer of anguish, the bringer of blessedness, guide to that final blissful state so much desired by a suffering world.[6]

Included in this notion is also the sense that the "Buddha personality" permeates every person and the whole of reality.

Berry also finds elements of the notion of the savior-personality in the thought of the neo-Confucian scholar Wang Yang-ming (1472–1529). He says that Wang "tells us that a truly developed person is someone who realizes that we form one body with heaven, earth and all living things."[7]

However, despite the provocative and interesting insights of thinkers like Berry and Teilhard, I think that they, like a number of other contemporary theologians, ultimately drive too sharp a wedge between the cosmic Christ and the Jesus of history, as though they were two distinct realities. By emphasizing the cosmic Christ, the awkward problem of Jesus' limited historical and cultural reality is neatly, if unconsciously, side-stepped. But I think that this is too easy a solution. The historical Jesus is not so easily dismissed.

So how do we make sense of the man Jesus in this context?

What is the importance of the historical Jesus?

While the notion of the cosmic Christ has a real appeal to those of us who are trying to develop a theology of ecology, nowadays there is also no denying the importance of the historical Jesus, the man who existed two thousand years ago in Judea and Galilee. He is not only a model for Christians. He also attracts many unbelievers. Skeptics and even atheists often say that they admire both him and his teaching. It is belief in God that is seen as *the* modern problem for unbelievers and even for Christians. Jesus' historical presence makes him attractive because for many the problem is the seeming absence of God. God is no longer needed to explain the world's intelligibility, and, as we have seen, the natural world is no longer viewed as a theophany but merely as a storehouse of materials and energy that can be used to attain superficial human self-sufficiency. It was this secularization of the world that led directly to the conclusions of the so-called "death of God" theologians of the 1960s.[8] There is a real sense in which "God" continues to be a problem for many today.

Often enough, the problem of God comes to the fore through a discussion of how a "good God" can permit Auschwitz, or Somalia, or Rwanda, or the suffering of the innocent, or the death of children. In a debate arranged by the Jewish community of Melbourne, Australia, God was "put on trial." Melbourne has more holocaust survivors than any place outside Israel. The key question was: where was God when six million people died?[9] The primary focus is on the problem of suffering and evil and the reconciliation of this with human freedom and the existence of God's goodness.

Yet assertions about the problem of God are often followed by expressions of admiration for Jesus, his teaching, and his example of good living and gentleness. Among contemporary unbelievers there is widespread interest in Jesus Christ. The English critic A.N. Wilson, who some years ago solemnly announced his loss of faith and departure from the church, still felt the need to produce an unusual and somewhat inaccurate portrait of Christ in the book *Jesus*.[10] Barbara Thiering's maverick and tendentious interpretation of Jesus' life and work was widely reviewed and discussed in the world-wide media.[11] Both these books (plus another by Bishop John Spong) have been thoroughly appraised by N.T. Wright in his *Who Was Jesus?*[12] He is particularly critical of both Wilson and Thiering.

Two far better contemporary books on Jesus are those by John Dominic Crossan, *The Historical Jesus* and *Jesus: A Revolutionary Biography*, which have caused considerable discussion in scholarly circles.[13] The important study of Jesus by Edward Schillebeeckx continues to exercise a major influence on theological discussion.[14] These well-known books represent only a tiny proportion of the vast published output about Jesus over the last few decades. It is also easy to forget that there is an enormous fundamentalist and evangelical publishing industry focused on Jesus. At the other end of the spectrum there is the serious study of christology—the theological investigation of the historical and biblical issues that are raised by the person of Jesus and his significance. Thus there is a vast contemporary theological literature that examines him and his importance and his relationship and relevance to our world.

So there is no doubt that there is great interest in Jesus Christ. Vast claims are made by his followers about his influence on individual and communal life. Traditional Christianity has always viewed Christ as the pivotal point of human history and the central focus of God's revelation. Without him Christianity would lose its *raison d'etre*. For Christians of an evangelical stamp, the focus is on the discovery of the historical Jesus through the Bible and faith and the continuing impact of Christ through the experience of his relationship with the self. Often this will come in a moment of conversion leading to personal commitment. For those at the Catholic end of the spectrum, the stress has been much more on the church as the body of Christ, and the focus has been on the triumphant and risen Christ who is experienced in worship, the Mass, and the sacraments, as well as in prayer and a serious commitment to spirituality. Liberal Protestants have focused more on religious feeling and experience and loosely related them to the Bible, the Christian community, and, together with Catholics, a serious commitment to social justice. Some evangelicals also express their commitment to Christ through involvement in social justice—as, for instance, in the Methodist tradition.

In fact, so great is the focus on Jesus in some Christian circles nowadays that Matthew Fox has correctly spoken about the distinct danger of what he calls "Jesusolatry"—the idolatry of Jesus. By this Fox means that attention is so focused on Christ that it distorts the doctrine of the Trinity by losing all sense of the transcendence of God and the work of the Spirit. Fox uses this distortion to reinforce his emphasis on the cosmic Christ. "Jesusolatry" is rooted in a distorted notion of the trinitarian God. As both Karl Rahner and the Oxford theologian John Macquarrie have warned, it is the unity and oneness of God that is most often under threat from a kind of "Christian tritheism" which absolutizes the separate and individualized notion of the persons of the Trinity and loses all sense of the unity of God.

Macquarrie holds that this is primarily due to the different meaning given to the word "person" in our culture. In the Greek trinitarian formulas of the fourth and fifth centuries when the doctrine was clarified, the word "person" was used in a rather impersonal sense! Today the word "person" is defined in terms of separate individuality. So it is easy to see why we end up with a form of tritheism:

> This is partly due to the modern connotations of the word "person", for while it would be true to say that a person in the fullest sense can only come into being in interaction with other persons, nevertheless a person always remains a separateness,

for there would seem to be an inevitable privacy and impenetrability in personal being ... One might also mention what theologians call "appropriation", language which ascribes to one "person" of the Trinity an activity or character that belongs to all three.[15]

Significantly in our context, Macquarrie refers to the issue of creation and to the way in which this is attributed solely to the Father. He cautions: "Creation is not the work of the Father alone ... the New Testament often speaks of the work of the Son or Logos in creation."[16] In order to maintain our sense of the unity of God while acknowledging the different experiences that we have of God's presence, Rahner uses the language of modality to try to explain himself:

> Insofar as the modes of God's presence for us as Spirit, Son and Father do not signify the same modes of presence, insofar as there really are true and real differences in the modes of presence for us, these three modes of presence for us are to be strictly distinguished ... But insofar as these modes of presence of one and the same God for us may not nullify the real self-communication of God as the one and only and same God, the three modes of presence of one and the same God must belong to him as one and the same God, they must belong to him in himself and for himself.[17]

It is only when we return to this primal Christian doctrine of the Trinity that we realize how distorted much of the church's teaching about Jesus has become. At times one has the feeling that modern Christianity has lost a sense of the transcendence of God in its excessive preoccupation with Jesus.

What does Jesus have to offer to ecological theology?

Nevertheless, the reality of the historical Jesus remains, and the personal and unbreakable connection between the man who lived two thousand years ago and the pre-existent and now glorified Christ cannot be lost without totally distorting orthodox christology. So we are back to the problem with which I started this chapter: how can a man who lived in an obscure part of the Roman Empire just two thousand years ago really be the central figure of all history? How can someone whose whole life was culturally and historically conditioned, no matter how revolutionary his teachings have been, become a major influence on the formation of a new ecological vision of life and spirituality? This problem is reinforced if we are to take seriously the conclusion of scholars like Crossan who say that in his own time Jesus would have been seen as a "peasant nobody."[18] What does a "peasant nobody" from Roman Judea have to offer to our time, when extraordinary shifts in our relationship to the world and reality itself are occurring? What does the historical Jesus have to do with a whole new ecological vision of life and in what sense is Jesus normative for faith and belief?

The problem with contemporary Christian theology is that it does not take these questions seriously enough. Of course, I am not really sure that I can answer my own questions either. It is just that I believe that the awkward link between the historical Jesus and the cosmic Christ must be maintained. While I agree that the *emphasis* in an ecological theology might need to shift to the cosmic Christ and in trinitarian theology toward a more unitive sense of the Godhead, the intimate connection between all of this and the man Jesus cannot be lost. I, for one, refuse to retreat from the importance of the historical and the factual. Religion can never afford to lose its rootedness in and contact with historical reality. Yet at the same time, I do agree with Matthew Fox that the present distorted over-emphasis on Jesus is actually a symptom of the last gasp of the nineteenth century's almost manic search for the historical man Jesus who lived in Roman Judea in the first century.

Perhaps a clue to the solution of the problem of the apparent unimportance of the historical Jesus in the history of the cosmos is suggested by Denis Edwards.[19] Drawing on the thought of Karl Rahner, Edwards sees Jesus as the most important person in history, who, in his own flesh, expresses the essence of God's self-revelation and who, at the same time, expresses in his crucified body the essence of the cosmic longing for the transcendent.

> He is the self-transcendence of the world of matter reaching out to God ... This self-transcendence of the cosmos, in its highest and final stage, is identical with the absolute self-communication of God.[20]

Edwards points in the right direction: the real, historical, material existence of Jesus is a clue to his pivotal role in world history.

Paradoxically and curiously, the doctrine of the incarnation was lost in the search for the historical Jesus. Theologians and biblical scholars became so focused on the historical facts of Jesus' biography that they actually lost the significance of his human existence. The unique characteristic of Christianity as a religion is the importance it places on the material, on the flesh, on that which most roots us in the processes of the earth. This is clearly the attitude of the New Testament. The First Letter of John, for instance, makes belief in the identity between the physical, human Jesus and the divine son of God normative for Christian belief: "By this you know the Spirit of God: every spirit that confesses that Jesus Christ has come in the flesh is from God" (1 John 4:2). The author of John's gospel refuses to back away from the reality of Jesus' physicality and the facticity of his human existence and history. He will not compromise with those who want to spiritualize and turn Jesus into an abstraction. It is in the human face and body of Jesus that we discover God, and this is reinforced when Jesus' flesh is made the touchstone of continuing in his company:

> Unless you eat the flesh of the Son of Man and drink his blood, you have no life in you. Those who eat my flesh and drink my blood have eternal life (John 6:53–54).

This was too much for many of Jesus' disciples and they turned away. The simple fact is that most people are gnostics at heart and find a false spirituality much more attractive than a genuine commitment to the corporeal and physical.

The word "flesh" is a key one in biblical anthropology. In the Bible God alone is "Spirit." All else is flesh. But the biblical word does not just refer to the "meat" of the person, the material and animal side in contradistinction to the spiritual. It has no relationship to the Greek idea of a body of flesh animated by a spiritual soul. For the Bible a person does not *have* a body; he or she *is* a body. Each of us is a psycho-spiritual unity that is summed up by the word "flesh." In the New Testament, the word also refers to the sense of the physical as destined for sickness and death, to the vulnerable and mortal aspects of life.

In fact, the notion of flesh rather than the notion of "soul" is central to New Testament theology. It teaches that God became one of us in the flesh of Jesus Christ. Thus God takes the material world profoundly seriously. Paul states the paradox of the incarnation starkly: "For our sake God made the sinless one into sin, so that in him we might become the goodness of God" (2 Corinthians 5:21, Jerusalem Bible). This extraordinary text uncompromisingly claims that Christ embraced all of the consequences of enfleshed, human existence—physical limitations, frustrations, sickness, sexuality, and the psychological and physical parameters that are built into the fabric of human life. The New Testament is consistently insistent that Christ in Jesus assumed our human condition in the fullest sense.[21] It is crystal clear that the flesh of Jesus is basic to the definition of who Christ is. It was only when Christianity moved out of its Jewish matrix into the wider Greco-Roman world that this integrated anthropology was largely lost in the Hellenistic Neo-Platonist philosophical dualism which permeated Christian theology and has continued to dominate the Christian tradition until our own time.

I have already indicated that I believe that theology has to jettison this debilitating dualism. Simultaneously it has to realize that a strong incarnational emphasis on Jesus' historicity and physicality has real significance for the development of a theology of ecology. The doctrine of the incarnation literally means that God takes the flesh, matter, and the world seriously—so seriously, in fact, that in Jesus the transcendent enters into the very processes of material existence.

The consequences of this are patently obvious. If God takes matter so seriously that God becomes actually identified with matter, then surely we too must take it profoundly seriously. The incarnation of God assumes its central symbolic role: "God so loved the world that he gave his only Son" (John 3:16). It is only a thorough-going incarnational theology that will rid Christianity of its seemingly ineradicable vestiges of dualism and contempt for the world and matter. The incarnation means that it is incumbent on Christianity to take the cosmos seriously. For it is in matter that God is revealed. I see Christ not as the center of history, but as the ultimate symbol that God takes God's material world seriously. It is matter that is sacramental, for God alone is spirit and everything else is matter. Matter is the symbol of the Ultimate. The incarnation is profoundly about ecology.

This is reinforced by the often misunderstood Christian doctrine of the resurrection of the body. It is commonly forgotten that a doctrine is primarily a symbol and is more important symbolically than it is literally. In its oddly anthropocentric way, Christianity is saying that the body and the flesh are so important that it is in and through the body that each will come to what Paul calls the *pleroma*, the fullness of experience in God. But Paul also applies this notion of fullness to the world itself, which, he says, has been "groaning in labor pains" until the world and each of us achieves "the redemption of our bodies" (Romans 8:22–23).

There are actually two images of the end of the world in the New Testament. One is represented in the twenty-fifth chapter of the Gospel of Matthew: in this image the world is destined for a destructive, fiery cataclysm and a vast and frightening scene of judgment. This reflects the Jewish apocalypticism of the intertestamental period which deeply influenced the gospels. But there is another end-of-the-world scenario in the New Testament and this is represented in the Pauline writings. In this the world is not destroyed but brought to completion and fullness. Cosmic history is seen as "one great act of giving birth" as it moves toward "the glory, as yet unrevealed, which is waiting for us" (Romans 8:18, Jerusalem Bible).

This is a very different picture to that presented by elements of mainstream Christianity and especially by Christian fundamentalism, which sees the divine destruction of the world as a kind of cleansing moment from which those who are saved will emerge. In contrast, in Paul's image the idea of the completion and fulfillment of the world process is intimately linked to human salvation itself. You cannot have one without the other. In this scenario, if we destroy the world or even large parts of it, we will destroy ourselves and our chance of salvation.

It is these neglected elements of christology which need to be emphasized as we move toward the development of an ecological theology. Yet I still have to admit that personally I find myself dissatisfied with christology and far more preoccupied with the search for God in the world than I do with the quest for Jesus. The sense of transcendent presence that one finds in the wilderness and in the sea and among the wild animals and in the beauty of the stars and the vast history of the cosmos is far more pervasively influential on me than all the theological talk and deep reflection on the "Cosmic Christ." In my view, theology in our time needs almost to reinvent itself. It must discover a new starting point. It must look outward from its historical preoccupations with Christ, the Bible, salvation, and the church to focus on the history and reality of the cosmos. It is here that the elusive presence of the transcendent God is to be found. It is in the environment of the world and its cosmic context that the ultimate meaning of existence is to be discovered. It is the natural world which is the primal revelation of God and the place where the transcendent is most sacramentally present.

Theology in a new context

At the core of Hans Küng's theology is one word: ecumenism. His entire theological output constantly comes back to the practice of dialogue in the most democratic sense between people of differing views. From the time of his original work on Karl Barth, through his emphasis during and after the Second Vatican Council on inter-Christian dialogue, to his present preoccupation with the wider ecumenism of Christian dialogue with the other great world religions, he always comes back to the importance of an ecumenical attitude.

In his recent book *Theology for the Third Millennium* Küng uses the word "ecumenical," in its broadest sense, to describe the emerging cultural epoch. He says that he prefers this term to the modern cultural buzz-words "postmodern" and "post-enlightenment" or the French term *posthistoire* to describe what is happening socially and culturally in the contemporary world:

> I would prefer to call this emerging epoch of ours ecumenical, in the sense of a new global understanding of the various denominations, religions and regions ... We have reached a crisis which some today would understand apocalyptically as an "end time", which others, unwilling to abandon all hope, would see as a time of transition.[22]

Küng stresses that this new ecumenical culture is only just starting to emerge and argues that it will lead us to a new understanding of ourselves and our relationship to the world. We need to construct an *oikoumene* which is characterized by a transnational world-view and is able to reach across the particularities of religion, culture, and nation to give us a sense of being citizens of the whole earth. Küng suggests that while the epoch of modernity was boringly secular in outlook and characterized by the fatuous "God is dead" debate, the new ecumenical world-view has rediscovered that religion and spirituality are an essential part of being human. God is alive today and is being found anew.

Despite the ravages of rabid fundamentalism in all the great religious traditions, it is basically important for the sake of peace and the survival of the world that genuinely religious people tackle the task of which Küng speaks.[23] This task is the deeply ecumenical work of discovering that which binds the world together rather than emphasizing that which separates. Küng actually takes this further when he questions whether it is in fact possible to ask if there is "one true religion," let alone "one true church." This is a frightening question for certain types of Christians, given the traditional emphasis on the exclusivity of Christ. Actually, the question sits squarely between fanaticism and indifference and is of profound importance.

> Blind zeal for truth has brought on unrestrained injury, burnings at the stake, destruction, and murder at all times and in all churches and religions. Conversely, fatigued forgetfulness of truth has as its consequence disorientation and anomie, so that many people no longer believe in anything at all.[24]

The Catholic Church has come a long way in dealing with this question. It clearly recognized at the Second Vatican Council that the other great world religions are genuine vehicles of grace and salvation: "The Catholic religion rejects nothing of all which is true and holy in these religions" (*Declaration on Non-Christian Religions*, 2). Catholic theology has moved right away from the notion that one has to be, in that odd phrase, an "anonymous Christian" to attain salvation. The same cannot be said for many branches of Protestantism. Despite vigorous debate in the World Council of Churches at several general assemblies, the Protestant tradition generally still has got a long way to go to recognize the importance of this question and the fact that the majority of the human race come to grace and truth through their own religions.

Deep ecumenism has much to offer to deep ecology. That is why developmental fanatics are so suspicious of it. What is needed is a truly ecumenical theology that can underpin a trans-religious approach to caring for the natural world. That world is the deepest and most pervasive symbolic image of that which all religions seek—the transcendent. At the heart of all religion is the restless search for God, for the God that transcends all of the revelations of the religious books—Bible, Qu'ran, Bhagavad-Gita—for the God who is more often found in music, in art, in the wilderness, and above all in the natural world than in the self-engrossed and sad faces of the followers of particular revelations and saviors.

There is only one non-negotiable, and that is that we only have *one* world—this one—and it is here and nowhere else that we will find God. If we destroy the world, we destroy not only ourselves but the most important symbol of God that we have.

Notes

Introduction

1   Karol Wojtyla, *Love and Responsibility*, English edn, London: Collins, 1981, p.121.

Chapter One : ARE WE THE CENTRE ?

1   For information on Weddell seals, see Ronald Strahan (ed.), *The Australian Museum Complete Book of Australian Mammals*, North Ryde: Cornstalk Publishing, 1991, p.471.

2   Timothy Weiskel, "In Dust and Ashes: The Environmental Crisis in Religious Perspective," *Harvard Divinity Bulletin*, 21/3 (1992), p.8.

3   Thomas Berry, *The Dream of the Earth*, San Francisco: Sierra Club Books, 1988, p.21.

4   Cheryl Simon Silver for the National Academy of Sciences, *One Earth One Future: Our Changing Global Environment*, Washington, DC: National Academy Press, 1990, p.124. See also pp.123–130.

5   ibid., op. cit., p.117. See also Paul Harrison, *The Third Revolution: Environment, Population and a Sustainable World*, London: I.B. Tauris, 1992, p.88.

6   Harrison, pp.38–54.

7   Silver, p.76. See pp.63–77 for a discussion of global warming.

8   Thomas Berry, "The Dream of the Future: Our Way into the Future," *Cross Currents*, Summer/Fall, 1987, p.210.

9   Theodore Roszak, *Where the Wasteland Ends: Politics and Transcendence in Post-Industrial Society*, New York: Doubleday, 1973, pp.234–235.

10 Paul Collins, "What's New about the New Age?" *Saint Mark's Review*, Spring 1990, p.10.

11 ibid., p.13.

12 ibid., pp.10–11.

13 For a critical treatment of post-modernism, see Keith Tester, *The Life and Times of Post-Modernity*, London: Routledge, 1993.

14 C.D. Rowley, *The Destruction of Aboriginal Society*, Harmondsworth: Penguin, 1972; Noel Butlin, *Our Original Aggression: Aboriginal Populations of South Eastern Australia 1788–1850*, Sydney: Allen & Unwin, 1983;

Henry Reynolds, *The Other Side of the Frontier: Aboriginal Resistance to the European Invasion of Australia*, Ringwood: Penguin, 1982, and *Frontier: Aborigines, Settlers and the Land*, Sydney: Allen & Unwin, 1987; Roger Milliss, *Waterloo Creek: The Australia Day Massacre of 1838*, Ringwood: McPhee Gribble, 1992.

15 Butlin, p.147.

16 Milliss, pp.183–197. Milliss says that there is a dispute about the exact number of Aborigines killed at Waterloo Creek. It seems to have been between 200 and 300 persons.

17 George Grey, *Journals of Two Expeditions of Discovery in Northwest and Western Australia During the Years 1837, 38 and 39*, Vol.2. London, 1841, p.185. Quoted in Alan Atkinson & Marion Aveling (eds.), *Australians 1838*, Sydney: Fairfax, Syme & Weldon, 1987, p.24.

18 Paul Collins, "William Bernard Ullathorne and the foundation of Australian Catholicism," PhD thesis, Canberra, 1989, p.344.

19 Geoffrey Barraclough, *History in a Changing World*, Oxford: Basil Blackwell, 1957, p.223.

20 Herbert Spencer, *Social Statics; or the Conditions Essential to Human Happiness*, London, 1851.

21 Barraclough, p.224.

22 For Gordon Childe, see the *Australian Dictionary of Biography*, Vol.7, Melbourne: Melbourne University Press, 1979, pp.636–637.

23 Colman T. Barry (ed.), *Readings in Church History*, Vol.III, Paramus, N.J.: Newman Press, p.74.

24 Hugh Morgan, "A threat expert's view of the green movement," *The Age*, 30 December 1992, p.11.

25 Berry, "Dream of the Future," pp.212–213.

Chapter Two : HOW MANY CAN THE EARTH SUSTAIN?.

1 Al Gore, *Earth in the Balance: Forging a New Common Purpose*, London: Earthscan, 1992, p.307.

2 Colin McEvedy & Richard Jones, *Atlas of World Population History*, Harmondsworth: Penguin, 1978, pp.19, 123, 207, 271, 321.

3 Gore, p.308.

4 *The World Almanac and Book of Facts*, p.399.

5 Paul R. Ehrlich, *The Population Bomb*, London: Pan, rev. edn, 1972 (first published in the US in 1968); Paul R. Ehrlich & Anne H. Ehrlich, *The Population Explosion*, Simon & Schuster, New York: 1990.

6   Colin Clark, *The Myth of Overpopulation*, Melbourne: Advocate Press, 1973.

7   Julian Simon, *The Ultimate Resource*, Princeton, N.J.: Princeton University Press, 1981, and *The Theory of Population and Economic Growth*, Oxford: Basil Blackwell, 1986.

8   Silver, pp.80–81.

9   See Paul Collins, "Jeremiah O'Flynn: Persecuted Hero or Vagus?" *The Australasian Catholic Record*, 63 (1986), pp.87–95; 179–194.

10   Gore, p.307.

11   Jacqueline Sawyer:, "The Population Explosion," *The New Road*, Issue 16, Oct.–Dec., 1990, p.5.

12   Ehrlich, *The Population Explosion*, p.216.

13   Harrison, pp.288–291.

14   ibid., p.290.

15   *ANU Reporter*, 27 April 1994, p.12.

16   *The Lambeth Conference*, London: SPCK, 1958, p.147.

17   Basim F. Masallam in the *Encyclopedia of Bioethics*, ed. Warren T. Reich, New York: Macmillan, 1978, Vol.3. p.1268.

18   For Father Arthur McCormack, see *The Tablet*, 19/26 December 1992, p.1636, and 16 January 1993, pp.89–90.

19   ibid., 19/26 December, 1992, p.1636.

20   J. Bryan Hehir in the *Encyclopedia of Bioethics*, Vol.3, p.1254.

21   Quoted in Robert Blair Kaiser, *The Politics of Sex and Religion: A Case History in the Development of Doctrine*, Kansas City: Leaven Press, 1985, p.65.

22   Stanislas de Lestapis, *Family Planning and Modern Problems: A Catholic Analysis*, English trans., London: Burns & Oates, 1961.

23   ibid., p.74.

24   ibid., p.76.

25   ibid., p.181.

26   ibid, p.232. Emphasis in original.

27   ibid., p.264.

28   *Populorum progressio*, paragraph 37. Vatican trans. published by St Paul Publications, Homebush, 1967.

29   Hehir, p.1255.

30   ibid., p.1256.

31   See Kaiser, pp.143–145; 149–150; 214.

32   I have described the evolution of the encyclical *Humanae vitae* and its reception in my book *Mixed Blessings: John Paul II and the Church of the Eighties*, Ringwood: Penguin, 1986, pp.114–119.

33   *Solicitudo rei socialis*, paragraph 25. Vatican trans. published by St Paul Publications, Homebush, 1988.

34   Collins, *Mixed Blessings*, pp.167–172.

35   David Willey, *God's Politician: John Paul and the Vatican*, London: Faber & Faber, 1992, p.164.

36   ibid., p.165.

37   *Veritatis splendor*, paragraphs 80–81. See the *Catholic International*, 4/11 (1993), p.534.

38   Sean McDonagh, "Care for the Earth is a Moral Duty," *The Tablet*, 30 April 1994, p.514.

39   Reported in *The Tablet*, 1/9 April 1994, p.438.

40   David S. Toolan, "The Tempest Over Cairo," *America*, 27 August 1994, pp.3–4.

41   Reported in *Terra Viva*, an independent daily produced at the Cairo Conference, 6 September 1994.

42   Quoted in *Australian Population News*, 1/2 (1994), p.4.

43   A full text can be found in *The Tablet*, 17 September 1994, pp.1180–1182.

44   Quoted in the *National Catholic Reporter*, 9 September 1994.

45   The source of this and other quotations from the Conference is the *Earth Negotiations Bulletin* (Vol.6, No.39), published by the International Institute for Sustainable Development.

46   Editorial in *The Tablet*, 17 September 1994, p.1151.

47   Editorial in the *National Catholic Reporter*, 9 September 1994.

48   ibid.

49   Quoted by McDonagh, "Care for the Earth," p.514.

50   Christopher D. Stone, *Earth and Other Ethics: The Case for Moral Pluralism*, New York: Harper & Row, 1987. See also Eugene C. Hargrove, *Foundations of Environmental Ethics*, Englewood Cliffs, N.J.: Prentice-Hall, 1989.

51   Karol Wojtyla in *Love and Responsibility* and John Finnis, *Natural Law and Natural Rights*, Oxford: Basil Blackwell, 1980.

52   *Summa*, 1–2, q.71, a.3. (Quotations from the *Summa* are my own translation unless otherwise noted.)

53   ibid., 1–2, q.90, a.1.

54   ibid., 1–2, q.91, a.1.

55   ibid., 1–2, q.91, a.2. (Trans. by Timothy McDermott (ed.), *Summa Theologiae: A Concise Translation*, London: Eyre and Spottiswoode, 1989, p.281.)

56   ibid., 1–2, q.93, aa.4–5. (Trans. by McDermott, p.285.)

57   ibid., 2–2, q.47, a.2. (Trans. by McDermott, p.376.)

58   ibid., 1–2, q.95, a.2.

59   Reported in *The Tablet*, 23 April 1994, p.500.

60   Aristotle, *Nicomachean Ethics*, in *The Works of Aristotle* Vol.IX, ed. and trans. W.D. Ross, Oxford: Oxford University Press, 1915, 1133b–1134a.

61   Xavier Leon-Dufour (ed.), *Dictionary of Biblical Theology*, 2nd edn, London: Geoffrey Chapman, 1973, p.281.

62   ibid., p.282.

63   Quoted in the *ANU Reporter*, 27 April 1994, p.12.

64   *Encyclopedia of Bioethics*, Vol.3, pp.1244–1249.

Chapter Three : THE BIBLE, CHRISTIANITY AND ECOLOGY

1   Lynn White, "The Historical Roots of Ecological Crisis," *Science*, 155 (1967), pp.1203–1207.

2   Rupert Sheldrake, *The Rebirth of Nature: The Greening of Science and God*, London: Century, 1990, pp.25ff.

3   ibid., p.26.

4   Thomas Berry in an *Insights* interview, Radio National (Australia), recorded 30 June 1993.

5   Josephine Flood, *Archaeology of the Dreamtime: The Story of Prehistoric Australia and its People*. Pymble: Angus and Robertson, 1992, p.158. See pp.157–170 for the extinction of the mega-fauna.

6   ibid., p.170.

7   Clarence J. Glacken, *Traces on the Rhodian Shore*, Berkeley: University of California Press, 1967, p.151.

8   There has been much published over the last decade on the Bible and environmentalism, but see particularly John Austin Baker, "Biblical Views of Nature," in Charles Birch, William Eakin & Jay B. McDaniel (eds.), *Liberating Life. Contemporary Approaches to Ecological Theology*, Maryknoll, New York: Orbis, 1990, pp.9–26.

9   ibid., pp.19–20.

10   For an historical study of Christian attitudes to the body, see Frank Bottomley, *Attitudes to the Body in Western Christendom*, London: Lepus Books, 1979.

11   John Carmody, *Ecology and Religion: Toward a New Christian Theology of Nature*, New York: Paulist, 1983, p.166.

12   J.N.D. Kelly, *Early Christian Doctrines*, London: A. & C. Black, 1968, pp.24, 26. For a popular introduction to gnosticism, see Elaine Pagels, *The Gnostic Gospels*, New York: Random House, 1979.

13   Rosemary Radford Ruether, *Sexism and God-Talk: Toward a Feminist Theology*, Boston: Beacon Books, 1983, pp.79–80.

14   E.R. Dodds, *Pagan and Christian in an Age of Anxiety*, New York: W. W. Norton, 1965, pp.9–10.

15   Arthur O. Lovejoy, *The Great Chain of Being: A Study of the History of an Idea*, Cambridge, MA.: Harvard University Press, 1936, p.24.

16   ibid., p.25.

17   ibid., p.35. Pages 24–35 are highly recommended.

18   Dodds, p.29.

19   Referred to in Lovejoy, p.24.

20   Dodds, p.11.

21   Louis Bouyer, *A History of Christian Spirituality, Vol.1: The Spirituality of the New Testament and the Fathers*, New York: Seabury Press, 1963, p.351.

22   Jean Leclercq, F. Vandenbroucke & Louis Bouyer, *A History of Christian Spirituality, Vol.2: The Spirituality of the Middle Ages*, New York: Seabury Press, 1968, pp.231–234.

23   Margaret Miles, *Augustine on the Body*, Missoula: Scholars Press, 1979; *Fullness of life: Historical Foundations of a New Asceticism*, Philadelphia: Westminster, 1981.

24   Edward Schillebeeckx, *Ministry: Leadership.in the Community of Jesus Christ*, New York: Crossroad, 1981, p.86.

25   Wolfgang Lederer, *The Fear of Women*, New York: Harcourt, Brace, Jovanovich, 1968, p.26. On menstrual taboos, see pp.25–34.

26   Peter Brown, *The Body and Society: Men, Women and Sexual Renunciation in Early Christianity*, London: Faber & Faber, 1988.

27   ibid., pp.29–30.

28   ibid., p.438.

29   ibid., p.442.

30 ibid., p.442. See also Giuseppe Bovini's *Ravenna: Its Mosaics and Monuments*, Ravenna: A. Longo Editore, 1978.

31 This is the Jerusalem Bible translation.

32 Rosemary Rader, *Breaking Boundaries: Male / Female Friendship.in Early Christian Communities*, New York: Paulist Press, 1983.

33 ibid., p.114.

34 ibid., p.113.

35 Cicero, *De natura deorum*, 13:35, in Glacken, p.56.

36 Glacken, p.144.

37 See Jean Danielou, *The Origins of Latin Christianity: A History of Early Christian Doctrine before the Council of Nicaea*, London: Darton, Longman & Todd, 1977, Vol.III, pp.233–244.

38 Novatian, *De trinitate*, 2. Quoted in Danielou, p.238.

39 Quoted in Danielou, pp.240–241.

40 Denis Minns, *Irenaeus*, London: Geoffrey Chapman, 1994, p.135. This is an excellent introduction to the theology of Irenaeus.

41 ibid., p.25.

42 H. Paul Santmire, *The Travail of Nature: The Ambiguous Ecological Promise of Christian Theology*, Philadelphia: Fortress Press, 1985, p.35.

43 Friedrich Heer, *The Medieval World: Europe from 1100 to 1350*, London: Weidenfeld & Nicolson, 1962, p.96.

44 ibid., p.113.

45 ibid., p.289.

46 Matthew Fox, *Sheer Joy: Conversations with Thomas Aquinas on Creation Spirituality*, San Francisco: Harper, 1992.

47 ibid., pp.59–60. Here Fox is conflating two different texts of Aquinas— one from a sermon and the other from his *Commentary on the Romans*.

48 Glacken, p.175.

49 Sheldrake, pp.12, 33.

50 Jonathan Sumption, *Pilgrimage: An Image of Medieval Religion*, London: Faber & Faber, 1975. Rosalind & Christopher Brooke, *Popular Religion in the Middle Ages: Western Europe 1000–1300*, London: Thames & Hudson, 1984.

51 Heinrich Wolfflin, *Renaissance and Baroque*, London: Fontana/ Collins, 1964, p.38.

52 On Berulle and Olier, see William M. Thompson (ed.), *Berulle and the*

French School: Selected Writings, New York: Paulist Press, 1989. See also Louis Cognet, *Post-Reformation Spirituality*, London: Burns & Oates, 1959.

53   ibid., pp. 32–33.

54   Sheldrake, p. 37.

55   Charles Birch, *On Purpose*, Kensington: NSW University Press, 1990. John Polkinghorne, *Science and Creation: The Search for Understanding*, London: SPCK, 1988.

56   Denis Edwards, *Jesus and the Cosmos*, Homebush: St Paul Publications, 1991 and *Made from Stardust: Exploring the Place of Human Beings Within Creation*, North Blackburn: Collins Dove, 1992.

57   James Lovelock and Sidney Epton, "The Quest for Gaia," in *New Scientist*, 6 (1975), pp. 304ff. James Lovelock, *Gaia: A New Look at Life on Earth*, Oxford: Oxford University Press, 1979. *The Ages of Gaia: A Biography of Our Living Earth*. Oxford: Oxford University Press, 1988.

58   Jürgen Moltmann, *God in Creation: An Ecological Doctrine of Creation*, London: SCM, 1985.

Chapter Four : Contempory Thinkers

1   I.M. Bochenski, *Contemporary European Philosophy*, Berkeley: University of California Press, 1956, p. 103. See also Leszek Kolakowski, *Bergson*, Oxford: Oxford University Press, 1985.

2   Henri Bergson, *Creative Evolution*, English trans., London: Macmillan, 1911.

3   Frederick Copleston, *A History of Philosophy*, Vol. IX, London: Burns & Oates, 1977. p. 179.

4   Kolakowski, p. 58.

5   Henri Bergson, *The Two Sources of Morality and Religion*, English trans. London: Macmillan, 1935.

6   For an explanation of Blondel's thought, see *Maurice Blondel: Letter on Apologetics and History and Dogma*, trans. and introduced by Alexander Dru and Illtyd Trethowan, London: Harvill Press, 1964.

7   A whole literature has grown up around the relatively small collection of works which constitute Teilhard's corpus. I have found that the best introductions are Claude Cuenot's *Teilhard de Chardin: A Biographical Study*, Baltimore: Helicon Press, 1965, and Emile Rideau's *Teilhard de Chardin: A Guide to His Thought*, London: Collins, 1967.

8   Rideau, p. 53.

9   P. Teilhard de Chardin, *Toward the Future*, trans. Rene Hague, London: Collins, 1975, p. 171.

10   Rideau, p.117.

11   P. Teilhard de Chardin, *The Future of Man*, trans. Norman Denny, London: Collins, 1964, p.34.

12   This essay is found in *Toward the Future*, pp.163–208.

13   This essay is found in *The Hymn of the Universe*, trans. Gerard Vann, London: Collins, 1965, pp.59–71.

14   ibid., pp.64–65.

15   *The Divine Milieu: An Essay on the Interior Life*, English trans., New York: Collins, 1960.

16   Birch, *On Purpose*, p.xi.

17   William E. Hocking, "Whitehead as I Knew Him," in George L. Kline (ed.), *Alfred North Whitehead: Essays on his Philosophy*, Englewood Cliffs, N.J.: Prentice-Hall, 1963, pp.10–13.

18   A.N. Whitehead, *Process and Reality: An Essay in Cosmology*, Cambridge: Cambridge University Press, 1929.

19   Reproduced in F.S.C. Northrop & Mason W. Gross (eds.), *Alfred North Whitehead: An Anthology*, Cambridge: Cambridge University Press, 1953, pp.467–528.

20   *Process and Reality*, p.520.

21   Northrop & Gross, p.492.

22   ibid., p.493.

23   *Process and Reality*, p.39.

24   In what follows I have drawn on the unpublished paper "Whitehead and Plato" by Rev Dr Greg Moses of Saint Paul's National Seminary, Kensington, NSW.

25   ibid., p.5.

26   ibid, p.8.

27   ibid., p.4.

28   *Process and Reality*, pp.523–524.

29   Charles Hartshorne, "Whitehead's Novel Intuition," in Kline, p.24.

30   Charles Hartshorne, *Man's Vision of God*, Chicago: Willet Clark, 1941, p.117.

31   Charles Hartshorne, *Reality as Social Process: Studies in Metaphysics and Religion*, Boston: Free Press, 1953, p.24.

32   John B. Cobb, *Is it too Late? A Theology of Ecology*, Beverly Hills, CA: Bruce, 1962, p.vii.

33 Charles Birch and John B. Cobb, *The Liberation of Life: From the Cell to the Community*, Cambridge: Cambridge University Press, 1981.

34 ibid., p.152.

35 Jay B. McDaniel, *Earth, Sky, Gods and Mortals: Developing an Ecological Spirituality*, Mystic, CT: Twenty Third Publications, Second Printing, 1990.

36 Charles Birch, *Regaining Compassion: For Humanity and Nature*, Kensington: New South Wales University Press, 1993, pp.36–37.

37 Both are published by the New South Wales University Press.

38 *On Purpose*, pp.33ff.

39 ibid., p.174.

40 Birch in *Liberating Life*, p.63.

41 *Regaining Compassion*, pp.105–106.

42 A copy of the Report can be found in *Liberating Life*, pp.273–290.

43 Sallie McFague, "Imaging a Theology of Nature: The World as God's Body", Birch et al., in *Liberating Life*, pp.201–227. See also *The Body of God: An Ecological Theology*, Minneapolis: Fortress, 1993.

44 McFague in Birch et al., p.203.

45 In John Hick (ed.), *The Myth of God Incarnate*, Philadelphia: Westminster, 1977, p.42.

46 McFague in Birch et al., p.206.

47 ibid., p.204.

48 Tissa Balasuriya, *Jesus Christ and Human Liberation*, Colombo: Centre for Society and Religion Publications, 1976. Reprinted by Orbis, Maryknoll, NY, 1979.

49 McFague in Birch et al., p.205.

50 ibid., p.211.

51 ibid., p.213.

52 ibid., p.214.

53 ibid., p.214.

54 McFague, *Body of God*, pp.99–101.

55 ibid., p.101.

56 ibid., p.102

57 Geoffrey R. Lilbourne, *A Sense of Place: A Christian Theology of the Land*, Nashville: Abingdon Press, 1989.

58 Cavan Brown, *Pilgrim Through This Barren Land*, Sutherland, NSW: Albatross, 1991.

59   McFague in Birch et al., p.217.

60   Jürgen Moltmann, *God in Creation: An Ecological Doctrine of Creation*, London: SCM, 1985.

61   ibid., p.xi.

62   *Theology of Hope: On the Ground and Implications of a Christian Eschatology*, London: SCM, 1967.

63   *The Crucified God: The Cross of Christ as the Foundation and Criticism of Christian Theology*, New York: Harper & Row, 1974.

64   ibid., p.5.

65   Jürgen Moltmann, *The Trinity and the Kingdom of God*, English trans., London: SCM, 1981.

66   Jürgen Moltmann, *The Way of Jesus Christ*, English trans., London: SCM, 1989.

67   Thomas Fox, "Approaching the Ecozoic Period of Earth History," *National Catholic Reporter*, 6 September 1991, p.21.

68   Articles on a vast range of subjects related to ecology were published in *Cross Currents* right through the 1970s and 1980s.

69   Thomas Berry, *Buddhism*, 1989, and *Religions of India: Hinduism, Yoga, Buddhism*, 1992, both reprinted by Anima Publications of Chambersburg, PA.

70   Thomas Berry, *The Dream of the Earth*, San Francisco: Sierra Club Books, 1988. In 1991 Berry published the results of a theological dialogue with Thomas Clarke, *Befriending the Earth: A Theology of Reconciliation Between Humans and the Earth*, Mystic, CT: Twenty Third Publications, 1991.

71   Brian Swimme & Thomas Berry, *The Universe Story*, San Francisco: Harper, 1992.

72   Biographical details come from Anne Lonergan & Caroline Richards (eds.), *Thomas Berry and the New Cosmology*, Mystic, CT: Twenty Third Publications, 1987, pp.2–3, and a personal interview recorded in late 1990 and broadcast on the Radio National (Australia) program *Insights* on 27 January 1991. A further, more detailed personal interview was held on 30 June and 1 July 1993 at Riverdale. Further quotes from Berry in this section, unless otherwise indicated, are from the January 1991 *Insights* interview.

73   Quoted in Lonergan & Richards, p.3.

74   See especially Dawson's *Religion and the Rise of Western Culture*, London: Sheed and Ward, 1950.

75 Thomas Berry, "Contemporary Spirituality: The Journey of the Human Community," *Cross Currents*, Summer/Fall, 1974, pp.174–175.

76 McFague, *Body of God*, p.71.

77 *Dream of the Earth*, p.14.

78 ibid., p.17.

79 Paul Hazard, *The European Mind 1680–1715*. New York: Meridian. 1963, p.40. See also pp.198–216. For a theological treatment of Bossuet, see Owen Chadwick, *From Bossuet to Newman*, Cambridge: Cambridge University Press, 1957, pp.1–20.

80 *Dream of the Earth*, p.196.

81 "Cenozoic" is the American form of the term "Cainozoic" used in other English-speaking countries.

82 Thomas Berry, "The Ecozoic Period", unpublished paper, p.2.

83 *The Universe Story*, p.241.

84 ibid., p.243.

85 ibid., p.238.

86 ibid., p.237.

87 ibid., p.258.

88 ibid., p.260.

89 Matthew Fox, *On Becoming a Musical, Mystical Bear: Spirituality American Style*, New York: Paulist Press, 1972. *Whee! We, Wee All the Way Home: A Guide to a Sensual Prophetic Spirituality*, Sante Fe, NM: Bear and Co., 1976.

90 Matthew Fox, *Original Blessing: A Primer in Creation Spirituality*, Sante Fe, NM: Bear and Co., 1981. *The Coming of the Cosmic Christ*, Melbourne: Collins/Dove, 1989.

91 This summary is based on an interview I did with Fox which was first broadcast on the Radio National (Australia) program *Encounter* in 1989. Quotations in this section are from this interview unless otherwise stated.

92 A copy of the "Pastoral Letter" can be found in *Creation*, November/December 1988.

93 Sean McDonagh, *To Care for the Earth: A Call to a New Theology*, London: Geoffrey Chapman, 1986. *The Greening of the Church*, London: Geoffrey Chapman, 1990. *Passion for the Earth*, London: Geoffrey Chapman, 1994.

94 Sean McDonagh in Walter Schwarz (ed.), *Updating God*, Basingstoke: Marshall Pickering, 1988, p.140.

95 ibid., p.141.

96 *To Care for the Earth*, pp.3–11

Chapter Five : God's Earth.

1   McEvedy & Jones, *Atlas of World Population History*, pp.19, 123, 207, 271.

2   Quoted in Elizabeth Tooker (ed.), *Native North American Spirituality of the Eastern Woodlands*, New York: Paulist Press, 1979, p.27.

3   Interview with the author, 1993.

4   R.M. & C.H. Berndt, *The World of the First Australians*, 2nd edn, Sydney: Ure Smith, 1977, p.138.

5   William J. Lines, *Taming the Great South Land: A History of the Conquest of Nature in Australia*, Sydney: Allen & Unwin, 1991, pp.197ff.

6   ibid., p.196.

7   For the political attitude of the Tasmanian Hydro, see the views of former Tasmanian Premier, Doug Lowe, in Roger Green (ed.), *Battle for the Franklin*, Sydney: Fontana/Australian Conservation Foundation, 1981, pp.166–177.

8   Lines, p.211.

9   Berry: "Dream of the Future," p.210.

10   Martin Gilbert, *The Dent Atlas of the Holocaust: The Complete History*, 2nd edn, London: J.M. Dent., 1993, p.245.

11   Quoted in the paper "Can Only a God Save Us?" delivered at the World Council of Churches General Assembly, Canberra, February 1991, by Jan Van der Veken of the Catholic University, Leuven, Belgium. Emphasis added.

12   See Hugo Ott, *Martin Heidegger: A Political Life*, London: Fontana, 1993, and Victor Farias, *Heidegger and Nazism*, Philadelphia: Temple University Press, 1989.

13   John Macquarrie, *Heidegger and Christianity*, London: SCM, 1994, p.14.

14   George Steiner, *Heidegger*, 2nd edn, London: Fontana, 1992, p.83.

15   Steiner, p.136. Another excellent introduction to Heidegger can be found in William Barrett's *Irrational Man: A Study in Existential Philosophy*, New York: Doubleday, 1962, pp.206–238.

16   Christopher Manes, *Green Rage: Radical Environmentalism and the Unmaking of Civilization*, Boston: Little, Brown, 1990, p.143.

17   ibid., p.226.

18   Heidegger in 1955. Quoted in Gregory Tropea, *Religion, Ideology and Heidegger's Concept of Falling*, Atlanta, GA: Scholars Press, 1987, pp.97–98.

19   Steiner, p.62. Macquarrie, p.108.

20   Stephen Hawking, *A Brief History of Time: From the Big Bang to Black Holes*, London: Bantam, 1988, p.144.

21   ibid., p.8.

22   Paul Davies, *God and the New Physics*, London: Penguin, 1983, and *The Mind of God: The Scientific Basis for a Rational World*, New York: Simon & Schuster, 1992.

23   Carl Sagan in the Introduction to Hawking, p.x.

24   ibid., p.122.

25   ibid., p.149.

26   Davies, *The Mind of God*, p.73.

27   ibid., p.82.

28   ibid., p.92.

29   Paul Davies, "Before the Big Bang," *The Australian*, 9 March 1994, pp.25, 29.

30   St Augustine, *Concerning The City of God, Against the Pagans*, trans. Henry Bettenson, London: Pelican, 1972, Book XI, ch.6.

31   Davies, "Before the Big Bang," p.29.

32   Hawking, p.144.

33   ibid., p.125.

34   Owen Gingerich, "The Universal Rover," *Nature*, Vol.336, 17 November 1988, p.288.

35   H.R. Pagels, *Perfect Symmetry: The Search for the Beginning of Time*, Harmondsworth: Penguin, 1985, p.11.

36   Sheldrake, pp.102–104.

37   ibid., p.104.

38   Steiner, p.28.

39   Karl Barth, *The Epistle to the Romans*, trans. E.C. Hoskyns, Oxford: Oxford University Press, 1933. The key German edition is the second edition of 1921.

40   Steiner, p.x.

41   Herbert Hartwell, *The Theology of Karl Barth: An Introduction*, London: Duckworth, p.48.

42   Karl Barth, *Church Dogmatics*, Vol.I Pt 1, Edinburgh: T. & T. Clark, 1936–69, p.x.

43   Glacken, pp.42–44; 60–61.

44   Richard Dawkins, *The Blind Watchmaker*, Harmondsworth: Penguin, 1990.

45   Jacques Monod, *Chance and Necessity: An Essay on the Natural Philosophy of Modern Biology*, New York: Vintage Books, 1972.

46   John Polkinghorne, *Religion and Current Science*, Kensington: New College, University of New South Wales, 1993, p.17.

47   ibid., p.17.

48   This material is based on papers given by Professors Owen Gingerich and John Polkinghorne at the symposium *Science and Theology: Questions at the Interface* at the University of Otago, Dunedin, New Zealand, 15–21 August 1993. The papers have been edited by Murray Rae, Hilary Regan and John Stenhouse and published by T. & T. Clark, Edinburgh, 1994.

49   *Summa Theologiae*, 1, q.13, a.4–5. (Trans. McDermott, *Summa Theologiae*, pp.31–32).

50   George Duby, *The Age of the Cathedrals: Art and Society, 980–1420*, Chicago: University of Chicago Press, 1981, p.184.

51   Abraham Maslow, *Toward a Psychology of Being*, Princeton, NJ: Princeton University Press, 1968, chapters 6 and 7.

52   Rudolf Otto, *The Idea of the Holy*, Harmondsworth: Penguin, 1953. (First published in German in 1917.)

53   Romans 8:22. Here I have used the more vivid and expressive *Jerusalem Bible* translation. The *New Revised Standard Version* says that creation is "groaning in labor pains."

54   Karl Rahner, *The Foundations of Christian Faith: An Introduction to the Idea of Christianity*. New York: Seabury, 1978, pp.57–66.

55   Gregory of Nyssa, *The Life of Moses*, trans. Abraham J. Malherbe & Everett Ferguson, New York: Paulist Press, 1978, p.116.

56   ibid., p.95.

57   His major works were *The Celestial Hierarchy*, *The Divine Names*, *The Ecclesiastical Hierarchy* and *The Mystical Theology*. A full translation can be found in Colm Luibheid, *Pseudo-Dionysius: The Complete Works*, New York: Paulist Press, 1987.

58   *The Mystical Theology*, ch. 5. See ibid., p.141.

59   *De potentia*, q.7, a.5, ad 14. (Trans. Matthew Fox, *Sheer Joy*, p.196.)

60   *Poems of Saint John of the Cross*, trans. Roy Campbell. Harmondsworth: Penguin, 1960, p.11.

61   Ross Collings, *John of the Cross*, Collegeville, MN.: Michael Glazier/Liturgical Press, 1990, pp.26–49.

62   Aidan Kavanagh, *On Liturgical Theology*, New York: Pueblo, 1984, p.82.

63 Joan Lindsay, *Picnic at Hanging Rock*, Ringwood: Penguin, 1967.

64 John S. Dunne, *A Search for God in Time and Memory*, London: Sheldon Press, 1975, pp.1–31.

65 "Burnt Norton" from "Four Quartets" in T.S. Eliot, *Collected Poems 1909–1962*, London: Faber & Faber, 1963.

66 William James, *The Varieties of Religious Experience: A Study in Human Nature*, Collins/Fontana, reprinted 1960, pp.366–413.

67 R.C. Zaehner, *Mysticism Sacred and Profane: An Inquiry into some Varieties of Praeternatural Experience*, Oxford: Oxford University Press, 1957, p.33.

68 ibid., p.41.

69 Joseph Marechal, *Studies in the Psychology of the Mystics*, London: Burns Oates and Washbourne, 1927, p.103.

70 ibid., p.111.

71 ibid., p.98.

72 ibid., p.121.

73 Karl Rahner, *Nature and Grace and Other Essays*, London: Sheed and Ward, 1963, p.10.

74 Rahner, *Foundations of Christian Faith*, p.32.

75 Jean Dalumeau, *Catholicism Between Luther and Voltaire: A New View of the Counter Reformation*, Philadelphia: Westminster Press, 1977, p.154ff.

76 David Tracy, *The Analogical Imagination: Christian Theology and the Culture of Pluralism*, London: SCM, 1981. See especially pp. 405ff.

77 ibid., p.408.

78 Robert Bernard Martin, *Gerard Manley Hopkins: A Very Private Life*, London: Harper/Collins, 1992, p.205.

79 Norman H. MacKenzie, quoted in ibid., p.205.

80 ibid., pp.206ff.

81 ibid., p.207.

82 J.H. Newman, *An Essay in Aid of a Grammar of Assent*, ed. I.T. Ker, Oxford: Oxford University Press, 1985, pp.221ff.

Chapter Six : CHRIST, THEOLOGY & GOD'S EARTH

1 John L. McKenzie, *Dictionary of the Bible*, London: Geoffrey Chapman, 1966, p.146.

2 Fox, *Coming of the Cosmic Christ*, pp.75–79.

3 ibid., p.79. Author's emphasis.

4 Berry, *Religions of India*, pp.84–85; p.213.

5 Berry, *Buddhism*, p.31.

6 ibid., pp.32–33.

7 Berry, *Dream of the Earth*, p.15. On Wang see also Herrlee G. Creel, *Chinese Thought From Confucius to Mao Tse-Tung*, Chicago: University of Chicago Press, 1953, pp.213–216.

8 Thomas J.J. Altizer and William Hamilton, *Radical Theology and the Death of God*, Harmondsworth: Penguin, 1966.

9 This debate was broadcast on the Radio National (Australia) program *Encounter* on 24 July 1994.

10 A.N. Wilson, *Jesus*, London: Sinclair-Stevenson, 1992.

11 Barbara Thiering, *Jesus the Man: A New Interpretation from the Dead Sea Scrolls*, Sydney: Transworld, 1992. Published in the US as *Jesus and the Riddle of the Dead Sea Scrolls*. San Francisco: Harper, 1992.

12 N.T. Wright, *Who Was Jesus?* London: SPCK, 1993.

13 John Dominic Crossan, *The Historical Jesus: The Life of a Mediterranean Jewish Peasant*. Edinburgh: T. and T. Clark, 1991, and the popularization and development of the 1991 book, *Jesus: A Revolutionary Biography*, San Francisco: Harper, 1994.

14 Edward Schillebeeckx, *Jesus: An Experiment in Christology*, London: Collins, 1979.

15 John Macquarrie, *Principles of Christian Theology*, New York: Charles Scribner's Sons, 1977, pp.193–194.

16 ibid., p.194.

17 Rahner, *Foundations of Christian Faith*, pp.136–137.

18 Crossan, *The Historical Jesus*, p.xii.

19 Edwards, *Jesus and the Cosmos*, pp.79–93.

20 ibid., p.83.

21 There are a whole series of texts in the New Testament to support this contention: John 1:14–16; John 6:51–59; 1 John 4:2–3; 2 John 4; 1 Corinthians 15:35–49; 2 Corinthians 5:16; Philippians 2:6ff; 1 Timothy 3:16; Colossians 1:22.

22 Hans Küng, *Theology for the Third Millennium: An Ecumenical View*, New York: Doubleday, 1991, pp.3–4.

23 ibid., p.227.

24 ibid., p.228.

Bibliography

Altizer, Thomas J.J. & Hamilton, William, *Radical Theology and the Death of God*. Penguin, Harmondsworth, 1966.

Aristotle, *The Works of Aristotle*. Ed. & trans. W.D. Ross. Oxford University Press, Oxford, 1915, Vol.IX.

Atkinson, A. & Aveling, M., *Australians 1838*. Fairfax, Syme & Weldon, Sydney, 1987.

Augustine, *Concerning the City of God: Against the Pagans*. Trans. Henry Bettenson. Pelican, Harmondsworth, 1972.

Balasuriya, Tissa, *Jesus Christ and Human Liberation*. Centre for Society and Religion Publications, Colombo, 1976. Reprinted by Orbis, Maryknoll, NY, 1979.

Barraclough, Geoffrey, *History in a Changing World*. Basil Backwell, Oxford, 1957.

● Barrett, William, *Irrational Man: A Study in Existentialist Philosophy*. Doubleday, New York, 1962.

Barry, Colman T. (ed), *Readings in Church History*. Newman Press, Paramus, N.J., 1960.

Barth, Karl, *Church Dogmatics*. T. & T. Clark, Edinburgh, 1936–69.

Barth, Karl, *Epistle to the Romans*. Trans. E.C. Hoskyns. Oxford University Press, Oxford, 1933.

● Bergson, Henri, *Creative Evolution*. English trans. Macmillan, London, 1911.

Bergson, Henri, *The Two Sources of Morality and Religion*. English trans. Macmillan, London, 1935.

Berndt, R.M. & C.H., *The World of the First Australians*. Ure Smith, Sydney, 1977.

Berry, Thomas, *Buddhism*. Anima Publications, Chambersberg, PA, 1989.

Berry, Thomas, "Contemporary Spirituality: The Journey of the Human Community." *Cross Currents*, Summer/Fall, 1974. pp.172–183.

Berry, Thomas, *Religions of India: Hinduism, Yoga, Buddhism*. Anima Publications, Chambersberg, PA, 1992.

Berry, Thomas, *The Dream of the Earth*. Sierra Club Books, San Francisco, 1988.

Berry, Thomas, "The Dream of the Future: Our Way into the Future." *Cross Currents*. Summer/Fall, 1987, pp.200–215.

Berry, Thomas, "The Ecozoic Period." Unpublished paper.

Berry, Thomas & Clarke, Thomas, *Befriending the Earth: A Theology of*

Reconciliation Between Humans and the Earth. Twenty Third Publications, Mystic, CT, 1991.

Berry, Thomas & Swimme, Brian, *The Universe Story*. Harper, San Francisco, 1992.

Birch, Charles, *On Purpose*. New South Wales University Press, Kensington. 1990.

Birch, Charles, *Regaining Compassion for Humanity and Nature*. New South Wales University Press, Kensington, 1993.

Birch, Charles & Cobb, John B., *The Liberation of Life: From the Cell to the Community*. Cambridge University Press, Cambridge, 1981.

Birch, Charles, Eakin, William & McDaniel, Jay B., (eds.), *Liberating Life: Contemporary Approaches to Ecological Theology*. Orbis, Maryknoll, NY, 1990.

Bochenski, I.M., *Contemporary European Philosophy*. University of California Press, Berkeley, 1956.

Bonaventure, *Bonaventure: The Soul's Journey into God, The Tree of Life, The Life of Saint Francis*. Trans. Everet Cousins. Paulist Press, New York, 1978.

Bottomley, Frank, *Attitudes to the Body in Western Christendom*. Lepus Books, London, 1979.

Bouyer, Louis, *A History of Christian Spirituality, Vol. 1: The Spirituality of the New Testament and the Fathers*. Seabury, New York, 1963.

Bovini, Giuseppe, *Ravenna: Its Mosaics and Monuments*. A. Longo Editore, Ravenna, 1978.

Brooke, Rosalind & Christopher, *Popular Religion in the Middle Ages: Europe 1000–1300*. Thames & Hudson, London, 1984.

Brown, Cavan, *Pilgrim Through This Barren Land*. Albatross, Sutherland, NSW, 1991.

Brown, Peter, *The Body and Society: Men, Women and Sexual Renunciation in Early Christianity*. Faber & Faber, London, 1988.

Butlin, Noel, *Our Original Aggression: Aboriginal Populations in South Eastern Australia. 1788–1850*. Allen & Unwin, Sydney, 1983.

♦ Capra, Fritjof, *The Tao of Physics*. Fontana / Collins, London, 1976.

Carmody, John, *Ecology and Religion: Toward a New Christian Theology of Nature*. Paulist Press, New York, 1983.

Chadwick, Owen, *From Bossuet to Newman*. Cambridge University Press, Cambridge, 1957.

Clark, Colin, *The Myth of Overpopulation*. Advocate Press, Melbourne. 1973.

Cobb, John B., *Is It Too Late? A Theology of Ecology*. Bruce, Beverly Hills, CA, 1972.

Cognet, Louis, *Post-Reformation Spirituality*. Burns & Oates, London, 1959.

Collings, Ross, *John of the Cross*. Michael Glazier / Liturgical Press, Collegeville, MN., 1990.

Collins, Paul, "Jeremiah O'Flynn: Persecuted Hero or Vagus?" *The Australasian Catholic Record*. 63 (1986), pp.87–95; 179–194.

Collins, Paul, *Mixed Blessings: John Paul II and the Church of the Eighties*. Penguin, Ringwood, 1988.

Collins, Paul, *No Set Agenda: Australia's Catholic Church Faces an Uncertain Future*. David Lovell, Melbourne, 1992.

Collins, Paul, "What's New About the New Age?" *Saint Mark's Review*, Spring 1990, pp.10–15.

Collins, Paul, "William Bernard Ullathorne and the Foundation of Australian Catholicism 1815–1840." PhD thesis, ANU, Canberra, 1989.

Copleston, Frederick, *A History of Philosophy*, Vols.I–IX. Burns & Oates, London, 1946–1974.

Creel, Herrlee G., *Chinese Thought from Confucius to Mao Tse-Tung*. University of Chicago Press, Chicago, 1953.

Crossan, John Dominic, *Jesus: A Revolutionary Biography*. Harper, San Francisco, 1994.

Crossan, John Dominic, *The Historical Jesus: The Life of a Mediterranean Jewish Peasant*. T. & T. Clark, Edinburgh, 1991.

Cuenot, Claude, *Teilhard de Chardin: A Biographical Study*. Helicon Press, Baltimore, 1965.

Danielou, Jean, *The Origins of Latin Christianity: A History of Early Christian Doctrine Before the Council of Nicaea*. Vol.III. Darton, Longman & Todd, London, 1977.

Davies, Paul, "Before the Big Bang." *The Australian*. 9 March 1994.

Davies, Paul, *God and the New Physics*. Penguin, London, 1983.

Davies, Paul, *The Mind of God: The Scientific Basis for a Rational World*. Simon & Schuster, New York, 1992.

Dawkins, Richard, *The Blind Watchmaker*. Penguin, Harmondsworth, 1990.

Dawson, Christopher, *Religion and the Rise of Western Culture*. Sheed & Ward, London, 1950.

de Lestapis, Stanislas, *Family Planning and Modern Problems: A Catholic Analysis*. Burns & Oates, London, 1961.

Delumeau, Jean, *Catholicism Between Luther and Voltaire: A New View of the Counter Reformation*. Westminster Press, Philadelphia, 1977.

Dodds, E.R., *Pagan and Christian in an Age of Anxiety*. W.W. Norton, New York, 1965.

Dru, Alexander & Trethowan, Illtyd (eds.), *Maurice Blondel: Letter on Apologetics and History of Dogma*. Harvill Press, London, 1964.

Duby, Georges, *The Age of the Cathedrals: Art and Society, 980–1420*. University of Chicago Press, Chicago, 1981.

Dunne, John S., *A Search for God in Time and Memory*. Sheldon Press, London, 1975.

Edwards, Denis, *Jesus and the Cosmos*. St Paul Publications, Homebush, 1991. Published in the US by Paulist Press, New York, 1991.

Edwards, Denis, *Made from Stardust: Exploring the Place of Human Beings Within Creation*. Collins Dove, North Blackburn, 1992.

Ehrlich, Paul R., *The Population Bomb*. Pan, London, 1972.

Ehrlich, Paul R. & Anne H., *The Population Explosion*. Simon & Schuster, New York, 1990.

Eliot, T.S., *Collected Poems 1909–1962*. Faber & Faber, London, 1963.

Farias, Victor, *Heidegger and Nazism*. Temple University Press, Philadelphia, 1989.

Finnis, John, *Natural Law and Natural Rights*. Basil Blackwell, Oxford, 1980.

Flood, Josephine, *Archaeology of the Dreamtime: The Story of Pre-historical Australia and its People*. Angus & Robertson, Pymble, 1992.

Fox, Matthew, "Is the Catholic Church Today a Dysfunctional Family? A Pastoral Letter to Cardinal Ratzinger and the Whole Church." *Creation*. November/December, 1988, pp.23–37.

Fox, Matthew, *On Becoming a Musical, Mystical Bear: Spirituality American Style*. Paulist Press, New York, 1972.

Fox, Matthew, *Original Blessing: A Primer in Creation Spirituality*. Bear and Co., Santa Fe, NM, 1981.

Fox, Matthew, *Sheer Joy: Conversations with Thomas Aquinas on Creation Spirituality*. Harper, San Francisco, 1992.

Fox, Matthew, *The Coming of the Cosmic Christ: The Healing of Mother Earth and the Birth of a Global Renaissance*. Collins Dove, Melbourne, 1989.

Fox, Matthew, *Whee! We, Wee All the Way Home: A Guide to a Sensual Prophetic Spirituality*. Bear and Co., Santa Fe, NM, 1981.

Fox, Thomas, "Approaching the Ecozoic Period of Earth History." *National Catholic Reporter*, 6 September 1991.

Gilbert, Martin, *The Dent Atlas of the Holocaust: The Complete History*. 2nd edn. J.M. Dent, London, 1993.

Gingerich, Owen, "The Universal Rover." *Nature*, Vol.336, 17 November 1988, p.288.

Glacken, Clarence J., *Traces on the Rhodian Shore*. University of California Press, Berkeley, 1967.

Gore, Al, *Earth in the Balance: Forging a New Common Purpose*. Earthscan, London, 1992.

Green, Roger (ed.), *Battle for the Franklin*. Fontana/Australian Conservation Foundation, Sydney, 1981.

Gregory of Nyssa, *The Life of Moses*. Trans. Abraham J. Malherbe & Everett Ferguson. Paulist Press, New York, 1978.

Hargrove, Eugene C., *Foundations of Environmental Ethics*. Prentice-Hall, Englewood Cliffs, N.J., 1989.

Harrison, Paul, *The Third Revolution: Environment, Population and a Sustainable World*. I.B. Tauris, London, 1992.

Hartshorne, Charles, *Man's Vision of God*. Willet Clark, Chicago, 1941.

Hartshorne, Charles, *Reality as Social Process: Studies in Metaphysics and Religion*. Free Press, Boston, 1953.

Hartwell, Herbert, *The Theology of Karl Barth: An Introduction*. Duckworth, London, 1964.

Hawking, Stephen W., *A Brief History of Time: From the Big Bang to Black Holes*. Bantam, London, 1988.

Hazard, Paul, *The European Mind 1680–1715*. Meridian, New York, 1963.

• Heer, Friedrich, *The Medieval World: Europe from 1100 to 1350*. Weidenfeld & Nicolson, London, 1962.

• Hick, John (ed.), *The Myth of God Incarnate*. Westminster, Philadelphia, 1977.

• James, William, *The Varieties of Religious Experience: A Study in Human Nature*. Collins/Fontana, London, Reprinted 1960.

• John of the Cross, *Poems of St John of the Cross*. Trans. Roy Campbell. Penguin, Harmondsworth, 1960.

Kaiser, Robert Blair, *The Politics of Sex and Religion: A Case History in the Development of Doctrine 1962–1985*. Leaven Press, Kansas City, MO., 1985.

Kavanagh, Aidan, *On Liturgical Theology*. Pueblo, New York, 1984.

Kelly, J.N.D., *Early Christian Doctrines*. A. & C. Black, London, 1968.

Kline, George L. (ed.), *Alfred North Whitehead: Essays on His Philosophy*. Prentice-Hall, Englewood Cliffs, NJ, 1963.

Kolakowski, Leszek, *Bergson*. Oxford University Press, Oxford, 1985.

Küng, Hans, *Theology for the Third Millennium: An Ecumenical View*. Doubleday, New York, 1988.

Leclercq, J.; Vandenbroucke, F. and Bouyer, L., *A History of Spirituality, Vol.2: The Spirituality of the Middle Ages*. Seabury, New York, 1968.

Lederer, Wolfgang, *The Fear of Women*. Harcourt, Brace, Jovanovich, New York, 1968.

Leon-Dufour, Xavier (ed.), *Dictionary of Biblical Theology*, 2nd edn. Geoffrey Chapman, London, 1973.

Lilbourne, Geoffrey R., *A Sense of Place: A Christian Theology of the Land*. Abingdon Press, Nashville, 1989.

Lindsay, Joan, *Picnic at Hanging Rock*. Penguin, Ringwood, 1967.

Lines, William J., *Taming the Great South Land: A History of the Conquest of Nature in Australia*. Allen & Unwin, Sydney, 1991.

Lonergan, Anne & Richards, Caroline (eds), *Thomas Berry and the New Cosmology*. Twenty Third Publications, Mystic, CT, 1987.

• Lovejoy, Arthur O., *The Great Chain of Being: A Study of the History of an Idea*. Harvard University Press, Cambridge, MA., 1936.

Lovelock, James, *Gaia: A New Look at Life on Earth*. Oxford University Press, Oxford, 1979.

Lovelock, James, *The Ages of Gaia: A Biography of Our Living Earth*. Oxford University Press, Oxford, 1988.

Lovelock, James & Epton, Sidney, "The Quest for Gaia." *New Scientist*, 6 (1975). pp.304ff.

Macquarrie, John, *Heidegger and Christianity*. SCM, London, 1994.

Macquarrie, John, *Principles of Christian Theology*. Charles Scribner's Sons, New York, 1977.

Manes, Christopher, *Green Rage: Radical Environmentalism and the Unmaking of Civilization*. Little, Brown, Boston, 1990.

Marechal, Joseph, *Studies in the Psychology of the Mystics*. Burns, Oates & Washbourne, London, 1927.

Martin, Robert Bernard, *Gerard Manley Hopkins: A Very Private Life*. Harper/Collins, London, 1992.

• Maslow, Abraham, *Toward a Psychology of Being*. Princeton University Press, Princeton, NJ, 1968.

McDaniel, Jay B., *Earth, Sky, Gods and Mortals: Developing an Ecological Spirituality*. Twenty Third Publications, Mystic, CT, 1990.

McDermott, Timothy (ed.), *Summa Theologiae: A Concise Translation*. Eyre & Spottiswoode, London, 1989.

McDonagh, Sean, "Care for the Earth is a Moral Duty." *The Tablet*, 30 April 1994, pp.514–515.

McDonagh, Sean, *Passion for the Earth*. Geoffrey Chapman, London, 1994.

McDonagh, Sean, *The Greening of the Church*. Geoffrey Chapman, London, 1990.

McDonagh, Sean, *To Care for the Earth: A Call to a New Theology*. Geoffrey Chapman, London, 1986.

McEvedy, Colin & Jones, Richard, *Atlas of World Population History*. Penguin, Harmondsworth, 1978.

McFague, Sallie, *The Body of God: An Ecological Theology*. Fortress, Minneapolis, 1993.

McKenzie, John L., *Dictionary of the Bible*. Geoffrey Chapman, London, 1966.

Miles, Margaret, *Augustine on the Body*. Scholars Press, Missoula, Montana, 1979.

Miles, Margaret, *Fullness of Life: Historical Foundations for a New Asceticism*. Westminster, Philadelphia, 1981.

Milliss, Roger, *Waterloo Creek: The Australia Day Massacre of 1838*. McPhee Gribble, Ringwood, 1992.

Minns, Denis, *Irenaeus*. Geoffrey Chapman, London, 1994.

Moltmann, Jürgen, *God in Creation: An Ecological Doctrine of Creation*. SCM, London, 1985.

Moltmann, Jürgen, *The Crucified God: The Cross of Christ as the Foundation and Criticism of Christian Theology*. Harper & Row, New York, 1974.

Moltmann, Jürgen, *Theology of Hope: On the Ground and Implications of a Christian Eschatology*. SCM, London, 1967.

Monod, Jacques, *Chance and Necessity: An Essay on the Natural Philosophy of Modern Biology*. Vintage Books, New York, 1972.

Morgan, Hugh, "A threat expert's view of the green movement." *The Age*. 30 December 1992, p.11.

Moses, Greg, "Whitehead and Plato." Unpublished paper, Saint Paul's National Seminary, Kensington, NSW.

Newman, J.H., *An Essay in Aid of a Grammar of Assent*. Ed. I.T. Ker. Oxford University Press, Oxford, 1985.

Northrop, F.S.C. & Gross, Mason W. (eds.), *Alfred North Whitehead: An Anthology*. Cambridge University Press, Cambridge, 1953.

Ott, Hugo, *Martin Heidegger: A Political Life*. Fontana, London, 1993.

• Otto, Rudolf, *The Idea of the Holy*. Penguin, Harmondsworth, 1953.

• Pagels, Elaine, *The Gnostic Gospels*. Random House, New York, 1979.

Pagels, H.R., *Perfect Symmetry: The Search for the Beginning of Time*. Penguin, Harmondsworth, 1985.

Polkinghorne, John, *Religion and Current Science*. New College Lectures, Kensington, NSW, 1993.

Polkinghorne, John, *Science and Creation: The Search for Understanding*. SPCK, London, 1988.

Pseudo-Dionysius, *Pseudo-Dionysius: The Complete Works*. Trans.Colm Luibheid. Paulist Press, New York, 1987.

Rader, Rosemary, *Breaking Boundaries: Male/Female Friendship in Early Christian Communities*. Paulist Press, New York, 1983.

Rae, Murray, Regan, Hilary, Stenhouse, John (eds.), *Science and Theology: Questions at the Interface*. T. & T. Clark, Edinburgh, 1994.

Rahner, Karl, *Foundations of Christian Faith: An Introduction to the Idea of Christianity*. Seabury, New York, 1978.

Rahner, Karl, *Meditations on Priestly Life*. Sheed & Ward, London, 1973.

Rahner, Karl, *Nature and Grace and Other Essays*. Sheed & Ward, London, 1963.

Rahner, Karl, *Theological Investigations*, Vol.IV. Helicon Press, Baltimore, 1966.

Reich, Warren T. (ed.), *Encyclopedia of Bioethics*. Macmillan, New York, 1978.

Reynolds, Henry, *Frontier. Aborigines, Settlers and the Land*. Allen & Unwin, Sydney, 1987.

Reynolds, Henry, *The Other Side of the Frontier: Aboriginal Resistance to the European Invasion of Australia*. Penguin, Ringwood, 1982.

Rideau, Emile, *Teilhard de Chardin: A Guide to His Thought*. Collins, London, 1967.

Roszak, Theodore, *Where the Wasteland Ends: Politics and Transcendence in Post-Industrial Society*. Doubleday, New York, 1973.

Rowley, C.D., *The Destruction of Aboriginal Society*. Pelican, Ringwood, 1972.

Ruether, Rosemary Radford, *Sexism and God-Talk: Towards a Feminist Theology*. Beacon Books, Boston, 1983.

Santmire, H. Paul, *The Travail of Nature: The Ambiguous Ecological Promise of Christian Theology*. Fortress Press, Philadelphia, 1985.

Sawyer, Jacqueline, "The Population Explosion." *The New Road*, Issue 16, Oct.–Dec. 1990.

Schillebeeckx, Edward, *Jesus: An Experiment in Christology*. Collins, London, 1979.

Schillebeeckx, Edward, *Ministry: Leadership in the Community of Jesus Christ*. Crossroad, New York, 1981.

Schwarz, Walter (ed.), *Updating God*. Marshall Pickering, Basingstoke, 1988.

Sheldrake, Rupert, *The Rebirth of Nature: The Greening of Science and God*. Century, London, 1990.

Silver, Cheryl Simon (ed.), National Academy of Sciences, *One Earth One Future: Our Changing Global Environment*. National Academy Press, Washington, 1990.

Simon, Julian, *The Theory of Population and Economic Growth*. Basil Blackwell, Oxford, 1986.

Simon, Julian, *The Ultimate Resource*. Princeton University Press, Princeton, NJ, 1981.

Steiner, George, *Heidegger*. 2nd edn, Fontana, London, 1992.

Stone, Christopher D., *Earth and Other Ethics: The Case for Moral Pluralism*. Harper & Row, New York, 1987.

Strahan, Ronald (ed.), *Complete Book of Australian Mammals*. Cornstork Publishing, North Ryde, 1991.

Sumption, Jonathan, *Pilgrimage: An Image of Medieval Religion*. Faber & Faber, London, 1975.

• Teilhard de Chardin, Pierre, *The Hymn of the Universe*. Collins, London, 1965.

• Teilhard de Chardin, Pierre, *The Divine Milieu: An Essay on the Interior Life*. Collins, London, 1960.

• Teilhard de Chardin, Pierre, *The Future of Man*. Collins, London, 1964.

Teilhard de Chardin, Pierre, *Toward the Future*. Collins, London, 1975.

Tester, Keith, *The Life and Times of Post-Modernity*. Routledge, London, 1993.

Thiering, Barbara, *Jesus the Man: A New Interpretation from the Dead Sea Scrolls*. Transworld, Sydney, 1992. Published in the US as *Jesus and the Riddle of the Dead Sea Scrolls*. Harper, San Francisco, 1992.

Thompson, William M. (ed.), *Berulle and the French School: Selected Writings*. Paulist Press, New York, 1989.

Tooker, Elizabeth (ed.), *Native American Spirituality of the Eastern Woodlands*. Paulist Press, New York, 1979.

Toolan, David S., "The Tempest Over Cairo." *America*, 27 August 1994, pp. 3–4.

Tracy, David, *The Analogical Imagination: Christian Theology and the Culture of Pluralism*. SCM, London, 1981.

Tropea, Gregory, *Religion, Ideology and Heidegger's Concept of Falling*. Scholar's Press, Atlanta, GA, 1987.

Weiskel, Timothy, "In Dust and Ashes, The Environmental Crisis in Religious Perspective." *Harvard Divinity Bulletin*, 21/3 (1992), p. 8.

White, Lynn, "The Historical Roots of the Ecological Crisis." *Science*, 155 (1967), pp. 1203–1207.

Whitehead, Alfred North, *Process and Reality: An Essay in Cosmology*. Cambridge University Press, Cambridge, 1929.

Willey, David, *God's Politician: John Paul and the Vatican*. Faber & Faber, London, 1992.

Wilson, A.N., *Jesus*. Sinclair-Stevenson, London, 1992.

Wojtyla, Karol, *Love and Responsibility*. Collins, London, 1981.

Wolfflin, Heinrich, *Renaissance and Baroque*. Fontana/Collins, London, 1964.

Wright, N.T., *Who Was Jesus?* SPCK, London, 1993.

• Zaehner, R.C., *Mysticism. Sacred and Profane: An Inquiry into Some Varieties of Praeternatural Experience*. Oxford University Press, Oxford, 1957.

Index